SAINTS IN POLITICS

SAINTS
IN POLITICS

The 'Clapham Sect' and the
Growth of Freedom

ERNEST MARSHALL HOWSE

LONDON · GEORGE ALLEN & UNWIN LTD
Ruskin House Museum Street

First published in Great Britain in 1953
Reprinted 1971
This impression 1971, 1973, 1976

ISBN 0 04 942088 7

Printed in Great Britain by
Biddles Ltd, Guildford, Surrey

Preface

IN PARLIAMENT, during their lifetime, they were lampooned as "The Saints," and in history they have been remembered as "The Clapham Sect." They were not saints and they were not a sect, and they enjoyed with hearty zest the "savoury fleshpots" of this world; but they were a unique fraternity. History has had no other such "brotherhood of Christian politicians." By the liberality of their minds no less than of their purses, by their chosen causes, their concerted labours, their systematic research, their original methods of organizing public opinion, their persistent and triumphant campaigns, they made a permanent difference to the history not only of England but of the modern world.

It is strange that this significant story has not previously been told. For more than a century the Clapham Sect has been made familiar by an unceasing succession of references in histories and essays. Yet though the more celebrated of the men of Clapham have been the subjects of biographies—some of which, notably Coupland's *Wilberforce*, are of outstanding merit—no previous attempt has been made, on more than the most meagre scale, to collect and collate the dispersed information, and to picture the work of the group as a group. The present writer has endeavoured to provide in this volume a connected story of the concerted toil of the Clapham company in a mosaic pieced together from almost innumerable sources: biographies and histories; parliamentary debates; contemporary magazines and pamphlets; proceedings of societies; minutes of committees and organizations; and an immense variety of fugitive records now unavailable save to research students in a limited group of libraries.

The story which the mosaic reveals is an exciting and inspiring one. It shows a company of men, at first unknown to one another but individually moved by religious impulse, gathering around Wilberforce after his conversion, and, as a company, organizing movements that were then thought revolutionary, and that involved bitter conflict with contemporary sentiment, and with vested interests of gigantic power. It reveals further how these men, while they were inspired almost wholly by motives of religious origin, spoke in the vocabulary of religion, and engaged largely in enterprises of a specifically religious nature, yet by the principles they invoked and the methods they developed became a powerful indirect influence in wide ranges of social progress.

It is the fashion of some contemporary historians to minimize the significance of moral factors in history; to conclude that regardless of such men as Woolman and Wilberforce, Livingstone, and Lincoln, slavery would have disappeared anyway; and, indeed, that the errors of each generation of the past have been inexorably outmoded by the impersonal working of material forces. Such thinking is the vestigial remnant of a romanticism now sadly discredited, and its dangerous unreality has been made clear by contemporary experience. Nothing in human history promises that evil will ever be eliminated without toil, pain, and vicarious suffering, or without the inspiration of men animated by the noble insights of religion.

The story of the Clapham Sect remains a shining instance of how society can be influenced by a few men of ability and devotion. The change in the attitude of England toward slavery, for example, between the beginning of the story and the end cannot be adequately accounted for by change in economic situation, or by any material factors; it can be accounted for only by a change in moral judgments. And that change was effected chiefly by men inspired by the religious doctrine of the brotherhood of man in the fatherhood of God. The story is an illuminating reminder that spiritual factors in civilization may outweigh material factors, and that men of prophetic mind are still the hope of history.

More acknowledgments are due than I can make. First of all, I must thank Principal Hugh Watt, of New College, Edinburgh, who suggested to me the work that was waiting to be done, who directed my study for a Ph.D. thesis on the Clapham Sect, and who recommended its publication. Next, I must turn to Dr. Frank Klingberg, formerly head of the Department of History in the University of California at Los Angeles, who happened some years ago to read the MS and kept writing an insistent request that its material be given to the public. Finally, I must by no means omit the Social Science Research Council of Canada and the Publication Fund of the University of Toronto Press: they not only commended the MS, they provided the money to put it in print.

In the preparation of the book I availed myself of many helpers. In its first stages my wife patiently sat in the British Museum and other libraries, and copied out volumes of extracts and references. In the final stage she prepared the index. Many hands laboured with pencil and typewriter, among them Miss Bess Bowen in California and Miss Ethel Ross, Miss Emily Shields, and Miss Joan Peck in Toronto. I should also like to pay tribute to the skill and intelligent counsel of Miss Eleanor Harman and Miss Francess Halpenny of the University of Toronto Press. Apart from such assistance as these acknowledgments scantily suggest, I wrote the book.

E. M. H.

Acknowledgments

GRATEFUL ACKNOWLEDGMENT is made to the following publishers for permission to quote from copyright material: George Allen & Unwin, Ltd., *Lord Shaftesbury and Social-Industrial Progress* by J. Wesley Bready (1926); G. Bell & Sons, Ltd., *The Foreign Policy of Castlereagh, 1815–1822* by C. K. Webster (1925); Ernest Benn, Ltd., *History of the English People in 1815,* and *History of the English People, 1815–1830* by Elie Halévy (1924, 1926) and *England,* by William Ralph Inge (1926); Clarendon Press, *Wilberforce* by R. Coupland (1923); J. M. Dent & Sons, Ltd., and H. L. Stewart, *A Century of Anglo-Catholicism* (1929); Messrs. Drake, Son, & Parton, *The History of Liquor Licensing in England* by Sidney and Beatrice Webb (1903); Harvard University Press, *The Private Record of an Indian Governor-Generalship* edited by Holden Furber (1933); Longmans, Green & Company, *British History in the Nineteenth Century* by George M. Trevelyan (1922), and *The Life and Letters of Lord Macaulay* by Sir George O. Trevelyan (1876); Macmillan & Co., Ltd., and The Macmillan Company of Canada, Ltd., *Christian Socialism* by Charles E. Raven (1920); Oxford University Press, *Granville Sharp* by E. C. P. Lascelles (1928); George Philip & Son, Ltd., *A Short History of the British Commonwealth* by Ramsay Muir (1922); Yale University Press, *The Anti-Slavery Movement in England* by Frank J. Klingberg (1926).

Contents

CHAPTER ONE

Seed plot of history

"THE ENGLAND that is about us," said J. R. Green in 1874, "dates from the American War. It was then that the moral, the philanthropic, the religious ideas which have moulded English Society into its present shape first broke the spiritual torpor of the eighteenth century."[1] And of the period moulded by these ideas Professor G. M. Trevelyan adds the judgment that the first fifty years, stretching from the War of Independence to the Reform Bill, "compose a single epoch."[2]

That epoch was the period of transition between two civilizations. The civilization of the saddle and the pack horse gave way to that of the coach and the canal, the civilization of subsistence agriculture to that of machines and factories, the civilization of a paternal aristocracy to that of a political middle class. The transition was turbulent. The American Revolution was followed by the French Revolution; the gales of both blew over the troubled waters of the Industrial Revolution; and the shadow of Napoleon Bonaparte fell upon the whole scene and darkened the confusion.

The tumult of the time aggravated the worst features of the old civilization before they could be mitigated by the amenities of the new. The early liberalism—when the younger Pitt became the first prime minister to ask the House of Commons to reform itself; when Thomas Hardy founded the London Corresponding Society, and Earl Grey the Friends of the People; when Horace Walpole rejoiced with Hannah More over the fall of the Bastille; and Burns drank the jubilant toast to the "last verse of the last chapter of the Book of

---

[1] J. R. Green, *History of the English People*, IV, 272.
[2] G. M. Trevelyan, *British History in the Nineteenth Century*, Preface. Trevelyan speaks particularly of political history, but his observation is true in wider areas. The opening pages of this history contain a masterly survey of the England of this period.

Kings"—very soon became but an unreal memory. Britain greeted
the dawn of the Revolution but became affrighted by the shadows.
Her ruling classes were driven by the Terror across the Channel to an
extremity of panic, an almost literal madness, in which they "saw
Englishmen as Jacobins walking,"[3] and committed deeds of injustice
and savagery for which that madness is the sole and insufficient
excuse. The aristocracy of Britain believed that the French Revolution
was a microcosm portraying the inevitable and terrible end of any
movement toward democracy. Paris had clearly demonstrated, they
thought, that reform, even well-intentioned reform, was of its own
evil momentum irresistibly carried to chaos, and that the only safety
lay in grateful acquiescence in the existing order, and swift and ruthless measures with every would-be reformer.

Unfortunately in the generation in which it was so grimly determined that laws and institutions should not change, economic life
was changing at a rate unequalled for centuries; and the laws and
institutions of the old day were pitiably inadequate to meet the
exigencies of the new. The consequent disharmony was in large
measure the cause of the injustice and misery of a dark period of
English history.

To aggravate the evil, at a time when the victims of that disharmony needed most to make their wretchedness known, the liberty
even to protest was summarily denied. Though enclosure acts were
progressively taking from poor people the privileges that had made
existence possible,[4] though multitudes were being herded by the
factory towns into buildings that were not the "homes of a race" but
"the barracks of an industry," though even above the din of new
machinery there began to be heard the "crying of the children,"
who, driven by brutal taskmasters, dragged through weary lives of
factory toil "half-dressed but not half-fed";[5] though a hundred

---

[3]G. M. Trevelyan, *Clio*, p. 110.
[4]"Between 1700 and 1760 we have records of over 200 Enclosure Acts and
over 300,000 acres enclosed; between 1761 and 1800 of 2,000 Acts and over
2,000,000 acres enclosed; and in the first fifty years of the nineteenth century
of 2,000,000 more acres and nearly 2,000 more Enclosure Acts." G. D. H. Cole,
A Short History of the British Working Class Movement, I, 28, 57. See also
J. L. and B. Hammond, *The Village Labourer*, pp. 26-106. In 1801 Arthur
Young wrote, "By nineteen out of twenty Enclosure Bills the poor are injured
and most grossly." See G. M. Trevelyan, *British History in the Nineteenth
Century*, p. 146.
[5]Alfred, *History of the Factory Movement*, I, 99-100.

colliers might be killed in a Northumberland mine without even a coroner's inquest; though misery might be men's lot, and starvation their prospect, even the faintest protest was forbidden by laws specially enacted, and administered by the very people for whose advantage they were devised. Even the old safeguard of habeas corpus was at times denied,[6] and magistrates with a Bourbon mentality became unfettered arbiters of a nation's freedom. Ruthlessly the hard-won liberties of the past were discarded. Tyranny was dressed in ermine, and oppression slowly broadened down from precedent to precedent.

It is difficult to picture the England of those days. On the one hand were a central government which "did nothing to secure the public safety, provided no schools, made no roads, gave no relief to the poor,"[7] a parliament dominated by the owners of rotten boroughs, and an aristocracy at once cultured, magnificent, and dissolute; and on the other hand a lower class, illiterate, sodden with gin, given over to vicious living and brutal pastimes, and represented only too faithfully in Hogarth's "Beer Street" and "Gin Lane." Prison reform was only touched. In 1784 John Howard had to mark "no alteration" to most of the prisons he had visited ten years before. Public whipping of women was still permitted. And children could be condemned to death for petty theft. It was an England in which the promise of later days had scarcely begun to dawn.

In the present day it has become quite the fashion to gloss over the grim features of English life in the Georgian period. The modern reader may be almost beguiled into thinking that because Gainsborough sketched lovely English countrysides and Sir Joshua Reynolds painted the beautiful children of England's stately homes therefore the times could not have been so bad. Undoubtedly there is a measure of truth in the epigram of Dickens concerning the Revolution era: "it was the best of times; it was the worst of times." But the distinguished rationalist, Mr. Cotter Morison, who could scarcely be accused of undue partiality to piety, looking back in 1884 has this to say of conditions even after the turn of the century:

---

[6]E.g. in 1794 and 1817.
[7]Elie Halévy, *England in 1815*, p. 32. There was of course no real police force until the time of Sir Robert Peel.

The scandals of the Court were bad enough; but no Court, however bad, can compromise a nation. The mass of the population was coarse, insolent, and cruel, and permitted things which would not be tolerated for a moment now. That there were exceptions, not only of individuals, but of whole though small classes, no one would deny. The Clapham Sect was a conspicuous example in a corrupt world; and many of the dissenters were truly pious, God-fearing people, who had turned away from the prevailing grossness. But these were only fractions of the nation. The general tone was low, violent, and brutal. The drinking, gambling, prize-fighting, bull-baiting England of the Regency is hardly to be realized in these decorous days.[8]

The external miseries were perhaps not the worst features of the times. Spiritual resources were wanting. The mighty impact of the Wesleyan revival had stirred new life in the Methodist mission but for the most part the church "had no light of its own for the awakening or the guidance of the age."[9] Whether Anglican or Non-Conformist the churches lacked spiritual vitality and served mainly as auxiliary props for the state's conservatism. What life there was survived chiefly in the parishes of the despised Evangelical clergymen, of whom, till John Newton came in 1780, Romaine—preaching at evenings in a darkened church, by the light of the candle in his own hand—was the only representative in all London.[10]

The wider fields of Empire looked no better. By the Quebec Act the British Parliament had just granted in Canada a religious toleration at that time unexampled. But on the other side of the world Australia was taking its place as a convict colony fitted to make yet more terrible the strengthened weapon of English criminal law. India had recently produced fearful witness to the iniquities which might fester under cover of the white man's rule in distant places where political power was divorced from political responsibility. And outraged Africa seemed to be assuming an inexhaustible role as a human game preserve for captive labour.

A dark time! And yet, said Green, this was the time from which came the moral, the philanthropic, the religious ideas which transformed later England. For the brutal and obvious forces were not

---

[8]*The Service of Man*, p. 53.
[9]J. L. and B. Hammond, *The Rise of Modern Industry*, p. 253.
[10]The church officials could not prohibit Romaine from preaching, but they could, and did, refuse to provide lighting.

the only forces at work. When social and economic life reached their nadir, intellect and imagination reached their zenith. Cowper, Burns, Blake, Coleridge, Wordsworth, Scott, Landor, Byron, Keats, and Shelley, a group of poets which the age did not match elsewhere in the world, lifted their voices in "the greatest burst of inspired song" since the Renaissance, and gave new power to the humanitarian tradition which their predecessors in English letters had already established in poetry and prose.[11] Of still more importance, the Evangelical revival grew in power, at a period critically opportune, and created a moral sentiment that permanently changed England's attitude to distant and defenceless peoples, and to her own brutal and degraded masses at home. Within a lifetime, like a group of mountain springs, there appeared in England a series of religious and humanitarian movements which altered the whole course of English history, influenced most of Europe, and affected the life of three other continents.

These movements sprang out of a new doctrine of responsibility toward the unprivileged, a doctrine which received its chief impulse from the Evangelical emphasis on the value of the human soul, and hence, of the individual. The first expression was in the abolition of the slave trade. Then the implications of the doctrine of responsibility widened. Britain took a new attitude to India, removed the restrictions against missionaries, initiated a system of education, and prepared the way for reforms such as the abolition of suttee. A still further implication followed, and the British people, in a time of national stringency, laid upon themselves a tax of £20,000,000 to give freedom to the Negroes of the British possessions. The influence of this enthusiasm was not confined to Britain; it was felt by every slave-trading nation in Europe. And in several nations it was British influence, British pressure, and even British money, which led to the abolition of the legal slave trade, and the long efforts to end the subsequent slave smuggling.[12]

While these movements of humanity and religion were being undertaken for distant peoples, movements of scarcely less significance

[11]An excellent study of humanitarian sentiment in eighteenth-century literature is contained in *The Negro in English Romantic Thought* by Eva Beatrice Dykes.

[12]Great Britain spent an additional £10,000,000 trying to end the illegitimate traffic.

were affecting the course of life in England itself. Among the most important was that for popular education. A new era commenced with the spreading of the Sunday schools, and continued with the founding of societies for national education. The support for popular education was derived in large degree from the religious conviction that every person had a sacred right to be able to read his Bible. The increase in literacy was therefore paralleled by the formation of great tract and Bible societies which diligently distributed religious literature, especially the Bible.

All these movements had secondary effects. Literacy was the necessary prelude to democracy. And the Sunday schools awakened interest in children, revealed conditions of child life, and, in their teachers, raised up to do battle for the oppressed child a host of spokesmen, who supplied the knowledge and created the sympathy which made possible the subsequent victories of the children's champions.[13]

But these movements were not all. The terrible injustice of the criminal law stirred up opponents who commenced the reform of the whole penal and judicial ·system. The growing knowledge of the conditions of factory life led to the first Factory Act, and the beginning of industrial reform. The dragging opposition of Parliament led to a sweeping reform of Parliament itself. The new spirit of tolerance led to Roman Catholic Emancipation. And, finally, the misery that inevitably remained in this period of transition was alleviated by the growth of a new and more sensitive philanthropy, a philanthropy defective indeed in its attitude to the *cause* of the misery, but nevertheless showing, as did all the other movements, an increased feeling of responsibility to the underprivileged.

In short, this turbulent epoch, ushered in beneath such dark and ominous clouds, witnessed the beginning of so many movements which profoundly affected future generations that, for all its grim

---

[13]". . . society has never yet realized how great is her debt to this voluntary organization of religious zealots for the part they played in breaking industrial serfdom. . . . Hundreds of Sunday School teachers signed petitions protesting against the fatigue inflicted upon factory children whom they tried to instruct; and the semi-religious agitation of such popular champions as Oastler and Rev. Rayner Stephens would have missed fire without the sympathetic atmosphere created by the Sunday School, the sworn champion of the outcast child." J. W. Bready, *Shaftesbury*, pp. 174-5.

and terrible features, it must ever be regarded as a seed plot in English history.

But, though progress be broad its impulse is always narrow. Professor Gilbert Murray reminds us that "the moving force in human progress is not widespread," that "the uplifting of man has ever been the work of a chosen few."[14] And the Chosen Few in this generation included a peculiar company sometime labelled "The Clapham Sect."[15]

[14]Gilbert Murray, *Religio Grammatici*, p. 28.

[15]See Appendix. In their lifetime the group were not known as the Clapham Sect. They were, in fact, not popularly known by that name until after the publication of Sir James Stephen's essay by that title. In their own day they were derisively known as the "Saints" and commonly so called. See *inter alia* (1) *Christian Observer*, 1813, p. 617; 1839, p. 798; (2) *John Bull*, Nov. 10, 1823, p. 356 (a virulent article on Macaulay, "Saint Zachariah"); (3) *The Times*, May 16, 1833; (4) *Parliamentary Debates*, 2nd series, IX, 255 ff.; New series, X, 1157; XI, 1167, 1234; (5) *Greville Memoirs*, II, 125, 278, 371.

CHAPTER TWO

Brotherhood of Christian politicians

"Some rivers spring from . . . a group of pools."[1]
This analogy to which Gladstone had recourse in describing the
Evangelical movement may be used not less appropriately to describe
that section of the movement which acquired the nickname "The
Clapham Sect." But in both the greater and the lesser movements
though there are many sources there is one from which issues the
dominant stream: in the former John Wesley; in the latter William
Wilberforce. And with both the spring must be sought in an
Evangelical conversion.

The conversion of Wilberforce occurred, oddly enough, while at
the age of twenty-six, he was making the conventional tour of the
Continent. His companion was a former tutor of his, the Reverend
Isaac Milner, afterward Dean of Carlisle. By chance they included in
their luggage Dr. Philip Doddridge's *Rise and Progress of Religion in
the Soul*. The reading of this book led Wilberforce to a study of the
New Testament and resulted in a conversion as significant as that of
John Newton or John Wesley.

The news of the conversion brought dismay to many of Wilberforce's friends; but it brought hope to other men, and centred their
thoughts on him as the promising advocate for their various causes.
In 1785 when Wilberforce was on his tour of the Continent a young
Cambridge graduate, Thomas Clarkson, had just read to the Senate
his prize essay *Anne liceat invitos in servitutem dare?* (Is it lawful to
make slaves of others against their will?) He had begun that essay
with his mind dwelling on academic distinction; he had finished it overwhelmed by the iniquities which his studies had convinced him were
true, and his conscience had told him were intolerable. While Wilber-

[1] W. E. Gladstone, *Gleanings of Past Years*, VII, 205.

force was in Europe reflecting on Doddridge's *Rise and Progress* Clarkson used to wander in the woods near his home, haunted by the facts he had discovered, and repeating to himself the conviction, "Then surely some person should interfere." He determined to do something himself, and resolved, as a preliminary move, to publish his essay. In the course of publication he came in contact with some interested Quakers who introduced him to Granville Sharp, already celebrated for having in 1772 won the decision that made slavery illegal in England. Clarkson and Sharp and these Quakers began to think much and to consult often about the possibility of ending the slave trade. They were in no wise afraid to face any difficulties or to undertake any labours. To this end in the summer of 1787 they formally constituted themselves an Abolition Committee. But their battle could be won only through Parliament. And their great need was for the right parliamentary champion, a man whose distinction and ability the House would not be able to ignore nor find it easy to overcome.

While they were eagerly exploring for possible sources of assistance Clarkson came in contact with Wilberforce and learned of his recent conversion. He immediately recognized that Wilberforce, with his wealth, his popularity, his eloquence, and his newly avowed dedication to religious aims, was just the man they wanted. Clarkson set to work to win Wilberforce to the cause. After their first conversation in the spring of 1787 he reported: "The manner in which Mr. Wilberforce had received me . . . tended much to enlarge my hope, that [the trade] might become at length the subject of a parliamentary inquiry." He soon added the determination that he "should never lose sight of Mr. Wilberforce, but, on the other hand, . . . should rather omit visiting some others, than paying a proper attention to him." Shortly afterwards he wrote that his friends "were of opinion that the time was approaching when we might unite, and that this union might prudently commence as soon as ever Mr. Wilberforce would give his word that he would take up the question in parliament."[2]

Though Clarkson did not know it he was but adding another appeal to many previous ones. Wilberforce had first become interested

[2]Thomas Clarkson, *History of Abolition*, I, 243, 244, 250.

in the slave trade when he was a boy, and when only fourteen years
of age he had written a precocious letter to a Yorkshire paper de-
nouncing the "odious traffic in human flesh."[3] Later, though still in
his unregenerate days, he had begun to gather information about the
state of slavery in Antigua. In 1783 he had consulted with the
Reverend James Ramsay, a retired missionary who was one of the
earliest champions of the West Indian slaves. During these years,
however, Wilberforce's interest in slavery, he later confessed, was
that of a dilettante, and "my own distinction was my darling object."[4]
But following his conversion and his new passion to devote his life
to some worthy cause, he had determined to champion abolition.
An important impulse in this direction was his meeting in 1786 with
Sir Charles Middleton and Lady Middleton; the latter had been
shocked by revelations about the slaves in the West Indies and
was looking for someone to take up the matter in Parliament.[5] His
consultation with Pitt was persuasive. Wilberforce's account of this
has become classical. "Pitt recommended me to undertake its conduct,
as a subject suited to my character and talents. At length, I well
remember, after a conversation in the open air at the root of an
old tree at Holwood just above the steep descent into the vale of
Keston, I resolved to give notice on a fit occasion in the House of
Commons of my intention to bring the subject forward."[6] This
memorable interview occurred shortly before Wilberforce's first
meeting with Clarkson. But Wilberforce did not divulge his determination and Clarkson thereafter believed that his own appeal had
done more than in fact it had to win the great leader. Yet however
we may apportion the influences that moved Wilberforce to his life
work it is clear that his enlistment in the anti-slavery campaign was
the genesis of many crusades which history now associates with the
homes of Clapham.

Wilberforce, Sharp, and Clarkson were soon to have other com
rades. In 1783, the year in which Wilberforce had consulted with
James Ramsay about slavery in the West Indies, a young Scottish
lawyer, James Stephen, *en route* to St. Christopher, happened to be
at Barbados, a port of call, during a so-called "trial" of Negroes,

³*Life of Wilberforce*, I, 9.   ⁴*Ibid.*, pp. 147-9.
⁵*Ibid.*, pp. 142-6.   ⁶*Ibid.*, pp. 150-1.

trial marked equally by the injustice of the proceedings, and the barbarity of the punishment—a Negro was burned alive. The young lawyer conceived at that trial an undying hatred of slavery. He held an important position at St. Christopher; but, contrary to general custom, he refused to own slaves, and endeavoured whenever possible to free those who served him.[7] In 1794 he returned to England still burning with indignation at the iniquities which festered under the slave system.

Naturally enough he turned for guidance to the man already becoming known in England as the slave's champion. He sought out William Wilberforce to discuss slavery with him. At that time there seemed little that Stephen could do, for his practice and his livelihood depended on the goodwill of the West Indians. He agreed, however, to make some use of his position by collecting information for Wilberforce—an unintentional augury of the future. Five years later he gave up his practice in the West Indies, and returned permanently to England, where his great gifts as a lawyer soon were to make him a leading figure in the Prize Appeal Court of the Privy Council. From that time he openly threw in his lot with Wilberforce, and from the first his trumpet gave no uncertain sound.

Meanwhile the West Indies had brought another important figure in touch with Clapham. In 1785, the year of Clarkson's dedication to the cause of the slaves and of Wilberforce's conversion, another Scot, Zachary Macaulay, a mere lad, who had gone to the West Indies as overseer of a Jamaica estate, wrote home to his family that he found himself growing "callous and indifferent" to the suffering of the Negroes whom he used to see in the fields about him "cursing and bawling" under the incessant cracks of the drivers' whips. He did his best, however, "to render the bitter cup of servitude as palatable as possible."[8] But in 1789, the year in which Wilberforce made his first and most eloquent speech on the slave trade, young Macaulay, having attained his majority, put aside "really great offers" and left forever the slave plantations which he hated. He returned to England to visit a sister who during his absence had married a Mr. Thomas Babington of Rothley Temple, Leicestershire. Babington was a man of high character and evangelical piety, and

[7] James Stephen, *Slavery Delineated*, pp. liii-lv.
[8] *Christian Observer*, 1839, p. 759.

his influence on Macaulay at an impressionable period deeply affected Macaulay's whole life.[9] Babington also, as will shortly be seen, soon provided the link between Macaulay and Clapham.[10]

These men, the nucleus of the later Clapham Sect, were first drawn together by a common interest in slavery, but slavery was not to exhaust the energies of the men of Clapham. Other interests were already drawing other figures into the growing circle. India as well as the West Indies had been looking to Wilberforce.

At the time Wilberforce was writing his boyish letter to the Yorkshire paper two young Scotsmen, John Shore (later Lord Teignmouth) and Charles Grant, youthful appointees of the East India Company, were beginning in India careers that were to lead the one to be Governor-General of India and the other to be the most powerful member of the East India Council in England, "the real ruler of the rulers of the East, the Director of the Court of Directors."[11] At that time the two young officials were unacquainted with each other, and a suggestion to either of them of association with such enterprises as afterward occupied their attention would have merely provoked derision. But in 1776 (the year in which Wilberforce went to Cambridge), Charles Grant, after a severe family tragedy, was converted, and commenced a friendship which was to be intimate and life-long with John Shore, who was then also "at the beginning of his own Christian career."[12] Ten years later, in 1786—the year of beginnings—when Wilberforce was taking his first communion, and Clarkson deciding to print his *Anne liceat,* Grant began to be occupied with the possibility of establishing in India, under the sanction and patronage of the government, an extensive scheme of Christian missions. He was much encouraged in this project by a new friend, David Brown, who had just come out to India as chaplain to the military orphanage in Calcutta. Brown had been a friend of an Evangelical clergyman, Charles Simeon of Cambridge, who could keep him informed in what quarters in England

---

[9]In 1795 Macaulay said of Rothley Temple, "To this place I owe myself. If there be in me . . . any desires superior to those of the beasts which perish, here were they first called into action." Viscountess Knutsford, *Zachary Macaulay,* p. 90.

[10]*Infra,* p. 18.

[11]Sir James Stephen, *Essays in Ecclesiastical Biography,* II, 217.

[12]Grant sailed for India in 1767, and arrived in 1768. Shore sailed in 1768 and arrived in 1769. They did not become acquainted till 1774.

sympathy for Grant's scheme might probably be found. Hence, when he and Grant had completed their mission plan, and were making appeal for it to England, they confined their hopes of practical results among the clergy to Simeon himself, and among the laity to the now notable William Wilberforce. In 1790 Grant returned to England and met Wilberforce, to whom later he was careful to introduce John Shore, when Shore also returned to England.

Beginning, then, in 1785 there were three men in England: Wilberforce, Sharp, and Clarkson; two men in the West Indies: Stephen and Macaulay; and two men in India: Grant and Shore, who were destined to labour in Clapham. And in Clapham others would be waiting.

Clapham is now a part of London; but until the beginning of the last century it was still a "village of nightingales" separated from the city by three miles of pleasant driving. It was this village which became the country residence of the group of wealthy men who figure in this story. Of that group a number, as the following pages will show, owned their own magnificent houses situated in the proximity of each other. Others of the group who did not own houses in Clapham visited and lived with their co-labourers—especially during the heat of the crusades—with an easy informality which seems almost incredible in this day.

The most permanent element in the Clapham Sect is to be found in the Thornton family. An uncle of William Wilberforce, John Thornton, was already living in a spacious mansion at Clapham when in 1756 Henry Venn, one of the most distinguished of the early Evangelicals, began his ministry there. John Thornton had three sons,. Samuel, Robert, and Henry, who all became members of Parliament. The father was descended from a long line of Yorkshire clergymen but had turned his talents to business, and Henry said of his own generation, "We are all City people and connected with merchants, and nothing but merchants on every side."[13] It was in the house of John Thornton that Wilberforce found a retreat in his first weeks of sober thought after his conversion. It was there that he and Henry drew close, and there that the Clapham Sect began to

[13]Henry Thornton, *Enquiry into Paper Credit,* Introduction by F. A. von Hayek, p. 12.

form around them. Looking back many years later Thornton wrote:

Few men have been blessed with worthier and better friends than it has
been my lot to be. Mr. Wilberforce stands at the head of these, for he
was the friend of my youth. I owed much to him in every sense soon
after I came out in life, for my education had been narrow, and his
enlarged mind, his affectionate and understanding manners and his
very superior piety were exactly calculated to supply what was wanting
to my improvement and my establishment in a right course. It is chiefly
through him that I have been introduced to a variety of other most
valuable associates, to my friends Babington and Gisborne and their
worthy families, to Lord Teignmouth and his family, to Mrs. Hannah
More and her sisters; to Mr. Stephen and to not a few respectable
members of Parliament. Second only to Mr. Wilberforce in my esteem
is now the family of Mr. Grant.[14]

After Henry had married, his house at Clapham was the chosen
meeting place of the brotherhood, and his famous library, designed
by Pitt, oval in shape, and "curiously wainscotted with books,"
became the G.H.Q. of the Clapham campaigns.

In 1792 the influence of the Thorntons brought another important figure to Clapham. John Thornton, having become an
intimate friend of Henry Venn, not only presented him with the
living at Huddersfield but paved the way for a son, John Venn,
later to become rector of Clapham.[15] John Venn, "a man of culture,
judgment, and sanctified common sense,"[16] and, like his father, an
ardent Evangelical, was offered the living of Clapham in 1792. He
began residence in Clapham in 1793 and won the following comment
in Wilberforce's diary: "Venn preached an excellent introductory
sermon. I received the sacrament and had much serious reflection."
Venn remained in Clapham until his death in 1813 and became the
fellow conspirator, the personal friend, and the spiritual guide of the
Clapham brotherhood, "the most notable congregation in all England."[17]

In 1797 Wilberforce married and took a house on Thornton's
estate. Wilberforce, however, acquired several houses, one of which,
in Palace Yard, was the London headquarters of the Sect during

[14]*Ibid.*, pp. 19-20.   [15]John Venn, *Annals,* p. 127.
[16]Eugene Stock, *History of the C.M.S.,* I, 41.
[17]G. R. Balleine, *History of the Evangelical Party,* 147.

parliamentary campaigns. In 1808 Wilberforce gave up his house in Clapham and took one at Kensington Gore, a mile from Hyde Park, where he had as neighbours Stephen, and later Macaulay, who moved so as to be near Wilberforce. Macaulay went to Clapham in 1803 and stayed till 1819. Lord Teignmouth, following his maxim "seek a neighbour before you seek a house," went to Clapham in 1802 and remained till 1808. James Stephen and Charles Grant both lived at Clapham for periods not precisely noted in any available literature about them.

In Clapham also lived valiant associates of the brotherhood: Charles Elliott of Grove House, Clapham; Edward James Eliot, brother-in-law of Pitt, who lived on Thornton's estate in the house which Wilberforce was afterwards to own, and who, until his early death in 1797, was to be a valuable link between Pitt and Wilberforce; and William Smith, member for Norwich, who, though not an Evangelical but "an avowed Socinian,"[18] was welcomed none the less heartily by the others, and entered with no less enthusiasm into their cherished projects.

The roll is not yet complete. The Clapham Sect had "non-resident" members, some of whom were scarcely less important than those who actually had local habitation within the "holy village." But, though the circle grows wider, the ties remain hardly less intimate.

The intellectual centre of the Evangelical party was Cambridge University, where the two chief leaders were Isaac Milner and Charles Simeon. Milner, Wilberforce's companion on the continental tour, was "an Evangelical Dr. Johnson," a "sort of Grand Lama"[19] of the Evangelical party. His influence was by no means negligible in Clapham, but he did not enter much into the practical labours, and hence, will play little part in the following pages. The other great leader was Charles Simeon, "St. Charles of Cambridge," who, if he had not quite the intellectual distinction of Milner, had an even greater practical influence. Lord Macaulay wrote in 1844: "As to Simeon, if you knew what his authority and influence were, and how they extended from Cambridge to the most remote corners of Eng-

---

[18]Venn, *Annals*, p. 145.
[19]J. H. Overton, *The English Church in the Nineteenth Century*, pp. 61, 63.

land, you would allow that his real sway in the church was far
greater than that of any primate."[20] Simeon was more directly linked
than Milner to the Clapham group. In his student days at Cambridge
he had been the friend of John Venn, and through the son had come
to know the father, Henry Venn, by whose influence he had been
brought into the Evangelical fold. From the first therefore he entered
the Clapham group as a member of their spiritual family.

Cambridge provided still other links with Clapham. While Wilberforce was at St. John's College his next-door neighbour and near
friend was one Thomas Gisborne. After leaving college the friends
had lost touch with one another. But the news that Wilberforce had
taken up the cause of abolition prompted Gisborne, now a clergyman
at Yoxall, Staffordshire, to join hands again with his old friend. He
therefore wrote to Wilberforce, and so recommenced a friendship that
lasted till death. Gisborne, indeed, became so intimately associated
with the Clapham activities that Yoxall Lodge, his home, became
almost a second Clapham; and because the Claphamites could not
always be at Yoxall Lodge, Gisborne "resided a large part of each
year with Wilberforce." Sir James Stephen later gave his considered
opinion that Gisborne was one of the supreme orators in the history
of the English pulpit, and wrote of him that "Among the sectaries of
that village [Clapham] he took his share in labour and in deliberation,
whether the abolition of the slave trade, the diffusion of Christianity,
the war against vice and ignorance, or the advancement of evangelical
theology, was the object of the passing day."[21] But, to gather up the
threads, Gisborne married the sister of Thomas Babington, and introduced Babington to Wilberforce. And Babington, it will be remembered, married the sister of Zachary Macaulay, and in turn introduced
Macaulay to the brotherhood.

There were still others whose influence and aid were to count for
much in Clapham enterprises. Mention may be made of Claudius
Buchanan, Henry Martyn, and Josiah Pratt. Claudius Buchanan was
another Scot, a young prodigal who had been wandering around
Europe, having for his sole stock in trade, "a lie and a violin,"[22] when
he was converted and came under the influence of the common friend
of the Sect, John Newton. As he seemed a promising convert the

[20]G. O. Trevelyan, *Life of Lord Macaulay,* I, 68.
[21]Sir James Stephen, *Essays in Ecclesiastical Biography,* II, 199.
[22]Sir John Kaye, *Christianity in India,* p. 166.

friends became interested in him. Henry Thornton sent him to Cambridge, where Simeon watched over him. Later Grant inspired him with the desire to go to India, and provided him with a chaplaincy in the East India Company. In consequence Buchanan was able to render powerful assistance to Clapham causes both in India and at home. Henry Martyn was "Simeon's spiritual son." Under the counsels of that eminent teacher, the guidance of Wilberforce, and the active aid of Grant he became an heroic missionary delegate of the Clapham Sect. Josiah Pratt was an Evangelical minister, a close friend of the Claphamites, the first editor of the *Christian Observer*, and one of the founders of the Church Missionary Society and of the British and Foreign Bible Society.

In time also there came the second generation of Claphamites, of whom the most distinguished were James and George Stephen, Robert and Charles Grant—all afterwards knighted—and Lord Macaulay. And one must remember that in 1786, the year in which Wilberforce decided to take up the cause of slavery, there was born in Castle Hedingham, Essex, Thomas Fowell Buxton, to whom nearly forty years afterwards Wilberforce was to pass the mantle of leadership in the last campaign for the emancipation of the slaves. And, finally, no account of the Clapham Sect can overlook the eminent Mrs. Hannah More, the "Queen of the Methodists,"[23] and the appointed agent of Wilberforce and Thornton in their philanthropic activities. "Equally with Wilberforce and Simeon, she was one of the 'great men' of the party."[24]

In time the Clapham Sect developed subsidiary ties of blood and kinship. As we have seen, Henry Thornton was Wilberforce's cousin; Gisborne married Babington's sister; and Babington married Macaulay's sister. In addition Charles Elliott married John Venn's sister; Stephen married Wilberforce's sister; and, all the available sisters having been taken, Macaulay married a pupil of Hannah More.[25] Soon, too, the next generation added its ties, and the son of James Stephen married the daughter of John Venn.

The group, in 1785 so widely scattered but soon to be gathered

[23]I.e., the Evangelicals. Cobbett called her "the Old Bishop in Petticoats." She was never married, but, in the custom of the day, assumed the "Mrs." as a title of respectability.

[24]Elie Halévy, *England in 1815*, p. 381.

[25]In addition to all this, the Babingtons, it is suggested, did some gentle planning so that Thornton married a close friend of their family. Knutsford, *Zachary Macaulay*, pp. 85, 100-3, 108.

in the Clapham mansions and to share in Clapham "Cabinet Councils," consisted of no ordinary persons. Granville Sharp, the oldest of the band, was, like John Venn, "the product of an unbroken line of theologians."[26] And a most remarkable product he was. Through poverty in his family he was in early youth apprenticed to a draper; but his humble start did not prevent rapid and distinguished attainments. He studied Hebrew to confute a Jew, and Greek to confute a Socinian, and to such effect that he made original contributions to the study of both languages. But Greek and Hebrew did not exhaust his versatile energies. While an apprentice he heard one of his masters mention a claim to some barony. Sharp at once "buried himself in pedigrees, feoffments, and sepulchral inscriptions," and, incredible as it may sound, actually established the title and sent the draper to sit in the House of Lords as Baron Willoughby de Parham.[27]

Still more remarkable was Sharp's achievement in the momentous legal battle over the Negro slave, James Somerset. In the year 1770 when there were about 14,000 Negroes in England held as slaves mostly by families with interests in West Indian plantations Granville Sharp selected Somerset to make a test case and contended that slavery was illegal under English law. His argument challenged judgments by Yorke, Talbot, and Blackstone, and was overwhelmingly opposed by the legal opinion of the time. Sharp gave two years to legal research on the relation in English law of property and persons. His labours produced for his counsel an exhaustive and impregnable brief. And when in 1772 the case was fought in court Lord Mansfield gave his famous judgment endorsing Sharp's proposition that "as soon as any slave sets his foot on English ground, he becomes free."[28]

Sharp in fact was never dismayed by any task. The more formidable the enemy the more courageously would he enter the lists against him. He had not the gifts of a leader: he was emotional and erratic, and strangely occupied with Old Testament prophecies; but he had great capacity for patient labour, and he was of a singularly attractive nature. Sir James Stephen presented him with no unearned

[26]E. C. P. Lascelles, *Granville Sharp*, p. 1.
[27]Sir James Stephen, *Essays in Ecclesiastical Biography*, II, 204.
[28]Prince Hoare, *Memoirs of Granville Sharp*, p. 92.

accolade: "As long as Granville Sharp survived it was too soon to proclaim that the age of chivalry was gone."[29]

Thomas Clarkson, less versatile and not so winsome, was nevertheless like Sharp gifted with a prodigious capacity for patient, laborious investigation; and, like Sharp, though unfitted to lead made an admirable henchman. Once when Clarkson was on a visit to Paris he wrote to Mirabeau every day for a month a letter containing sixteen to twenty pages to make sure that Mirabeau was kept fully informed about the slave trade. Another time to get some evidence he needed he sought a sailor whom he had once seen, but whose name he did not know. He systematically searched the ships of port after port till at last he found the sailor on the 317th ship he had visited. For tirelessly pursuing the trail of evidence, for stirring up committees and corresponding societies, for wielding a dull but voluminous pen, for faithfully performing the long drudgery essential to the ultimate success, he was suited to a high degree.

Zachary Macaulay, "the austere and silent father of the greatest talker the world has ever known,"[30] took up the work of Clarkson and developed it in ways of which Clarkson would have been quite incapable. Indeed, while Macaulay was meagrely furnished with the gifts which commend themselves to popular acclaim, he was above all others the man, who, with no concern for his own advantage and with no thought of any rewarding glory, uncomplainingly, year in and year out, bore the burden and heat of the day. His companions made the evenings eloquent; but he was the man who "rose and took pen in hand at four o'clock in the morning."[31] He sifted the evidence, gathered the facts, and presented the arguments from which his associates massed the terrible indictments which moved anti-slavery audiences to tumultuous applause. He was, said Fowell Buxton, the anti-slavery tutor of them all. And he laboured not only tirelessly but with extraordinary efficiency. His powers of analysis were astonishing, and his memory at once ecumenical and accurate.

Blue books and state papers were child's play to him, however dull or voluminous; he would attend half a dozen charitable committees . . .

[29]*Essays in Ecclesiastical Biography,* II, 204.
[30]F. W. Cornish, *The English Church in the Nineteenth Century,* I, 13.
[31]G. W. E. Russell, *The Household of Faith,* p. 225.

during the day, and refresh himself after dinner with a parliamentary
folio that would have choked an alderman by the sight of it alone. His
memory was so retentive, that, without the trouble of reference, he could
collate the papers of one session with those of three or four preceding
years; he analysed with such rapidity that he could reduce to ten or
twenty pages all that was worth extracting from five hundred; his acute-
ness was so great that no fallacy of argument escaped him, and no
sophistry could bewilder him; and more than that he was accuracy and
truth itself. . . . Every friend to slavery knew Macaulay to be his most
dangerous foe.[32]

When the brotherhood were at a loss for some needed information
they would say, "Let us look it up in Macaulay," and from long
experience they laid down the dictum, "Whatever Macaulay says,
may be taken for gospel, and quoted."[33] When Buxton was preparing
a dictionary for private reference he called it "My Macaulay."
Buxton indeed paid no unconsidered tribute when he said in Parliament: "If the Negro should be emancipated he would be more indebted to Mr. Macaulay than to any other man living."[34] And in
1833 on the passing of the Emancipation Bill he wrote to Macaulay:
"My sober and deliberate opinion is, that you have done more towards
this consummation than any other man."[35]

The intimate friend and fellow labourer of Macaulay was the
other West Indian, James Stephen, who, with gifts of speech far
greater than Macaulay's, with the relentless logic of a great lawyer,
with a fiery and terrible temper that all Macaulay's steadiness could
scarcely keep in check, with fervour that did not, like Macaulay's,
glow unchanged for years but rather flared intermittently into white
fury, was another Clapham giant whom the enemy always recognized
as one of their really formidable foes. Once when Stephen had burst
into indignation at the inactivity of the government, Macaulay turned
to young George Stephen, as the elder Stephen left, and said, "In
anger, your father is terrific."[36] Stephen, moreover, like Macaulay,
wielded an assiduous and powerful pen. He was described as "the

[32]George Stephen, *Antislavery Recollections,* pp. 51-2.
[33]*Christian Observer,* 1839, p. 804.
[34]*Parliamentary Debates,* 3rd series, XVIII, 519.
[35]Charles Buxton, *Memoirs of Sir Thomas Fowell Buxton,* p. 282.
[36]George Stephen, *Antislavery Recollections,* p. 33.

ablest pamphleteer of his day," and he and **Macaulay** together were considered "authors-general for our cause."[37]

Charles Grant and John Shore were another notable couple. They brought to Clapham the authoritative knowledge about Indian affairs that Stephen and Macaulay brought about West Indian. Grant became the most distinguished director of the East India Company, "the headpiece of the Company in Leadenhall Street, the mouthpiece of the Company in St. Stephen's, the oracle on all subjects of Indian import," and "the authority from whom Wilberforce derived at once the impulse and the knowledge" for the East Indian battles.[38] George Smith called Grant "the purest and ablest statesman whom Scotland . . . has ever sent to India."[39] In the East India Company he was celebrated not only for his masterly understanding of the "entire range and the intricate combinations" of the Company's affairs, but also "for nerves which set fatigue at defiance"; and at Clapham he was held in awe for piety which "though ever active, was too profound for speech"—a praise "to which, among their other glories, it was permitted to few of his neighbours there to attain or to aspire."[40] Besides leading the movement to establish Christian missions in India, Grant wielded the influence through which Buchanan, Henry Martyn, Thomas Thomason, David Corrie, and other Evangelical chaplains secured appointment to India.

In his labours for India Grant was aided by John Shore. Lord Macaulay, who had lived in India for four years as a member of the Supreme Council, wrote in 1844, "Lord Teignmouth governed India at Calcutta. Grant governed India in Leadenhall Street." Shore lacked Grant's strength but he was methodically competent and he was no less distinguished than Grant for his inflexible integrity. "John Shore was that comparatively rare political phenomenon in British-Indian history at this period, an honest man."[41] The confidence he inspired induced the East India Company to break its rule of appointing none but military men to the highest post in India, and to select Shore to succeed Lord Cornwallis as Governor-General. "The in-

---

[37]*Life of Wilberforce*, V, 207.
[38]Stock, *History of the C.M.S.*, I, 54.
[39]*Twelve Indian Statesmen*, p. 1.
[40]Sir James Stephen, *Essays in Ecclesiastical Biography*, II, 217.
[41]Holden Furber, *The Private Record of an Indian Governor-Generalship*, p. 4.

credible happened. A man who had no great name, no military reputation, no great political influence, nothing in fact but an unblemished private character and long years of meritorious service behind him, was appointed to what had then become the highest and most responsible post in the British Empire."[42] In that post Shore proved to be cautious and well intentioned but of no marked distinction in statesmanship. The *Cambridge Modern History* says disparagingly, "After the utmost allowance has been made for the difficulties of Sir John Shore's position, . . . no very great praise can be bestowed upon his conduct of affairs."[43] Furber's more recent study suggests that this judgment may be unnecessarily severe. Whatever his limitations of statesmanship, however, Shore had a concern, not too conspicuous in many contemporary officials, for the native peoples of India. He was also, like Grant, a man of genuine piety and on his return to England became an unflagging enthusiast for Clapham causes. In 1797, at the conclusion of his term as Governor-General, Shore was made Baron Teignmouth, and brought to the Clapham Sect its sole title.

Henry Thornton, dean of the brotherhood, in many ways resembled Charles Grant. He was calm and judicial but resolute and capable. He had the practical sagacity of a successful man of business. He was not, as is generally recorded, a Governor of the Bank of England. This error seems to have originated in a confusion with Samuel Thornton, Henry's oldest brother, who was a Governor. For a century it has been repeated almost invariably in reference to Thornton and it has found its way even into Leslie Stephen's article on Henry Thornton in the *DNB*. Hayek has shown that this tradition is entirely without foundation.[44] Though not a Governor of the Bank Henry did possess the wide grasp of abstract problems of finance which enabled him to write a classic *Enquiry into Paper Credit*. Long after it was written John Stuart Mill gave his judgment that it was the clearest exposition of the subject written in English; and when, in 1939, 136 years after its first edition, the book was republished, some economists considered that Mill's judgment was still correct.

An unusual company these men were, a group "whose brains and

[42]*Ibid.*, p. 6.
[43]*Cambridge Modern History*, IX, 721.
[44]In his introduction to Henry Thornton's *Enquiry into Paper Credit*, p. 14.

brilliancy could not be denied even by those who sneered at their religion,"[45] and withal a well-balanced group. Sharp and Clarkson and especially Macaulay brought monumental capacity for research; Stephen, destined to be Master in Chancery, expert legal knowledge, and, with Macaulay, first-hand knowledge of the slave trade; Thornton, business sagacity; Grant and Shore, extensive and intimate acquaintance with India, and valuable influence at the source of control; and the retinue of eager associates the necessary personnel to take care of the endless details of the Clapham campaigns.

Having listed all these, it is necessary to return to William Wilberforce, "the Agamemnon of the host . . . the very sun of the Claphamic system."[46] With all the gifts of the others, without Wilberforce they would never have been called a "Sect." Wilberforce needed the others to make him what he was; but the others needed Wilberforce to make a river from a group of pools. Wilberforce was a leader to the manner born. With an ample fortune, a liberal education, and high talents; with a natural eloquence that Pitt declared to be the greatest he ever knew; with a voice that in the melodious beauty of its tones has seldom been surpassed in the history of Parliament, that "resembled an Eolian harp controlled by the touch of a St. Cecilia,"[47] and that earned for him the sobriquet, "the nightingale of the House of Commons"; with graces of personality that made him the darling figure of society, and wit that shone even in the most brilliant company of his brilliant day; with an overflowing capacity for friendship, and yet a fidelity to conscience against which the interests of himself and his friends appealed in vain; with religious convictions that made him indeed harsh with his own infirmities, but that by their transparent sincerity made him the spiritual monitor of men who knew him best; with standards in public life that won for him the adherence of the highest moral feeling of the nation, and marked him as "the authentic keeper of the nation's conscience";[48] with the additional advantage of being the intimate friend of one of Britain's greatest prime ministers;[49] with—it must be admitted—conservative tenden-

---

[45]Balleine, *History of the Evangelical Party,* p. 147.
[46]Sir James Stephen, *Essays in Ecclesiastical Biography,* II, 194.
[47]*Ibid.,* II, 135.
[48]R. Coupland, *Wilberforce,* p. 346.
[49]In the early days of their political life Pitt and Wilberforce were "exactly like brothers." *Life of Wilberforce,* I, 158. Each lived at the other's house as casually as at his own.

cies which sometimes blinded him as to where oppression might lie, but with a burning passion to end oppression where he saw it; with a genuine love of man for himself, and "none of Society's uneasy distaste for the 'lower orders' ";[50] with a mind as wide as the world, and a sympathy which reached out to people not previously considered within the pale of humanity—with all these gifts and graces of character Wilberforce seemed providentially prepared for the task and the time. It was to Wilberforce that Sharp and Clarkson looked when they needed a leader for their cause; it was to Wilberforce that Stephen turned when he came back from the West Indies; it was to Wilberforce that Grant looked to find a champion for his mission schemes. Without Wilberforce all the other men would have been little rivulets in some section of their times; but without Wilberforce the rivulets would never have been gathered into one mighty stream, and harnessed for so many memorable enterprises.[51]

This group of Clapham friends gradually became knit together in an astonishing intimacy and solidarity. They planned and laboured like a committee that never was dissolved. At the Clapham mansions they congregated by common impulse in what they chose to call their "Cabinet Councils" wherein they discussed the wrongs and injustices which were a reproach to their country, and the battles which would need to be fought to establish righteousness. And thereafter, in Parliament and out, they moved as one body, delegating to each man the work he could do best, that their common principles might be maintained and their common purposes be realized.

In private intercourse they lived and acted almost as if they all belonged to an inner circle of one large family. They dwelt in one another's houses almost as a matter of course. Gisborne from Staffordshire, Babington from Leicester, and Simeon from Cambridge lived in the houses at Clapham, just as Wilberforce, Thornton, and Macaulay lived at Yoxall Lodge and Rothley Temple, the homes of Gisborne and Babington. Yoxall Lodge, indeed, was almost a second Clapham, and Wilberforce in 1803 wrote to Gisborne, "I longed to assist in the Cabinet Councils which must have been held at the lodge

[50]Coupland, *Wilberforce*, p. 194.
[51]"Could any moral chemist have compounded an extract of humanity selecting all its choicest and most useful elements, he could not have prepared a being so admirably adapted for the peculiar service he was to render as Wilberforce." George Stephen, *Antislavery Recollections*, p. 78.

when Henry Thornton was with you."[52] With intimate information from those who knew Clapham well, Lady Knutsford wrote:

> It was the custom of the circle . . . to consider every member of that coterie as forming part of a large united family, who should behave to each other with the same simplicity and absence of formality, which, in the usual way, characterizes intercourse only among the nearest relatives. They were in the habit of either assembling at the same watering places during what may ironically be called their holidays, or else spending them at one another's houses, taking with them as a matter of course their wives and children.[53]

They even invited any one they pleased, knowing that whoever would be acceptable to one would be acceptable to all. Then when the holidays were over they assembled as frequently as possible to breakfast at each other's houses, or to discuss plans far into the night. And even when the rush of their busy campaigns kept them in the city during the week they regularly retired to Clapham for the week-end to enjoy the quiet in their exclusive circle, and to listen to the earnest sermons of John Venn, or occasionally to an inspired oration from Gisborne. "It was a remarkable fraternity," says Coupland,

> remarkable above all else, perhaps, in its closeness, its affinity. It not only lived for the most part in one little village; it had one character, one mind, one way of life. . . . It was doubtless this homogeneity, this unanimity that gave the group its power in public life. They might differ on party issues; but on any question of religion or philanthropy the voice of the "Saints" in Parliament or in the press, was as the voice of one man. It was, indeed, a unique phenomenon—this brotherhood of Christian politicians. There has never been anything like it since in British public life.[54]

Yet remarkable as this "brotherhood of Christian politicians," this group of "Saints" might be, it was, as will soon be seen, a very tiny company to stem the current of the times, and to wage the battles that were to come.

[52] *Correspondence of William Wilberforce*, I, 253.
[53] Knutsford, *Zachary Macaulay*, p. 271. E.g., in 1809 Wilberforce casually tells of "halting for five or six days with Henry Thornton, where I carried Mrs. Wilberforce and my six children to the same house in which were now contained his own wife and eight." *Life of Wilberforce*, III, 419. Their houses, in fact, were as near as may be to common property. Thornton died in Wilberforce's house, and Wilberforce's daughter died in Stephen's house. See picture of the Clapham families given *infra*, pp. 168–70.
[54] Coupland, *Wilberforce*, p. 251.

CHAPTER THREE

Am I not a man . . .

THE GREATEST LABOURS of the Clapham Sect
centred on anti-slavery campaigns. The first movement was for the
abolition of the slave trade, that is, the capturing of Negroes in Africa,
and shipping them for sale to the West Indies. The stupendous
difficulty of banning this business can be understood only by knowing
how powerful and how deeply entrenched were the vested interests
which "the Trade"[1] at that time represented.

The English had entered this trade in 1562 when Sir John
Hawkins took a cargo of slaves from Sierra Leone and sold them in
St. Domingo. The English attitude, however, wavered for a while.
In 1618 an agent of the African Chartered Company when offered
slaves declared that the company would not buy "any that had our own
shapes." But after the Restoration Charles II gave a charter to a
company—of which his brother, James, later King of England, was a
member—which proceeded to take 3,000 slaves a year to the West
Indies. From that time the trade grew to enormous proportions. In
1770 out of a total of 100,000 slaves a year from West Africa, British
ships transported more than half; and in 1787 when Wilberforce
began his crusade that percentage was still maintained.

During the latter years of the eighteenth century the slave trade
was thought to be inseparably associated with the commerce and
welfare, and even the national security of Great Britain. It had
brought to British ports a prosperity they had never before known;[2]
it had returned fabulous profits to ship owners and slave traders; it

---

[1] Just as in England "the Trade" now means the Liquor Trade, so then it
meant the Slave Trade.

[2] After the American War the port of Liverpool was making £300,000 a year
from the slave trade. P. A. Brown, *The French Revolution in English History*,
p. 4. "Beyond a doubt it was the slave trade which raised Liverpool from a
struggling port to be one of the richest and most prosperous trading centres of
the world." Ramsay Muir, *History of Liverpool*, p. 195.

had built up an immense plantation system in the West Indies; and it had provided, so the nation believed, admirable training for British seamen, and an essential recruiting ground for the British navy. It alone, according to general conviction, made possible the prosperity and even the solvency of the herring and Newfoundland fisheries, "those great nurseries of seamen,"[3] and of sugar refining and ship building and other associated industries.

In 1791 Colonel Tarleton declared in the House of Commons that "abolition would instantly annihilate a trade, which annually employed upwards of 5,500 sailors, upwards of 160 ships, and whose exports amount to £800,000 sterling; and would undoubtedly bring the West India trade to decay, whose exports and imports amount to upwards of £6,000,000 sterling, and which gave employment to upwards of 160,000 tons of additional shipping, and sailors in proportion."[4] In 1799 the Duke of Clarence said in the House of Lords that "in 1788, the British West India capital amounted to seventy millions sterling; employing 689 vessels, 148,176 tons, navigated by 14,000 seamen. . . . The gross duties to the British empire, £1,800,000. . . . the present British capital in the West Indies, is equal to 100 millions sterling."[5]

The slave trade, in fact, was regarded as peculiarly suited to the necessities of Great Britain. It had been pronounced by statute as "very advantageous to the nation"; it had been patronized by royalty—after the Jacobin scare George III became strongly opposed to the abolitionists; it had been welcomed by the nation as the most coveted reward of successful warfare;[6] it had been legalized by charters (1631, 1633, and 1672), by act of Parliament (1698), and by treaty (1713, 1725, and 1748); and even more significantly, it had flung its far-reaching tentacles around the interests and ambitions of multitudes of ordinary folk. "Almost every order of people," said a Liverpool writer in 1795, "is interested in a Guinea cargo! . . . It is well known that many of the small vessels that import about an hundred slaves are fitted out by attorneys, drapers, ropers, grocers,

[3]Bryan Edwards, *Speech,* delivered in Jamaica, Nov. 19, 1789.
[4]*Parliamentary History,* XXIX, 281.
[5]*Ibid.,* XXXIV, 1105.
[6]In 1713 the *Assiento* of the Treaty of Utrecht, which secured for Britain the right to furnish 4,800 slaves yearly to America, was hailed as a national triumph.

tallow-chandlers, barbers, tailors, etc. . . . Some have one-eighth, some a fifteenth, some a thirty-second share."[7]

The proposal to abolish a trade on which such a wide share of Britain's good fortune seemed directly or indirectly dependent appeared to people of the latter part of the eighteenth century to be prompted by nothing but the wildest and most impracticable idealism.

The slave trade had not then become associated with moral obloquy. In 1783 when Granville Sharp took up the case of the *Zong*, the vessel from which 132 sickly slaves had been thrown overboard so that the owner might profit by the insurance, the Solicitor-General reprobated the "pretended appeals" to "humanity," and asserted that the slaves were "property," and that the master therefore had an unquestioned right to throw overboard as many as he wished without " '*any shew or suggestion of cruelty*,' or a '*surmise of impropriety*.' "[8] The trial demonstrated that after the murder of 132 men the only issue which an English court allowed was the "precise distribution of costs and losses."[9] In 1789 Lord Penrhyn in the House of Commons indignantly maintained that a man might engage in the trade without even an "imputation of inhumanity."[10]

Even people more humanitarian in temper easily reconciled themselves to the unfortunate features of the trade, on the ground of its sheer economic necessity. A London publicist expressed no solitary opinion when he wrote in 1764: "The impossibility of doing without slaves in the West Indies will always prevent this traffic being dropped. The necessity, the absolute necessity, then, of carrying it on, must, since there is no other, be its excuse."[11] In 1791 Mr. Grosvenor in the House of Commons said that the slave trade "was not an amiable trade, but neither was the trade of a butcher an amiable trade, and yet a mutton chop was, nevertheless, a very good thing."[12] And in 1807 Mr. Anthony Brown said in the House of Commons that the slave trade was an evil, but an evil "interwoven with the most important interests of the country."[13] John Wesley in his pamphlet

[7]Muir, *History of Liverpool*, p. 194.
[8]Prince Hoare, *Memoirs of Granville Sharp*, pp. 239-45.
[9]J. Le B. Hammond, *Charles James Fox*, p. 234.
[10]*Parliamentary History*, XXVII, 582.
[11]R. Coupland, *Wilberforce*, p. 75.
[12]*Parliamentary History*, XXIX, 281.
[13]*Parliamentary Debates*, VIII, 1046.

Thoughts upon Slavery had said as early as 1774, "I deny that villainy is ever necessary,"[14] but Wesley's words found no great echo in popular opinion.

Naturally the slave trade had not been prosecuted without protest. Other churchmen than Wesley had denounced it. George Fox had raised his voice against it in 1671, and Richard Baxter in 1680. John Woolman had inspired the Quakers in America with an undying hatred of the idea of slavery. In 1772 the English Quakers had joined with Granville Sharp to establish the principle that in England at least slavery was illegal. Following Wesley's anti-slavery pamphlet the Methodist Conference in 1780 had compelled all their overseas ministers to free their slaves. Dr. Porteus, Bishop of London, in 1783 had preached against slavery to the Society for the Propagation of the Gospel. The Society, however, caught little of the Bishop's spirit. In the next year it decided to forbid Christian instruction to slaves.

Men of letters, too, had spoken as strongly as the churchmen. James Thomson, Daniel Defoe, Adam Smith, William Godwin, Mrs. Aphra Behn, Richard Savage, and Samuel Johnson—all had either directly or indirectly been advocates for the unhappy Negro. And in 1776 David Hartley, son of the metaphysician, had introduced into Parliament the first motion against slavery.

All these did necessary work in cultivating the humanitarian sentiment in which the later movements were to find some starting ground. But they had no sensible effect upon the triumphant progress of the trade itself. They raised, as Wilberforce was later to raise, the considerations of religion and humanity. But not even humanity, much less religion, was then supposed to invade the spheres of commerce and national necessity. "Humanity," exclaimed the Earl of Abingdon in reply to Wilberforce, "is a private feeling, and not a public principle to act upon."[15]

The hard temper of the eighteenth century accepted without qualm that the slave trade itself, whatever incidental evils might be associated with it, was an inevitable part of the economic order, and far too powerful to be overthrown by considerations of abstract principle. Edmund Burke had been afraid to make the trade an issue lest

---

[14]John Wesley, *Thoughts upon Slavery*, p. 35.
[15]*Parliamentary History*, XXX, 657.

it should ruin his party.[16] Pitt, too, with all his early enthusiasm could not venture to make it a party question. Even John Wesley at first did not imagine that it could be legally outlawed; his *Thoughts upon Slavery* advocated only individual action. When Wilberforce first spoke, appeals to justice and mercy, and "enthusiastic" preaching about the worth of souls, seemed pitiably weak to counter the material advantages which the trade returned to its titanic interests. "The sacrifice of Africa was still a 'necessity' for Europeans across the Atlantic. The Trade, indeed, could never satisfy the planters' needs. Conditions of slave-life on the plantations were not conducive to any large natural increase in the stock. Always more imported slaves were wanted, and some day more islands might be British, more land available for cultivation. There seemed no reason why the Trade should ever come to an end."[17]

"Necessity" indeed was presumed to confront every humanitarian objection with an invincible gesture, and while individual protests rose and died away "the Trade" stalked remorselessly on "with a step steady as time, and an appetite keen as death."[18]

OPENING MOVES OF THE CAMPAIGN

Such was the position of the slave trade, and such the mind of England, when, in 1787, William Wilberforce calmly wrote in his diary, "God Almighty has set before me two great objects, the suppression of the slave trade and the reformation of manners." Yet, incredibly enough, never did warrior enter the lists more confidently than Wilberforce. He was optimistic even about a plan to persuade France to agree jointly with England to abolish the trade. He wrote to Sir William Eden, British ambassador in Paris, about negotiations. But Eden was more worldly wise, and replied that he was not "sanguine as to the success of any proposition, however just and right, which must militate against a large host of private interests."[19] Wilberforce was strangely unaware of the real power of the interests he opposed. He thought that he could detect in the Commons "a universal disposition" in his favour, and early in his campaign he

[16]*Life of Wilberforce*, I, 152-3.   [17]Coupland, *Wilberforce*, pp. 84-5.
[18]*Life of Wilberforce*, I, 231.   [19]*Ibid.*, I, 157.

wrote with confident italics, "On the whole . . . *there is no doubt of the success.*"[20]

That early optimism soon suffered rude jolts. In 1788 Wilberforce was extremely ill, so ill that he was not expected to live; and in his place Pitt agreed to introduce to Parliament the matter of the slave trade. On May 9 Pitt moved a resolution binding the House to consider the circumstances of the slave trade early the following session. He spoke in a purposely noncommittal manner. Some members, he said, held that the slave trade should be abolished, others that it only needed different regulations; at least, the question should be considered, and by the next session members would have opportunity to be informed. Pitt's resolution stirred a perfunctory debate. The West Indians[21] remained complacently silent. But their real character was soon revealed. The charges against the slave trade induced some members of Parliament to inspect a slave ship lying in harbour. The sight of the slave quarters, and the apprehension of the unspeakable miseries which the tightly packed slaves must endure in the "Middle Passage,"[22] led Sir William Dolben, one of the party and a close friend of Wilberforce, to introduce into Parliament in the same session a bill to regulate the number of slaves that could be transported in a given tonnage.[23]

A bill of regulation was different from a vague resolution; and the West Indians immediately stirred into action. Lord Penrhyn said that the proposed measure would "abolish the Trade . . . [on which] two-thirds of the commerce of this country depended,"[24] and assured the Commons that the tales of the Middle Passage were begotten in fanaticism and nurtured in falsehood, and that the captive slave looked upon the voyage from Africa as "the happiest period of his life."[25] But they made a tactical error. Their haughty assumption that the trade must not be subject to any legislation whatever was more than Pitt could stand. He spoke indignantly against this attitude

[20]Coupland, *Wilberforce,* p. 100.
[21]The agents and connections of the slave trade were called the "West Indians" in contrast with the "Nabobs" who represented the powerful vested interests of East India.
[22]The route of the slave ships from the Guinea Coast to the West Indies lay entirely within the tropical belt, in the "Middle Passage."
[23]*Parliamentary History,* XXVII, 573.
[24]*Ibid.,* p. 589.   [25]*Ibid.,* p. 592.

in the Commons, he browbeat the Lords by threatening to resign from the cabinet, and thus forced the bill through both houses.

That unexpected defeat awakened the slave interests to the new danger, and created a storm of opposition to the abolitionists. Wilberforce was assaulted on all grounds, political and moral. Gisborne wrote to him: "I shall expect to read in the newspapers of your being carbonadoed by West Indian planters, barbecued by African merchants, and eaten by Guinea captains; but do not be daunted, for—I will write your epitaph."[26] The virulent attack opened the eyes of the abolitionists to the nature of the task they were undertaking.

Undaunted, however, Wilberforce, on recovering from his illness, continued to pursue his campaign, and on May 12 of the next year, 1789, he introduced his motion on the slave trade in his first speech to Parliament on the subject.[27] As an illustration of the ground of his indictment against the slave trade and the method of his attack upon it, it is well to quote from Hansard his opening sentences and some characteristic passages:

When I consider the magnitude of the subject which I am to bring before the House—a subject, in which the interests, not of this country, nor of Europe alone, but of the whole world, and of posterity, are involved: and when I think, at the same time, on the weakness of the advocate who has undertaken this great cause—when these reflections press upon my mind, it is impossible for me not to feel both terrified and concerned at my own inadequacy to such a task. But when I reflect, however, on the encouragement which I have had, through the whole course of a long and laborious examination of this question, how much candour I have experienced, and how conviction has increased within my own mind, in proportion as I have advanced in my labours;—when I reflect, especially, that however averse any gentleman may now be, yet we shall all be of one opinion in the end;—when I turn myself to these thoughts, I take courage—I determine to forget all my other fears, and I march forward with a firmer step in the full assurance that my cause will bear me out, and that I shall be able to justify, upon the clearest principles, every resolution in my hand, the avowed end of which is, the total abolition of the slave trade. . . . I mean not to accuse any one, but to take the shame upon myself, in common, indeed, with the whole parliament of Great Britain, for having suffered this horrid trade

26 *Life of Wilberforce*, I, 218.   27 *Parliamentary History*, XXVIII, 41-67.

to be carried on under their authority. We are all guilty—we ought all to plead guilty, and not to exculpate ourselves by throwing the blame on others; and I therefore deprecate every kind of reflection against the various descriptions of people who are more immediately involved in this wretched business. . . .

In a terrible indictment of conditions on slave ships Wilberforce stated that the mortality during the passage and in the "seasoning" period after landing amounted to "about fifty per cent. and this among negroes who are not bought unless quite healthy at first, and unless (as the phrase is with cattle) they are sound in wind and limb." "As soon as ever I had arrived thus far in my investigation of the slave trade . . . so enormous, so dreadful, so irremediable did its wickedness appear that my own mind was completely made up for the abolition. A trade founded in iniquity, and carried on as this was, must be abolished, let the policy be what it might. . . ." He then went on to deal with the argument that the abolition would ruin the West Indies. "If the ruin of the West-Indies threatened us on the one hand, while this load of wickedness pressed upon us on the other, the alternative, indeed, was awful" but he was prepared to "prove, by authentic evidence, that, in truth, the West Indies have nothing to fear from the total and immediate abolition of the slave trade." After an extensive review of West Indian trade Wilberforce launched his final appeal for the Negroes.

When we consider the vastness of the continent of Africa; when we reflect how all other countries have for some centuries past been advancing in happiness and civilization; when we think how in this same period all improvement in Africa has been defeated by her intercourse with Britain; when we reflect it is we ourselves that have degraded them to that wretched brutishness and barbarity which we now plead as the justification of our guilt; how the slave trade has enslaved their minds, blackened their character, and sunk them so low in the scale of animal beings, that some think the very apes are of a higher class, and fancy the ourang-outang has given them the go-by. What a mortification must we feel at having so long neglected to think of our guilt, or to attempt any reparation! It seems, indeed, as if we had determined to forbear from all interference until the measure of our folly and wickedness was so full and complete: until the impolicy which eventually belongs to vice,

was become so plain and glaring, that not an individual in the country
should refuse to join in the abolition; it seems as if we had waited until
the persons most interested should be tired out with the folly and
nefariousness of the trade, and should unite in petitioning against it.

Let us then make such amends as we can for the mischiefs we have
done to that unhappy continent: let us recollect what Europe itself was
no longer ago than three or four centuries. What if I should be able to
show this House that in a civilized part of Europe, in the time of our
Henry 7 there were people who actually sold their own children? what, if
I should tell them that England itself was that country? what, if I
should point out to them that the very place where this inhuman traffic
was carried on, was the city of Bristol? Ireland at that time used to
drive a considerable trade in slaves with these neighbouring barbarians;
but a great plague having infested the country, the Irish were struck
with a panic, suspected (I am sure very properly) that the plague was a
punishment sent from Heaven, for the sin of the slave trade, and therefore abolished it. All I ask, therefore, of the people of Bristol, is, that
they would become as civilized now, as Irishmen were four hundred
years ago.

Sir, the nature and all the circumstances of this trade are now laid open
to us; we can no longer plead ignorance. . . . it is brought now so directly
before our eyes, that this House must decide, and must justify to all the
world, and to their own consciences, the rectitude of the grounds and
principles of their decision. A society has been established for the
abolition of this trade, in which dissenters, quakers, churchmen . . . have
all united. . . . Let not parliament be the only body that is insensible to
the principles of national justice. Let us make reparation to Africa . . .
and we shall soon find the rectitude of our conduct rewarded, by the
benefits of a regular and a growing commerce.

These imperfect fragments from a report which Wilberforce
himself declared was inaccurate cannot reproduce more than the
feeblest echo of a speech which was accounted one of the finest in
the golden age of parliamentary oratory. Burke said that "the House,
the nation, and Europe, were under great and serious obligations
to the hon. gentleman for having brought forward the subject in a
manner the most masterly, impressive, and eloquent. The principles
were so well laid down, and supported with so much force and order,
that it equalled any thing he had heard in modern times, and was

not perhaps to be surpassed in the remains of Grecian eloquence."[28]

Eloquence was not enough. The West Indians had summoned the resources at their control, and, although Wilberforce was supported by Pitt, Fox, and Burke, even such giants could not prevail against the interests of commerce. The Commons voted to postpone action—an expedient that was to find ample imitation in the years that followed.[29]

In his defeat Wilberforce had learned one useful lesson. He had no body of informed opinion to which he could appeal, and no adequate source of reliable information. His campaign would not prosper as long as men could talk about the Middle Passage as providing the "happiest period" of a slave's life. The first condition of success was wider knowledge. And it was in his search for knowledge that Wilberforce began to gather about him his "Clapham Sect."

Clarkson had been invaluable from the beginning, both for gathering evidence and for writing letters and pamphlets and spreading information. But Wilberforce needed still other labourers. He had already called in William Smith to help in watching the inquiries which the Privy Council and the House of Commons had instituted into the conduct of the slave trade. Together with Smith he had hovered around watching and assisting his witnesses, until he had been almost exhausted by the labour.[30] And when the inquiries were ended there were hundreds of pages of evidence to be read and analysed, and sifted for future use. With the multitudinous other calls upon his time Wilberforce was overwhelmed. So gradually he began to enlist a larger company of co-workers.

In October 1790 he joined with Babington and went to Gisborne's house, Yoxall Lodge, where the two remained for a month working together in retirement nine hours a day, reading and abridging evidence. In November he was called back to London to enter again into the old political life and bustle. But early in the spring he retired once more, this time to the "rural fastness" of Thornton's house at Clapham where he resumed his work on the evidence. He even continued working through Sunday. "Spent Sunday as a work-

---

[28]*Life of Wilberforce*, I, 219.   [29]*Parliamentary History*, XXVIII, 101.
[30]"I am almost worn out, and I pant for a little country air, and quiet."
Life of Wilberforce, I, 271.

ing day—did not go to church—Slave Trade" is an unusual entry in his diary.[31] Soon he wrote for further help from Babington: "Without shame or remorse I call on you to assist us in epitomizing the evidence. . . . You may be allowed a little . . . discretion . . . but you must be very reserved in the exercise of it. . . . In about a month I conceive I shall make my motion. Let me know how your engagements stand, that I may contrive to avail myself of your help whether in town or country."[32]

After exhaustive preparation Wilberforce composed a speech which he delivered in the House in 1791 in moving for "leave to bring in a Bill to prevent the further importation of slaves into the British islands in the West Indies." The speech bore witness to the long labours of investigation. It was, says Coupland, "the clearest, most circumstantial, and yet most succinct account, given then or since, of the case against the Slave Trade."[33] As usual, he began in a conciliatory tone (the report in *Parliamentary History* is, as so often, largely in the third person):

He wished to treat the subject with all the candour and fairness possible, and had always distinguished that which belonged to the cause from that which belonged to the persons. He was free to say, and he wished rather to say it then, when he was cool, lest it might be supposed afterwards that, in the warmth of debate, he maintained a contrary doctrine, that the parties immediately concerned, had conducted themselves towards him with great candour, and he thanked them for the fairness with which they had considered his propositions; and even those who had taken the most active part in the business, had shown that liberality of mind, which, at the same time that it was most grateful to his feelings, was a good omen to the cause.

Wilberforce then made a comprehensive survey of the nature and extent of the slave trade. He dealt once more with the manner in which the slaves were obtained on the coast of Africa, with the "oppression, fraud, treachery and blood" which corrupted the moral principles of those who carried on the trade. After a bitter indictment of a trade so evil that it was good to "turn our eyes for relief to some ordinary wickedness" he proceeded to make a survey of slave conditions in the West Indies. He made ample use of the material col-

[31]*Ibid.*, p. 290.   [32]*Ibid.*, p. 289.   [33]Coupland, *Wilberforce,* p. 141.

lected by his researchers in presenting a terrible sequence of authenticated facts. Among the instances he cited was one "where a master had cruelly cut the mouth of a child of six years old, almost from ear to ear, yet so strange and so novel a doctrine did it appear to the jury that a master was liable to punishment for any act of cruelty exercised on a slave that they brought in a conditional verdict 'Guilty, subject to the opinion of the court, if immoderate correction of a slave by his master be a crime indictable.' "

Wilberforce went on to declare that he was comparatively indifferent as to the immediate decision of the House. Great Britain, he was confident, would abolish the slave trade when its injustice and cruelty should be clearly known.

Let us not . . . despair; it is a blessed cause, and success, ere long, will crown our exertions. Already we have gained one victory; we have obtained, for these poor creatures, the recognition of their human nature, which, for a while, was most shamefully denied. This is the first fruits of our efforts; let us persevere, and our triumph will be complete. Never, never will we desist till we have wiped away this scandal from the Christian name, released ourselves from the load of guilt, under which we at present labour, and extinguished every trace of this bloody traffic, of which our posterity, looking back to the history of these enlightened times, will scarce believe that it has been suffered to exist so long a disgrace and dishonour to this country.[34]

Once again eloquence was not enough and though Wilberforce again had the support of the giants—Pitt, Burke, and Fox all gave powerful speeches in his support—the trade was still too strong. Drake, an anti-abolitionist, warned the House to beware of being carried away by "the meteors they had been dazzled with." "The leaders, it was true," he said, "were for the abolition; but the minor orators, the dwarfs, the pigmies, would . . . this day carry the question against them."[35] "Commerce clinked its purse,"[36] and after a two-day battle Wilberforce was defeated.

With that defeat Wilberforce and his workers began a new phase of their labour. Their first aim had been to convince Parliament, and, by dint of their combined labour, they had drawn from authentic

[34]*Parliamentary History*, XXIX, 250-78.
[35]*Ibid.*, p. 358.   [36]*Letters of Horace Walpole*, XIV, 418.

evidence a damning picture of the slave trade. But they were painfully aware that Parliament had been little moved by their laborious attempt. Their efforts had recoiled helplessly against the "multitude of silent votes," subservient to vested interests. Once after General Tarleton had defended the interests of the slave owners in Parliament he pointed to some of his Liverpool constituents in the gallery and exclaimed, "There are my masters."[37]

All the workers were being gradually convinced that their only hope lay in an appeal from Parliament to the people, an appeal that would be viewed with little favour in eighteenth-century England. Wilberforce at first had been suspicious of such tactics. He approved of promoting petitions to Parliament, and had encouraged Clarkson in that work. He also had kept his house in Palace Yard open to friends of abolition, and had neglected no means of winning persons of distinction. In his first labours, however, Wilberforce "distrusted and disowned the questionable strength which might be gained by systematic agitation." He did not then favour the use either of corresponding societies or of public meetings. But he was to be taught by his cause. He found that his hope lay only in the people; and in a short time he and his friends became the most persistent agitators in all Britain. "It is on the general impression and feeling of the nation we must rely," Wilberforce confessed early in 1792. "So let the flame be fanned. . . ."[38]

The flame was fanned accordingly. New experiments were attempted. Even before this time the abolitionists had adopted unusual methods of propaganda. One of Wilberforce's friends had suggested the employment of Gibbon as an anti-slavery propagandist, observing that "a fee would be a sufficient motive." This experiment, however, seems not to have been tried. But Cowper's poem, *The Negro's Complaint,* had been printed on expensive paper and circulated by the thousand in fashionable circles, and afterwards set to music and sung everywhere as a popular ballad. Wedgwood, the celebrated potter, had made another effective contribution to the cause. He designed a cameo showing, on a white background, a Negro kneeling in supplication, while he utters the plea to become so famous, "Am I not a man and a brother?" This cameo, copied on such articles as snuff boxes

[37]*Life of Wilberforce,* II, 147.
[38]*Ibid.,* I, 334.

and ornamental hairpins, became the rage all over England and specimens can still be seen in the ceramics section of the British Museum.

Clarkson now set out on a tour of the country, stirring up petitions, circulating pamphlets, arranging public meetings, and leaving in his wake a trail of corresponding societies.[39] "Great pains were taken by interested persons in many places to prevent public meetings. But no efforts could avail. The current ran with such strength and rapidity, that it was impossible to stem it."[40] It is difficult now to think that public meetings in themselves could be opposed as radical, but they were. Wilberforce wrote to Gisborne in 1792, "Consult topic 'Aristocratism,' and you will find that all great men hate public meetings."[41]

The more enthusiastic campaigners began also to organize a boycott of slave-grown sugar. Babington and William Smith were strongly in favour of the boycott, and themselves maintained it strictly; but Wilberforce remained doubtful of such a policy. The novel tactics, however, had unexpected success. Following his tour in 1792 Clarkson said that there was no town through which he passed in which some persons had not left off the use of sugar. He estimated that 300,000 people had abandoned its use.[42]

All these devices created for the abolitionists publicity which they were now determined to exploit to the full. "The best course," Wilberforce had written, "will be to endeavour to excite the flame as much as possible in a secret way, but not to allow it more than to smother until after I shall have given notice of my intention of bringing the subject forward. This must be the signal for the fire's bursting forth."[43] Like well-oiled machinery the organization was set in readiness, and when Wilberforce gave the signal it was set in motion. As by magic, petitions multiplied all over Britain; and with admirable timeliness on the day, April 2, 1792, on which Wilberforce introduced a definite motion that the slave trade "ought to be abolished," there was laid on the table of the House of Commons the last of 519 petitions for the total abolition of the slave trade.[44] "Never before had the politically passive, quiescent, oligarchic Britain of the eighteenth century witnessed such a lively and widespread movement. It had shown how

---

[39]Thomas Clarkson, *History of Abolition*, II, 351-2.   [40]*Ibid.*, p. 353.
[41]*Life of Wilberforce*, I, 336.   [42]Clarkson, *History of Abolition*, II, 349-50.
[43]*Life of Wilberforce*, I, 333-4.   [44]Clarkson, *History of Abolition*, II, 355.

much could be done to mobilize public opinion outside the walls of Parliament, yet strictly within the liberties of the constitution. It was a new and a great fact in British politics."[45]

But a new and formidable obstacle had been created. The French Revolution had begun to arouse in the ruling classes of England a reaction of terror. Moreover in the French colony of St. Domingo the Negroes had broken out in a terrible revolt. In English minds the talk of freedom for slaves seemed too closely associated with the "Liberty, Equality, Fraternity," hoarsely shouted in the streets of Paris. The aristocratic House of Commons had no liking whatever for the public meetings, the corresponding societies, the boycott, and the petitions of the preceding weeks. The majority of its members felt that all the talk about freedom and brotherhood was a dangerous business; and they were determined to establish an effective barrier to the whole movement.

They were obliged, however, to change their method. The patient researches of Wilberforce and his "white Negroes" had been so effectively stripping the coverings from the iniquities of the slave trade that even its defenders could no longer deny the conditions. They chose a more subtle expedient. They now admitted that the trade itself was undesirable, and pleaded only that a too sudden prohibition would create a calamitous dislocation of business, and run counter to "the sacred attention parliament had ever shown to the interests of individuals."[46] So in 1792 when Wilberforce introduced in Parliament his motion for abolition he found himself met not by opposition to his aim, but by a plea against the perils of a too hasty move towards it.

His speech was powerful enough to disturb even his most obstinate opponent. It was perhaps more horrifying than any previous one in its detailed description of the inhumanities of the trade. As usual, he began on a note of conciliation. "He professed himself desirous of now holding no other language than that of conciliation. . . . He wished not to be misunderstood, so as that it should be supposed, when he reprobated a system, he also reprobated individuals; he hoped that the cause of justice and humanity would be kept distinct from all personal considerations." Nevertheless he went on to declare that

the more he deliberated on the subject of this nefarious traffic the
more he was convinced that it ought to exist no longer. He called
once more on the discoveries of his researchers and massed a terrible
indictment of the slave trade.

In the year 1788 in a ship in this trade, 650 persons were on board, out
of whom 155 died. In another, 405 were on board, out of whom were
lost 200. In another there were on board 450, out of whom 200 died; in
another, there were on board 402, out of whom 73 died. When captain
Wilson was asked the causes of this mortality, he replied, that the slaves
had a fixed melancholy and dejection; that they wished to die; that they
refused all sustenance, till they were beaten in order to compel them to
eat; and that, when they had been so beaten, they looked in the faces of
the whites, and said, piteously, "Soon we shall be no more." They sometimes threw themselves overboard; but were in general prevented by the
high netting placed on purpose to restrain them; and such a death they
called an escape. This melancholy, and its attendant disorders mocked
all attempts at relief. The wretches on board the ships died sometimes
of insanity, sometimes of starvation; and sometimes they were drowned.
. . . He could have wished to drop for ever all recital of facts which
tended to prove the cruelty of those who dealt in this abominable traffic;
but there was an instance which he could not omit. . . . The instance . . .
was the case of a young girl of fifteen, of extreme modesty, who finding
herself in a situation incident to her sex, was extremely anxious to conceal
it. The captain of the vessel, instead of encouraging so laudable a disposition, tied her by the wrist, and placed her in a position so as to make
her a spectacle to the whole crew. In this situation he beat her; but not
thinking the exhibition he had made sufficiently conspicuous, he tied
her up by the legs and then also beat her. But his cruel ingenuity was
not yet exhausted, for he next tied her up by one leg, after which she
lost all sensation, and in the course of three days she expired. This was
an indisputable fact, [Name, name, name! resounded from all parts of
the House] Captain Kimber was the man. . . . this was not a singular
instance, there were proofs, beyond all dispute, of many others. . . .

   Mr. Wilberforce concluded by saying, that, in his exertions for the
present cause, he had found happiness, though not hitherto success . . .
that he . . . had the bliss of remembering, that he had demanded justice
for millions, who could not ask it for themselves.[47]

   All in vain was the powerful plea. Though Fox once more brought

[47]*Ibid.*, 1055-73.

his lurid eloquence to the battle, though Pitt, at six in the morning, concluded the debate with the greatest speech of his career, again the power of vested interests prevailed, and the House voted that Wilberforce's motion in favour of abolition should be qualified by the word *gradually*. Knowing full well the possibilities of that word a majority then voted cheerfully for the amended motion.[48]

Here was another defeat for Wilberforce. Yet the defeat was not absolute. Gisborne and Babington, who were watching their master from the gallery, hailed it as an omen of success. For the first time a motion for abolition had actually been carried in the House of Commons. And the defenders of the trade, formerly so confident, had been, as Isaac Milner wrote to Wilberforce, "plainly overawed and ashamed." Moreover, something was retrieved from the defeat. When the question was again discussed in the Commons on April 23 and 27 amendments were introduced which set definite dates, at first the year 1800 and finally 1796, only four years ahead, for abolition.[49] "On the whole," wrote Wilberforce, "matters have turned out better than I expected. . . ."[50]

The first success was not to be continued. Unfortunately for Wilberforce's brotherhood, at the very time they had determined to pit the strength of the people against the power of the vested interests in Parliament, the people themselves succumbed to the fear which had first manifested itself in the upper classes. After the horror of the "September Massacres" in 1792 the dread of revolution spread even to liberal sections of English opinion, and there again expressed itself in immediate and unreasoning fear of all reform. The agitation of 1792 could not be maintained in 1793. Wilberforce reported that "a damp and odium" had fallen on the idea of "collective applications."[51] The voice of England, which had spoken so strongly a few months before, was now strangely silent—and where it was not silent it was often tinged with a suspicious accent. "I do not imagine," wrote a correspondent from Yorkshire, "that we could meet with twenty persons in Hull at present who would sign a petition, that are not republicans."[52] It seemed, indeed, that many of the enthusiasts for abolition were people of Jacobinical tendencies. At any rate the

[48]*Ibid.*, 1158.   [49]*Ibid.*, 1293.
[50]*Life of Wilberforce*, I, 347.   [51]*Ibid.*, II, 19.
[52]*Ibid.*, p. 18.

abolitionists had shown a disturbing insensibility to the sacredness of property; and they had been audaciously endeavouring to repudiate the considered decisions of Parliament. Encouragement of such a temper was exceedingly dangerous. The eager whisper of the trade magnified the suggestion. The Revolution, in fact, had furnished the trade with just the weapon it needed. As in our day a common strategy to discredit a social programme is to call it Communistic, so at that time a common strategy was to call it Jacobinical. Under the taint of that label the abolition movement lost caste. In 1793 the Commons were not defying public opinion when they rejected Wilberforce's motion for further consideration of abolition of the trade.[53] And the Lords were merely capitalizing on the current temper when they made a savage attack on the whole question of abolition, as a subversive manifestation of republican principles. "What does the abolition of the slave trade mean?" asked the Earl of Abingdon fiercely, "more or less in effect, than liberty and equality? what more or less than the rights of man? and what is liberty and equality; and what the right of man, but the foolish fundamental principles of this new philosophy?"[54]

The cloud of republicanism had settled upon the Clapham Sect, and, though they did not know it, many long years were to elapse before they would be able to move from out its shadow.

THE SIERRA LEONE EXPERIMENT

Meanwhile far away from Paris and Westminster the Clapham Sect were engaged in another enterprise closely linked with their labours for abolition.

Some of the results of Granville Sharp's victory in freeing the slaves in England had not been anticipated. About 14,000 slaves were freed, and many of them, seeking a livelihood in the cities, were soon reduced to utter poverty. The streets of London began to swarm with black beggars, and about four hundred appealed personally to Sharp for assistance.[55] In 1786 a Committee for Relieving the Black Poor was formed to look after some of these unfortunates. During that year

[53] *Parliamentary History*, XXX, 520.   [54] *Ibid.*, p. 564.
[55] Hoare, *Memoirs of Granville Sharp*, p. 260. A good account of the Sierra Leone settlement, and especially of Granville Sharp's connection with it, is given in pp. 257-379.

a Dr. Henry Smeathman, who had spent some time in Sierra Leone, conceived the idea of establishing a colony of these Negroes in that place. The idea appealed to the abolitionists because it offered a means of demonstrating how Africa could develop under civilization and Christianity, and to the Government because it provided an un-expected means of getting rid of an awkward problem. Government aid was therefore given to the project, and in the spring of 1787 Sharp despatched a contingent of four hundred Negroes to establish a colony on the coasts of Sierra Leone.

All the ills that naturally beset a new colony were aggravated by the dissolute nature of the colonists and the unfortunate blunders of the promoters. By the end of the first year nearly half the settlers had died, and the remaining half were saved from starvation only by a cargo of provisions sent out chiefly at Sharp's personal charge. Toward the end of the second year, 1789, in revenge for the atrocities of British slave raiders, a native chief burned the settlement to the ground.

Even these reverses could not daunt the intrepid Sharp. He merely summoned his Clapham friends to recommence the work. In 1790 they formed the St. George's Bay[56] Association, which in the next year was incorporated as the Sierra Leone Company. Of this company Sharp was President and Henry Thornton, Chairman; Wilberforce, Grant, Lord Teignmouth, and Babington were among the directors,[57] and Simeon, Gisborne, and Charles Elliott among the interested members.[58]

Wilberforce's diary for 1791 shows his concern with the Company:

[October] "17th, Monday. Grant dined with us at H. Thornton's, and we discussed Sierra Leone. 18th. Meeting of directors at H. Thornton's. Dined there together and sat evening till late. . . . 20th. Directors at H. Thornton's all morning. . . . Returned to meeting at Thornton's, where only excellent Granville Sharpe [sic]. . . ."

[December] "15th. At work on Sierra Leone business most of the day.

---

[56]St. George's Bay was the name given by the first expedition to the harbor of Sierra Leone.
[57]*Correspondence of Wilberforce*, II, 510.
[58]Charles Hole, *Early History of the C.M.S.*, p. 18.

H. Thornton has been at it the whole day for some months.[59] 16th. Worked at Sierra Leone business preparing the Report."

"All this week at Sierra Leone business, and therefore staid in the city with H. Thornton. . . . Grant with us always at Thornton's—chosen director on Tuesday."[60]

Thereafter the brotherhood cherished this Company as one of their most important and significant projects, and gave to it much care and labour, and many anxious consultations in the oval room at Thornton's. Sharp, Wilberforce, and Grant especially gave their attention to it; but, most of all, Henry Thornton took it up as his specific responsibility. He wrote in 1791: "The colony works me from morning till night; the importance of the thing strikes me, and fills my mind so much that, at present, business, politics, friendship, seem all suspended for the sake of it."[61] Later Colquhoun wrote: "His [Thornton's] was the directing mind. He devised the plan; he formed the Company; he collected the capital; he arranged the constitution; he chose, equipped, and despatched the settlers; he selected and sent out the governor. . . . In every difficulty the appeal was to him. He obtained grants of money from Parliament; . . . when the colony passed on to the Crown, it was he who arranged the terms."[62]

The Sierra Leone Company made a valiant attempt to retrieve the fortunes of the unhappy colony. They sent out an expedition in 1791 which gathered together the sixty-four survivors, and soon augmented them by over one thousand Negroes from Nova Scotia.[63] But Sierra Leone was to be the land of historic misfortune. Catastrophe after catastrophe—ants and malaria, fire and insurrection— successively devastated the settlement. Irretrievable disaster was avoided only by the resources of the Clapham Sect itself.

Zachary Macaulay had now returned from the West Indies, and, introduced by Babington, had commended himself favourably to the

[59] Wilberforce was then with Gisborne at Yoxall Lodge, and Grant and Thornton had come for him unexpectedly to take him back to the city about the Sierra Leone business.

[60] Life of Wilberforce, I, 316, 322, 325.

[61] Henry Morris, Founders of the Bible Society, p. 65.

[62] John C. Colquhoun, Wilberforce and His Friends, p. 286.

[63] These Negroes had fought for the British in the American War, and in return had been set free in Nova Scotia; they found the climate too rigorous, and begged to be transported to Africa. However, there are substantial numbers of Negroes now living and thriving in Nova Scotia, the descendants of those who fled to Canada for freedom in the days of the "Underground Railway."

group. Thornton especially seems to have been keeping his eye on the
young man and with Babington to have sent the new recruit to
Sierra Leone on a tour of inspection. The directors of the Sierra Leone
Company were favourably impressed with Macaulay's work. When he
returned from the tour in 1792 Wilberforce wrote to Babington: "I
will by no means forget Macaulay. I think highly of his understanding; he appears to have a manly, collected mind."[64] Shortly afterwards, the brotherhood sent Macaulay back as second member of the
Sierra Leone council. Soon after his arrival he became, at the age
of twenty-six, Governor of the colony.

Macaulay had to be not only Governor, but commercial agent,
paymaster, judge, clerk, and even chaplain.[65] He had to write long
official reports to the directors, and additional long private letters to
Thornton, which in the intimacy of the group Wilberforce considered
as sent equally to him. Macaulay was so constantly overworked that
his health began to suffer; yet he held on, foiled an attempted insurrection, and disciplined the colony into respectable order. But in 1794
came the consummation of calamity. A roving squadron of French
Jacobins, piloted by an angered American slave captain, attacked the
town, plundered its inhabitants, burnt most of the Company's property, and left the luckless colonists on the verge of starvation.
Macaulay acted with extraordinary self-possession and intrepid
courage, and succeeded in rallying the dismayed settlers to the work of
reconstruction. But the strain and the excessive labours injured his
health, so that shortly afterwards he was compelled to return to
England.

Characteristically Macaulay turned even this necessity to good
account. He had received from Wilberforce a letter asking for "damning proof" of the evil character of the slave trade. He now decided,
though at a risk which might well give pause even to the healthiest
man, to secure his own proof at first hand. By some means he
managed to arrange a passage to Barbados on a slave ship.[66] Thence,
furnished with information invaluable to the brotherhood, he found
other passage to England, where after such signal service "he was
admitted at once and for ever within the innermost circle of friends

[64]*Correspondence of Wilberforce,* I, 93; II, 510.
[65]*Christian Observer,* 1839, p. 761.
[66]*Ibid.,* 1804, p. 344.

and fellow labourers who were united round Wilberforce and Henry Thornton."[67] These two men took early opportunity of introducing their protégé to that associate member of their "little confederacy" Mrs. Hannah More. On a visit to Mrs. More Macaulay fell in love with one of her pupils, Miss Selina Mills, who before the end of his furlough became his betrothed, and who, on his final return from Africa, became his wife.[68]

Macaulay remained in England nearly a year, living mainly with the Babingtons, though, of course, he made "long and frequent" visits to Wilberforce and Thornton, both at their London houses and at Thornton's famous villa in Clapham, where Wilberforce and Thornton were then living together. Early in 1796 he returned again to his arduous labours in Sierra Leone, where he was fortified by numerous letters of advice and criticism, but also of unvarying kindness, from the brotherhood at home. Macaulay was the junior member of the Sect and all the others felt constrained to give him counsel. He told Miss Mills of a letter from Babington, and added, "Nor was it the less acceptable for containing much faithful admonition and kind reproof."[69] Again he mentioned a letter from Henry Thornton, "in which were only eight lines," but which was yet long enough to give him "the satisfaction of knowing that he had nothing particularly to blame; a negative, but from Henry Thornton no mean praise."[70]

After continuing his labour for three years Macaulay returned to England in 1799 to assume the duties of Secretary to the Company. He took with him twenty-one African boys and four girls, to be educated and returned to Africa as missionaries. The plan had been proposed and financed by Robert Haldane of Scotland, who intended to take the children to Edinburgh. But when Macaulay learned more fully of the religious and political views of Haldane "his conviction became irrevocable that under no circumstances should Mr. Haldane have any share in training the minds or influencing the fate of the children." Macaulay coolly proposed that Haldane should continue to meet the expense, and be allowed "due" weight in general direction of the scheme. But Haldane, not surprisingly, refused the gracious

[67]G. O. Trevelyan, *Life of Lord Macaulay*, I, 20.
[68]Knutsford, *Zachary Macaulay*, pp. 92-115.
[69]*Ibid.*, p. 170.
[70]G. W. E. Russell, *The Household of Faith*, p. 226.

offer, and washed his hands of the whole affair. The friends at Clapham then formed the Society for the Education of Africans, which, largely financed by themselves, undertook the care and the cost of the children's education. Unfortunately the majority of the children succumbed to the English climate; but with the survivors, "some good was accomplished. They carried out to Africa many of the arts of civilized life. Whilst at Clapham they convinced Mr. Pitt that the African race is not naturally inferior to the European." Haldane and Macaulay, it deserves to be said, worked cordially together in later years.[71]

Despite the series of reverses Macaulay had saved the colony from impending disaster and established it on a permanent basis. After the French raid the chastened Negroes became more amenable to discipline. Before Macaulay left there were in Freetown, the main settlement, three hundred houses and twelve hundred inhabitants, who had attained a comfortable measure of prosperity. Macaulay's experience, however, had shown the need of a different constitution, with more adequate provision for legislation and the administration of justice. The directors therefore made application for a charter, and in 1800 transformed their little venture into the first of those chartered companies that were in the next century to play such a significant part in the development of Africa. In 1808 they took a still further step: Henry Thornton arranged the transfer of Sierra Leone to the Crown, and made it the first Crown Colony in Africa.

Financially the Sierra Leone Company was not a success. Thornton himself lost £2,000 to £3,000 on the venture, but from what he saw accomplished felt that he was "on the whole a gainer."[72] The Company was indeed formed with "no expectation of mercantile advantage." It was "really a great Missionary Society."

When the colony passed from the immediate control of Clapham it did not, however, cease to be of service. It remained an important base for missionary enterprise. Later when the slave trade was made illegal it became the home for victims rescued from pirate slavers. Altogether 18,000 liberated slaves, the displaced persons of these

[71]Hoare, *Memoirs of Granville Sharp*, p. 296. Knutsford, *Zachary Macaulay*, p. 224. For a discussion of the Haldane controversy see *ibid.*, pp. 201, 223-5; Alexander Haldane, *Memoirs of Robert Haldane and James Alexander Haldane*, pp. 249-53.
[72]*DNB*, "Henry Thornton."

earlier days, were received in Sierra Leone by 1825. In 1821 the colony became the headquarters of the British colonial government along the west coast of Africa, "a government which was one day to prove the first and most powerful and most persistent instrument for the suppression of the Slave Trade throughout the dark interior of Africa."[73]

But even in the earlier days something had been achieved. In spite of all the calamities the Clapham Sect could with some justification boast that their project had "displayed the superior advantages of English law and English justice on a shore where England had been only known for crimes and named for execration."[74]

The Lean Years

Sierra Leone had not diverted the Clapham campaigners from their old battle for the abolition of the slave trade. After 1793, indeed, anti-slavery labour became increasingly difficult and unpopular. The decade from 1794 to 1804 was a long period of accumulating defeat. Even the Abolition Committee languished. It held only two meetings a year for 1795, 1796, 1797, and after that no meetings at all until it was reorganized in 1804. But year after year till 1800 in persistent defiance of unvarying defeat Wilberforce introduced into Parliament his annual motion for abolition. He knew that men disliked it, but he would not allow them to forget it. Through all the lean years, in ill report far more than good, he and his faithful company fought doggedly for their goal, often flatly defeated, but occasionally gaining some small ground.

In 1794 Wilberforce managed to carry in the Commons a bill to abolish the supplying of slaves to foreign nations. But the House of Lords, where Abingdon warned the bishops that the bill contained seeds of "other abolitions," and suggested that they might look to their own downfall, threw out the bill with only four votes in its favour.

The next year, 1795, brought a sudden change in Wilberforce's position in Parliament. Two years earlier the French Republic had

[73]Coupland, *Wilberforce*, p. 279.
[74]Hoare, *Memoirs of Granville Sharp*, p. 310. Ironically enough in the Protectorate of Sierra Leone (seven times larger than the colony) which came under British oversight but was not subject to British law "all efforts to bring about an abolition of slave-owning failed until 1928." Lady Simon, *Slavery*, p. 61.

declared war on England. At the time Wilberforce had supported
Pitt in the waging of the war. Wilberforce was not an extreme pacifist.
He was not for peace at any price; but he was for peace any time it
was possible. In 1794 after the fall of Robespierre and the end of the
Reign of Terror Wilberforce believed that the English Government
should immediately seek to negotiate a peace. He had much support
among the sect. Toward the end of the year the issue began to appear
in his diary.

[December] "19th. . . . strongly at present disposed to peace. Talked
much politics with Gisborne, who quite agrees with me. . . ."

"Dec. 26th. Much political talk with Grant and H. Thornton, making
up my mind. . . ."[75]

Wilberforce at length made up his mind that he would publicly
advocate a peace settlement. He was taking a serious step and knew
it. He was aware that he was creating an open breach with his friend
Pitt, who was all for continuing the war. And the breach was a bitter
experience for both men. It was said that in all the stormy years of
his administration only two events ever robbed Pitt of his sleep:
Wilberforce's break with him in 1795; and the mutiny at the Nore
in 1797. Wilberforce had not only to break with Pitt; he had to face
bitter public hostility. The King openly cut him at a levee and others
imitated in many ways the royal example. Even in Yorkshire some of
his own constituents refused to speak to him. But Wilberforce was
responsible to his own conscience and was not to be intimidated by
personal consequences. He even seems to have thought of forcing the
hand of the Government by the typical Clapham method of an appeal
to the country. "If I thought that the bulk of the middle class throughout the nation was against the continuance of the war, the effect of
their interference in stopping it might more than compensate for the
great evil of exciting a spirit of discontent. But it is not so yet."[76]

It was indeed not so. Wilberforce was, as he himself said, "an
object of popular odium." And the consequence was extended from
the problem of peace to the problem of slavery. When Wilberforce
tried to remind the Commons in 1795 that by its 1792 decision it had

[75]*Life of Wilberforce*, II, 64, 68.   [76]*Ibid.*, II, 73.

declared for abolition in 1796, the House abruptly cast out his motion.[77]

Happily the breach with Pitt was of brief duration, chiefly because Pitt became converted to Wilberforce's thinking. Before long Pitt was seeking Wilberforce's counsel on ways to negotiate a peace; and by the end of the year had openly stated his willingness to treat with the Republican government.

The renewed friendship with Pitt, and the swing of public sentiment toward peace, restored Wilberforce's influence in the House. When on February 18, 1796, he moved for leave to introduce a bill abolishing the trade he met a more cordial reception than he had known since the outbreak of the war. Unexpectedly he was given a majority.[78] "Surprise and joy," he reported, "in carrying my question."[79] But the triumph was short-lived. An unexpected and bitter defeat was to follow. By chance, it happened that on the evening when the bill was read for the third time a comic opera opened in London. While a dozen of Wilberforce's sure supporters were swelling the applause for a popular singer of the day the trade seized its opportunity and in a depleted House threw out the bill 74 to 70. Wilberforce's austere view of the theatre was confirmed by this frivolity of his supporters. "I am personally hurt," he said.[80]

In British history 1797 was a dark year, "the darkest and most desperate that any British minister has ever had to face."[81] Under the strain Pitt lost his old interest in abolition. Moreover, 1797 brought the death of Edward Eliot of Clapham, brother-in-law of Pitt, intimate friend of Wilberforce, and a link between the two—in Wilberforce's words, "a bond of connexion, which was sure never to fail."[82] Although in personal loyalty Pitt "stood stiffly" by Wilberforce in a losing battle in the Commons, Wilberforce could never again put quite the same faith in his friend, and others not so understanding

---

[77]*Parliamentary History,* XXXI, 1345. "Shameful," was Wilberforce's comment. And he added that the "infamous vote" had furnished him with another argument for parliamentary reform.

[78]*Ibid.,* XXXII, 763.

[79]*Life of Wilberforce,* II, 140. Zachary Macaulay was then at Portsmouth *en route* to Africa, and heard the joyful tidings. "I scarcely ever felt purer pleasure," he wrote, "than on seeing Mr. Wilberforce's success in yesterday's paper." Knutsford, *Zachary Macaulay,* pp. 113, 114.

[80]Coupland, *Wilberforce,* p. 225.

[81]Lord Rosebery, *Pitt,* p. 133.

[82]*Life of Wilberforce,* II, 234-8.

openly accused the Prime Minister of defection from the cause. ". . . Mr. Pitt, unhappily for himself, his country and mankind," said Stephen, "is not zealous enough in the cause of the negroes, to contend for them as decisively as he ought, in the Cabinet any more than in parliament."[83]

The next year proved somewhat better for the patient campaigners. A new issue brought a local victory. Trinidad had been taken by the British, and the Carib tribes transferred from St. Vincent to the mainland. The abolitionists were anxious that the new lands should not be stocked with added cargoes of slaves from Africa. But the West Indians persuaded Pitt to allow slaves already in the old colonies to be transferred to the new—which, Stephen knew, would mean only that new slaves would be taken from Africa to replace those transferred. Stephen was furious. "Lloyd's Coffee House," he wrote to Wilberforce, "is in a roar of merriment, at the dexterous compromise. . . ." Fortified by Stephen's thorough knowledge of the situation Wilberforce was able to convince Pitt of the necessity of abandoning the measure. Nevertheless, because Wilberforce made no public protest Stephen thought that he was too carefully tempering his zeal with consideration for political friends, and wrote a sharp letter of protest to him: "I still clearly think that you have been improperly silent, and that when you see the government loading the bloody altars of commerce . . . with an increase of human victims . . . you are bound by the situation wherein you have placed yourself to cry aloud against it. You are even the rather bound to do so, because those high priests of Moloch . . . are your political, and Mr. Pitt also your private friend." Wilberforce's reply was "angelic." "Go on, my dear sir, and welcome. Believe me, I wish not to abate any thing of the force or frankness of your animadversions. . . . For your frankness I feel myself obliged. . . . Openness is the only foundation and preservative of friendship."[84]

The year 1799 witnessed a constant series of minor skirmishes. In March Wilberforce brought forward his usual motion for abolition, and met his usual defeat.[85] But there was more to follow. William Smith carried a bill for further regulation of the Middle Passage. And

[83]*Ibid.*, p. 225.   [84]*Ibid.*, pp. 260, 265-6.
[85]*Parliamentary History*, XXXIV, 518-65.

then the indefatigable company proceeded with their most hopeful venture.

The Sierra Leone settlement had been continually disturbed by the activities of the slave traders. To relieve their little colony and at the same time to make some small advance toward their ultimate goal Thornton and the others "after long and careful consultation" concocted a sort of "local option" measure for slavery, a measure to make the region around Sierra Leone a closed area to slave hunters. Thornton now brought forward this Slave Trade Limitation Bill. He was disappointed by the coolness of Pitt, and Wilberforce wrote in his diary (March 13), "Pitt coolly put off the debate . . . and so left misrepresentations without a word. William Smith's anger, Henry Thornton's coolness—deep impression on me, but conquered I hope in a Christian way." Yet together they managed to guide the bill through the House of Commons. The Lords, however, played their usual part. They decided that they would need to gather more evidence.

Immediately all the brotherhood were in action. They watched the inquiry and prepared witnesses for examination at the bar, consulting incessantly with their legal counsel, of whom the chief was Stephen. In the midst of the excitement Macaulay arrived on his final return from Sierra Leone, and, though he was proceeding to see his fiancée from whom he had been absent three years, he was immediately commandeered by Thornton and Wilberforce, and detained in London to give evidence before the Lords. Macaulay's patience for once failed him, and he was constrained to remain only by the plea that his evidence might save the bill. To add to his misery he was stricken by an attack of African fever, and had to prepare and deliver his evidence in ill health. Finally the evidence was concluded and Stephen with his impressive logic and fiery eloquence summed up for the abolitionists. The friends were in high spirits. "We have," wrote Wilberforce, "the strongest probability of carrying the Slave Limitation Bill."[86] Their hopes were rudely shattered. The inexorable Lords renewed their opposition. Lord Chancellor Thurlow ridiculed the Sierra Leone Company, which would "send missionaries to preach in a barn of Sierra Leone to a set of negroes, who did not understand a

[86]*Life of Wilberforce*, II, 340.

single word of his language."[87] On the second reading the bill was
defeated.

Worse was to follow. In 1800 Wilberforce was adroitly inveigled
into compromise. To placate the abolitionists some of the West
Indians said that they would be willing to agree to a suspension of
the trade for a number of years. Wilberforce thought that it would be
better to win a part than to lose the whole, and hence did not renew
in Parliament his annual motion on the slave trade. Just as he had
come to hope the compromise was "going on prosperously" the West
Indians changed their minds. Wilberforce then tried to get the
Government to enforce suspension in spite of the West Indians; but he
could get no support.[88] Hence, after all the steadfast labours, the last
year of the century was the first from the commencement of the
campaign in which the question of abolition was completely ignored
by Parliament. Yet Wilberforce's patient optimism did not falter.
Despite the reverse he did not lose his confidence that he could see
in the distance "the streaks of light indicating the opening day."

The dawn of the new century, however, was dark and forbidding.
"What tempests rage around," says Wilberforce's journal in January
1801.[89] The war and the bad harvests had created widespread distress;
and the men of the Clapham Sect, in common with all philanthropists,
were busy with schemes to alleviate the miseries of the poor. Wilberforce that year gave away £3,000 more than his income.[90] The motion
for abolition having been deferred on the previous year it was now
easy to follow the precedent, and Wilberforce decided that "the state
of affairs. . . . rendered it prudent to forbear bringing forward the
question in any form."[91] The next year, 1802, the precedent was still
easier to follow, and once again Parliament was untroubled by the
old familiar motion. True, Wilberforce would not have deferred his
motion for so long had he not been occupied with larger hopes. The
tidings of peace in October 1801 had suggested to him a "grand
Abolition plan." He revived his first dreams of a general convention
of European powers which would reach a common agreement to
abolish the trade. In his occupation with the larger plan he allowed
the usual abolition motion to be passed over. He and his group did,

[87]*Parliamentary History*, XXXIV, 1139.
[88]*Life of Wilberforce*, II, 367-8.   [89]*Ibid.*, III, 1.
[90]*Ibid.*, p. 4.   [91]*Ibid.*, p. 30.

however, forestall a move of Addington (the new Prime Minister) to open to slavery the territories of Trinidad, so that the year was not without its victory.[92]

In 1803 Wilberforce had resolved to present the matter again, but he was taken seriously ill with influenza. And while he was still confined at home there came the alarming threat of a French invasion. "You can conceive what would be said," he writes to Babington, "if I were to propose the Abolition now."[93] Very soon indeed the thought of Napoleon's army at Boulogne put aside completely for that year any possibility of further occupation with the slave trade.

The Last Phase

More than ten years had now passed since the French Revolution had terminated so abruptly the initial hopes for the abolition of the slave trade. And all the intervening time had been a weary record of valiant struggle and almost unvarying defeat. The long labours seemed to have gone for nothing and the end to be as far as ever from attainment. But the struggle had not been as fruitless as it seemed. Parliamentary bills and motions had been defeated; but bills and motions were not all the battle.

The Clapham Sect were now united. Sharp, Thornton, Wilberforce, Macaulay, Stephen, Lord Teignmouth, Grant, Gisborne, Smith, and Babington had all become accustomed to working together for common ends. Following chapters will show some of the labours they had already performed. No prime minister had such a cabinet as Wilberforce could now summon to his assistance. Indeed since the old Abolition Committee had ceased this group of friends had constituted an unofficial Abolition Committee, which of its own enthusiasm had continued to meet and to carry on discussion during all the years. The entry in Wilberforce's diary June 13, 1804, is: "Brougham, Stephen, Babington, Henry Thornton, Macaulay, dining with us in Palace Yard most days of the Slave Trade debates."[94] In an article on Macaulay in 1839 the *Christian Observer* said that the absence of the Abolition Committee during the years of reaction "was more than compensated by the very frequent meetings which were held at Mr. Wilberforce's house, in Old Palace Yard, at which were generally

[92]*Ibid.*, pp. 26 ff.   [93]*Ibid.*, p. 88.   [94]*Ibid.*, p. 176.

present Mr. Wilberforce, Mr. Stephen, Mr. Henry Thornton, Mr. Macaulay, Mr. William Smith, Lord Brougham, and others." It is not difficult to guess who some of the "others" were. When the official Abolition Committee was reassembled in 1804, it was augmented by Lord Teignmouth, Stephen, Macaulay, and Robert Grant, son of Charles. As Gisborne had already been elected corresponding member, the Clapham Sect must have gone to the committee *en masse*.

In addition the brotherhood had circulated in England a formidable quantity of abolitionist literature, and had established their own magazine, the *Christian Observer,* which had gained a wide circulation, and every month carried propaganda to an important section of the religious public. Moreover, five of the group—Wilberforce, Thornton, Babington, Smith, and Grant—were now in Parliament, and were beginning to distinguish themselves as the party of Independents, the "Saints," and to exercise a moral influence out of all proportion to their numbers. Finally the Clapham Sect now benefited by adventitious assistance. In the first place the long-used cry of Jacobinism had been done to death, and had lost its terror. "Jacobinism happily was too much discredited either to render to the Abolition her destructive aid, or supply a convenient reproach for its supporters."[95] In the second place, the Act of Union had been passed, so that in the new Parliament to which appeal must now be made there would be one hundred Irish members not bound up with the old interests which had given the trade its hold on Parliament.

Under these circumstances, so different from those of 1787, the Clapham Sect in 1804 girded themselves for the final struggle. Pitt had just been returned to office; and in the new Parliament Wilberforce on May 30 introduced—for the first time since 1799—his bill for the abolition of the slave trade. His speech, he thought, was awkward and stiff. But the temper of the House had changed, and the members, in larger numbers than had attended in the old days, heard him with gladness. There was also a dramatic intervention in his support. More than thirty of the Irish members, whose favour the abolitionists had taken care to cultivate, arranged a great dinner at which they drank success to the cause, and from which they marched to the House to vote in a body for Wilberforce. But even without

[95] *Ibid.,* p. 163.

these Wilberforce would have been safe; the division gave him a majority of 124 to 49.[96]

The Saints were intoxicated with their unaccustomed success. Stephen, Macaulay, Thornton, Grant, and William Smith, together with their new ally Brougham, hurried over to Wilberforce's house to shower him with their congratulations, and to spend most of the night laying plans for further campaigns and settling the main lines of the bill. They had scented victory. Twice before the House had voted for abolition, but with small houses and narrow majorities. Now the vote was large and the majority decisive. "From that night the issue of the question was clear."

The progress, however, was not rapid. The House of Commons did pass the second and third readings, though with diminished majorities because the Irish had "been persuaded . . . that it is an invasion of private property."[97] But the trade still had a bulwark in the House of Lords. There the Lord Privy Seal, invoking the "wisdom of our ancestors," boasted that there was one house at any rate which would look after the interests of the merchants and the colonists. The bill found only three defenders, two lords and one bishop, while it met four opponents from the royal family alone.[98] Wilberforce saw that an immediate vote would be fatal. Consequently he had agreed that the bill should not come to a division and in due course the Lords adjourned it until the next session.[99] After the first promising success this obstruction was disheartening. "I own," wrote Wilberforce to Gisborne, "it quite lowers my spirits to see all my hopes for this year at once blasted." "To be sure," he adds, "one session in such a case as this is not much."[100]

Delay did not mean idleness. Seeking to gain a point where he could, Wilberforce used his influence with Pitt to get the promise of a proclamation prohibiting the importation of slaves in the newly acquired Dutch colonies. On obtaining Pitt's promise he held "a conference in Palace Yard—Brougham, Grant, Babington, William Smith, Henry Thornton, and Macaulay," and decided not to carry the question to Parliament but to depend on private negotiations with Pitt.[101]

[96]*Ibid.*, p. 168.
[98]*Parliamentary Debates*, II, 929.
[100]*Ibid.*, p. 181.
[97]*Ibid.*, p. 177.
[99]*Life of Wilberforce*, III, 180-3.
[101]*Ibid.*, p. 184.

This decision taken, Wilberforce, having moved for rest to Lyme in Dorsetshire, began making thorough preparations for the expected battle of the following year. Stephen was already writing a pamphlet on slavery in the West Indies, and Wilberforce was anxious that all the others should also be working. He allotted a certain amount of labour to himself, and then wrote to Macaulay urging the enlistment of the band. Clarkson, he suggested, might be employed gathering evidence, and even the young Grants could search the classical authors for apt material.[102] The next campaign was not to want for preparation.

But 1805 was not to see the end of the struggle, and this time the blame could not be laid on the Lords. On February 15 Wilberforce moved in the House of Commons for leave to reintroduce the bill. Pitt openly avoided entering the debate. Fox and Wilberforce were both below their usual standard in debate, the Irish "were absent or even turned against us," and the bill was rejected by a majority of seven. After the division Wilberforce was addressed by the worldly-wise Clerk of the House of Commons, "Mr. Wilberforce, you ought not to expect to *carry* a measure of this kind. . . . you and I have seen enough of life to know that people are not induced to act upon what affects their interests by any abstract arguments." "Mr. Hatsell," Wilberforce replied, "I *do* expect to carry it, and what is more, I feel assured I shall carry it speedily."[103] Yet, following the triumph of the previous year, this defeat hurt Wilberforce the more. "I never felt so much on any parliamentary occasion," his diary records. "I could not sleep after first waking at night. The poor blacks rushed into my mind, and the guilt of our wicked land." "Still I will do all I can," he wrote patiently in a letter to Lord Muncaster, "If we cannot stop the whole of this accursed traffic, it is much to stop half of it. . . ."[104]

To stop half of it the brotherhood now took up the matter of the order-in-council which Pitt had promised the year before and of which, since his promise, nothing had been heard. Many of the abolitionists were now convinced that Pitt had turned traitor to the

---

[102]*Ibid.*, pp. 191-205. On page 203 is a list of "Propositions to be proved by extracts from African travellers."
[103]*Ibid.*, p. 213.
[104]*Ibid.*, pp. 213-15.

cause.[105] Wilberforce could not share that belief, but he did think that Pitt had been strangely unconcerned. He now wrote to him "strongly." Three days later he went to see him, and took so unusual a stand as to threaten that, failing action, he would "positively bring [the question] into the House." Pitt had no desire to lose so valuable a supporter as Wilberforce. He promised the proclamation, and re̅quested Wilberforce to have it prepared. Wilberforce thereupon called in Babington and Stephen to devise suitable regulations. It was then March 11, but the draft proclamation though sent immediately to Pitt was not returned for Wilberforce's approval until May 11. And then, for all their efforts, it was "in a very unsatisfactory state," "so framed as to be worse than none." Wilberforce again called in Stephen, and the two assisted the Attorney-General to repair the errors. Still the proclamation was delayed, and was not finally issued until September 13, 1805.

That favour was the last Pitt was to grant the abolitionists. In January 1806 he died; and his ministry was succeeded by the Ministry of All the Talents. The change was unquestionably to the advantage of the Clapham Sect. Grenville, who was now Prime Minister, was a convinced abolitionist, and Fox, now Foreign Secretary, had long been one of the most powerful champions of the cause in Parliament. Both were anxious to distinguish the new administration by the passing of an abolition act. Moreover, for the first time abolitionists held a decisive majority in the Cabinet. And in the House Wilberforce could count on a following larger than he had known since 1792. Yet caution was still necessary, and for the first session the abolitionists thought it the part of wisdom not to introduce a bill, but to prepare the way by resolutions expressing disapproval of the slave trade. Fostered by Fox in the House of Commons and Gren-

[105]There have been wide differences of opinion about Pitt's loyalty to the cause of abolition. For the adverse criticisms see: W. E. H. Lecky, *History of England in the Eighteenth Century*, V, 64-6; Brougham's *Speeches*, II, 14; a letter in Holland Rose's *Pitt and Napoleon*, pp. 321-4 (though Rose himself supports Pitt—see *William Pitt and National Revival*, pp. 477-9); and the *Edinburgh Review*, July, 1808, pp. 367-8 (written by Coleridge). Preceding pages have shown that Stephen lost his faith in Pitt, and that others were at times angered with him. Sir James Stephen in "The Clapham Sect," in *Essays in Ecclesiastical Biography* was adverse to Pitt. It is of importance, however, to remember that Wilberforce never lost his faith in Pitt, and that Clarkson agreed with Wilberforce (*History of Abolition*, II, 503-6).

ville in the House of Lords, these resolutions were triumphantly carried.

With success almost in their grasp Wilberforce and Stephen made plans to forestall a sudden burst of slave trading in the last days of its existence. They prepared a temporary enactment which prohibited the employment in the trade of any ships not hitherto employed in it, and fortunately managed to steer it through both houses in the seven weeks before the session ended.

Abolition was now practically secure; but the wary veterans had learned too much to relax their vigilance. The Abolition Committee gathered regularly at Wilberforce's house, preparation was made for providing any required evidence, and "no measure was omitted which the most watchful prudence could suggest."[106] In August Wilberforce "slipped into the snug and retired harbour of Lyme, for the purpose of careening and refitting." He wished quiet to prepare a last vigorous pamphlet on the slave trade, which, he hoped, "thrown in just in such circumstances [i.e. published just before the subject was debated in the Lords], may be like a shot which hits between wind and water. . . ." "It will be well," he observed shrewdly, "to supply people who wish to come over, with reasons for voting for us."[107] His labours were abruptly terminated. In October he was interrupted by a letter from the Prime Minister announcing the dissolution of Parliament and the calling of an election. Immediately he was plunged into the turmoil of a political campaign which, once again, placed him at the head of the poll. He was not able to resume work on the pamphlet until December, and did not have it ready for the press until January, 1807.[108]

When the pamphlet appeared the battle had already auspiciously commenced. Grenville was the first Prime Minister to sit in the House of Lords since the beginning of the abolition campaign and after consultation with Wilberforce he had decided to reverse the usual procedure and to introduce the bill first into the upper house. There the bill met stormy opposition in the course of which the old prejudices were once more invoked. The Earl of Westmorland scented future danger to "tithes and estates" because with abolitionist principles "no property could be considered safe," and declared that though "the

---

[106]*Life of Wilberforce*, II, 271-3.   [107]*Ibid.*, p. 273.
[108]The tract was of four hundred pages, and was published as *A Letter on the Abolition of the Slave Trade* (London, 1807).

Presbyterian and the prelate, the Methodist and the field preacher, the Jacobin and the murderer" combined against British property, he at least would not yield to them.[109] Lord St. Vincent "entered his solemn and final protest against this measure of national ruin, and walked out of the house."[110] But the years had changed even the House of Lords, and in little over a month—by February 10—the bill was fought through.[111]

On the same day the first reading was carried in the House of Commons, though with the concession to the enemy that the second reading should be postponed for a fortnight.[112] The interval meant another burst of activity for the Clapham Sect. Wilberforce called together his Abolition Committee to check the lists of the House of Commons, and found "a terrific list of doubtfuls." Thereupon each member of the group selected the men to whom he might have access, and the whole company set out to win votes for abolition by a campaign of personal interviews. To the very day of the second reading, February 23, 1807, they laboured together, and then repaired to the House to take their places on the floor or to crowd the galleries. They knew that this was to be their test night, and they had confidence that at last they could win.

Their hopes were not belied; the evening was one of unalloyed triumph. The House, too, felt that the great moment had come, and betrayed "an astonishing eagerness." Six or eight members were on their feet at once to join in this last assault on the iniquity which Britain was now to abolish.[113] The enthusiasm mounted with the impassioned speeches to its moving climax at the peroration of Sir Samuel Romilly, the Solicitor-General. When Romilly reached his brilliant contrast of Wilberforce and Napoleon the staid old House cast off its traditional conventions, rose to its feet, burst into cheers, and made the roof of St. Stephen's echo to "an ovation such as it had given to no other living man"—while Wilberforce himself, overcome with emotion, "sat bent in his chair, his head in his hands, and the tears streaming down his face."[114] In a short while he rose to his feet and in "a splendour of eloquence" delivered his last abolition

[109]*Parliamentary Debates*, VIII, 667.
[110]F. J. Klingberg, *The Anti-Slavery Movement in England*, p. 127. See *Parliamentary Debates*, VIII, 693.
[111]*Ibid.*, pp. 701-3.   [112]*Ibid.*, pp. 717-22.
[113]*Life of Wilberforce*, III, 296.
[114]Coupland, *Wilberforce*, p. 341.

speech. And then the Sect watched the eventful division, and saw abolition carried by the tremendous majority of 283 to 16.[115]

That division settled the matter. There was no further hope for the opponents of abolition. The third reading passed smoothly, and on March 25, 1807, the Abolition Bill received the royal assent.

The Clapham Sect however did not need to wait for the third reading. They knew well enough that their victory had been won, and by a common impulse they gathered to share triumph together. Late as the hour was, they moved in a happy company to Wilberforce's house in Palace Yard, there to rejoice with their honoured leader. How many were there is not certain; but Henry Thornton is mentioned, and Granville Sharp, and Grant and his son Robert, and Macaulay, and a new-found friend Reginald Heber. And none was so happy as Wilberforce himself. Seeing Henry Thornton, his unfailing help and counsellor in all the years of weary struggle, standing alone with a grave look on his face, Wilberforce in his happy fashion went over and inquired, "Well, Henry, what shall we abolish next?"[116]

The Clapham Sect cannot, of course, claim the entire glory for the abolition of the slave trade. The history of abolition has wider reaches than the present chapter. "A long campaign of humanitarianism under able men; a readjustment of the economic interests of the West Indians; a growth of industry and commerce so that the slave trade was of smaller relative importance in the total commerce of the country, although absolutely greater; the prospect of carrying the commerce on under other flags or illicitly; the example of abolition by other countries; the prospect of gaining universal abolition at the next peace congress; the determination of Fox and Grenville; all these played their part. Without humanitarian leadership, however, there would have been failure."[117]

Without the Clapham Sect there would indeed have been failure. They not merely took part in the movement; they made the movement. There seems no reasonable ground for believing that without their leadership, their concerted labours, their infectious passion, their unwearying persistence, the abolition campaign could have been carried, at least in their generation, to its successful finish.

[115]*Parliamentary Debates*, VIII, 945-95.   [116]*Life of Wilberforce,* III, 298.
[117]Klingberg, *The Anti-Slavery Movement in England,* pp. 129-30.

CHAPTER FOUR

The English have no priests or chaplains

"WHAT SHALL WE abolish next?" The Clapham Sect did not need to seek out any new enterprises. Already they had committed themselves to other causes, involving conflict with vested interests not less influential and scarcely less intolerant.

The closing years of the eighteenth century were critical not only for Britain's relations with Africa, but also for her relations with India. Anglo-Indian affairs had degenerated to "dire scandal and confusion"[1] of which the purple eloquence of Edmund Burke had just presented an unforgettable picture, and to which Pitt's India Bill of 1784 had responded with at least partial acknowledgment that British power in India involved moral obligations on the British Parliament.

Yet both Pitt and Burke envisioned but a meagre relationship between Britain and India. They cherished a great respect for India's ancient civilization. They desired that the intercourse between the two civilizations should be based on the stern justice which was the pride of their own. But they had no thought, for instance, that Britain was obligated to promote education in India, or to encourage a less sanguinary morality. They thought that Britain's relations with India were commercial, and that her responsibilities to India were political. With education, morals, and religion they had as little concern as with fashion and etiquette. Though gross abominations might openly characterize the life under their rule they would feel no responsibility whatever. The British indeed generally prided themselves on such an outlook. They made public boast that they never propagated their own religion. In 1793 Lord Macartney at the court of China explained proudly that "the English . . . have no priests or chaplains with them,

[1] G. M. Trevelyan, *British History in the Nineteenth Century*, p. 46.

as have other European nations."[2] It is not surprising therefore that when statesmen were beginning to be troubled about the obligations which justice to India involved, Christians were beginning to be troubled about the further obligations which Christianity involved.

Anyone inclined to think that Christians in England who began the campaign for the admission of Christianity to India were not properly appreciative of her "ancient civilization" will do well to reflect upon the following account of what that civilization had made a commonplace incident, the burning of a widow after her husband's death. Wilberforce in 1813 added the narrative to the published edition of his speech on the East India bill saying that it had been written by a missionary Mr. Marshman, a man of the most established integrity.

A person informing us that a woman was about to be burnt with the corpse of her husband, near our house, I, with several of our brethren, hastened to the place: but before we could arrive, the pile was in flames. It was a horrible sight. The most shocking indifference and levity appeared among those who were present. I never saw any thing more brutal than their behaviour. The dreadful scene had not the least appearance of a religious ceremony. It resembled an abandoned rabble of boys in England, collected for the purpose of worrying to death a cat or a dog. A bamboo, perhaps twenty feet long, had been fastened at one end to a stake driven into the. ground, and held down over the fire by men at the other. Such were the confusion, the levity, the bursts of brutal laughter, while the poor woman was burning alive before their eyes, that it seemed as if every spark of humanity was extinguished by this accursed superstition. That which added to the cruelty was the smallness of the fire. It did not consist of so much wood as we consume in dressing a dinner: no, not this fire that was to consume the living and the dead! I saw the legs of the poor creature hanging out of the fire while her body was in flames. After a while, they took a bamboo ten or twelve feet long and stirred it, pushing and beating the half consumed corpses, as you would repair a fire of green wood, by throwing the unconsumed pieces into the middle. Perceiving the legs hanging out, they beat them with the bamboo for some time, in order to break the ligatures which fastened them at the knees, (for they would not have come near to touch them for the world). At length they succeeded in bending them upwards into the fire, the skin and muscles giving way, and discovering

2*Life of Wilberforce*, II, 28.

the knee sockets bare, with the balls of the leg bones: a sight this which, I need not say, made me thrill with horror, especially when I recollected that this hapless victim of superstition was alive but a few minutes before. To have seen savage wolves thus tearing a human body, limb from limb, would have been shocking; but to see relations and neighbours do this to one with whom they had familiarly conversed not an hour before, and to do it with an air of levity, was almost too much for me to bear.

You expect, perhaps, to hear, that this unhappy victim was the wife of some brahmin of high cast. She was the wife of a barber who dwelt in Serampore, and had died that morning, leaving the son I have mentioned, and a daughter of about eleven years of age. Thus has this infernal superstition aggravated the common miseries of life, and left these children stripped of both their parents in one day. Nor is this an uncommon case. It often happens to children far more helpless than these; sometimes to children possessed of property, which is then left, as well as themselves, to the mercy of those who have decoyed their mother to their father's funeral pile![3]

It was to transform the degraded conceptions of human life which such an incident revealed that Wilberforce and his informed companions desired to introduce Christianity to India.

Hitherto indeed the representatives of Christian England had done little to spread the contagion of Christian ideas. Rather it was said cynically that Christians were "unbaptised" on their way to India; and the pagan level of Anglo-India life did not belie the comment. True the English had never given any encouragement to the practice of suttee. But Job Charnock, the founder of Calcutta, became an avowed pagan, and annually sacrificed a cock on the tomb of his native wife. In 1802 the English officials went in procession to a heathen temple to present in the name of the East India Company a thank-offering to the sanguinary goddess Kali for the success which the English had previously obtained. Thousands of natives watched the English officials presenting offerings to this idol. The natives for long wondered whether the Englishman had any god, and suspected rather that his origin was in the devil. When, after eighty years in India, the Company built its first church, and it became fashionable to attend service on Christmas and Easter, natives came in throngs to see the strange spectacle of the white man worshipping his own god. The official acknowledgment, however, was not very convincing. An old comment of the natives could still be repeated: "Christian religion devil religion; Christian much drunk, much do wrong, much beat, much abuse others." Anglo-Indian society indeed largely abandoned the virtues of its own race, and added the vices of another. Sir John Kaye's *Christianity in India*, though not unsympathetic to the Nabobs, yet bears witness to the dissolute nature of white society in India previous to 1785. As late as 1810 a Captain Thomas Williamson who wrote a book to "promote the welfare" of the young man of the East India Company's service, and who dedicated his book to the Court of Directors, included as a matter of course a whole section about native mistresses, their ornaments and cosmetics, and the expense of their keep. He told amusedly of one elderly gentleman who maintained sixteen of varied age and appointments, and who, when asked how he looked after such a number, replied, "Oh, I give them a little rice and let them run about." No less than drinking, duelling and gambling, concubinage and nautch dances became the order of the day.[4]

The long monopoly of a trading company bent solely on commercial exploitation had provided for India a steady witness to the worst in white civilization, and no testimony of the best. When reform came it was a long, slow process, receiving impulses from many sources, but especially marking the influence of one great Anglo-Indian, who in a later day was called "the father and founder of modern missionary effort in Great Britain's Indian Empire"[5]— Charles Grant of the Clapham Sect.

When Charles Grant commenced his Indian career he fell so far into conventional habits that, in a few years, despite rapid promotion in the Company's service he found himself carried by extravagant living, unfortunate business deals, and reckless gambling into debts totalling £20,000. Yet in his early years in Scotland Grant had been under strong religious influence, influence which the years in India had not eradicated, and which, recalled by serious family tragedy,[6] led in 1776 to his conversion.

---

[4]*The East India Vade-Mecum,* pp. 412-58.
[5]Henry Morris, *Life of Grant,* p. 395.
[6]In 1774 Grant lost his "good uncle" who had much influence over him; in 1775 he lost his brother and close friend; in 1776 he lost both his children within nine days.

For a few years after his conversion Grant lived quietly in India, becoming close friends with his fellow official and kindred spirit, John Shore, then also beginning his religious life. In 1784, one year before Wilberforce's conversion, Grant first became concerned with what was to be the central passion of his life. He received from Dr. Coke, a coadjutor of John Wesley, a letter inquiring about the possibility of establishing Christian missions in India. Grant's journal for November 21, 1784, has this note: "Read two days ago a letter from Dr. Coke, in connection with Mr. Wesley, with a scheme for a Mission to this country, and queries for information and assistance. A great project! May it be well influenced. May I answer rightly." Correspondence followed; but Grant thought that a mission should be operated under official patronage, and John Wesley had no faith in such a method. Moreover, though Grant still urged them to commence their mission, the Methodists, burdened with missions in Newfoundland, the West Indies, and the United States, found themselves at the time unable to attempt an added one to India. Hence the first scheme came to nothing.

The idea, however, did not die. From that time Grant became absorbed in developing a possible scheme of missions in India. In 1786 he was joined by a young clergyman, David Brown, who had come to India to superintend the Military Orphan Asylum. Grant found in David Brown a congenial spirit, with a timely knowledge of the men in England who might be sympathetic to a missionary enterprise. Accordingly the next year the two friends worked out together a very careful "Proposal" for an Indian mission, which embodied Grant's old idea of a mission under sanction of the civil government, and sent copies to fourteen likely men in England. Among these the main hopes were centred on Charles Simeon to interest the clergy and William Wilberforce to interest the laity. "Our hopes are particularly fixed on Mr. Wilberforce," wrote Brown to Simeon. "It is to his influence alone that we hope the minister will regard such a project, and ask for it the countenance of majesty."[7]

The judgment was vindicated. Wilberforce actually carried the proposal to Pitt to bespeak his interest, and both he and Simeon thereafter made the introduction of Christianity to India one of the main

[7]William Carus, *Memoirs of Simeon*, p. 79.

interests of their lives, taking it under their charge as a cause "emphatically Claphamic."[8]

Nothing, however, was immediately accomplished. But—unfortunately with an injudicious choice of agent—Grant attempted to establish at his own expense a private mission in Gumalti. This, the first attempt by any Protestant to reach the native peoples of India, was soon abandoned. Early in 1790, after eighteen years' residence, Grant left India and returned to England, there to pursue further his cherished purpose.

In England Grant speedily made acquaintance with Wilberforce and Henry Thornton, and his name was soon appearing regularly in Wilberforce's diary. The first reference to Grant in the published section of Wilberforce's diary is in 1791: "[February] 24th. Breakfasted with Grant."[9] In October 1794 Grant moved out to Clapham, taking up residence in a home which he had built next to Henry Thornton's.

England did not give much encouragement to missionary schemes. "Faint hopes people have of Missions," Grant wrote in August 1790.[10] But, in approved Clapham fashion, he undertook to further his cause by spreading knowledge. In 1792 he prepared an elaborate and well-considered treatise, planned at first for private circulation, and designed to set forth with all possible strength and earnestness the case for Christian missions in India. The pamphlet, entitled *Observations on the State of Society among the Asiatic Subjects of Great Britain*, was published in 1797; it was later described by George Smith as "the noblest treatise on the Asiatic subjects of Great Britain, and the means of improving their moral condition, which the English language has even yet seen."[11] In the same year, 1792, Grant arranged for John Shore, now returned from India, also to meet Wilberforce, and later in 1792 joined Wilberforce in persuading Shore to return to India as Governor-General. He also endeavoured to interest in his scheme other persons of importance, and, with an introduction from

---

[8]In 1830 Simeon wrote on his copy of the "Proposal": "It merely shows how early God enabled me to act for India; to provide for which, has now for forty-two years been a principal and an incessant object of my care and labour." *Ibid.*, p. 75.

[9]But Morris says that they must have met about November 1790. *Life of Grant*, p. 168.

[10]*Ibid.*, p. 184.   [11]*Twelve Indian Statesmen*, p. 2.

Wilberforce, interviewed the Bishop of London and the Archbishop of Canterbury—a preparatory move opening the way for later progress.

All this was minor skirmishing. The first opportunity for real action came in 1793 with the renewal of the East India Company's charter. The Clapham brotherhood had been eagerly anticipating the opportunity—Grant providing in this cause the local knowledge that Macaulay and Stephen had provided in the abolition cause. Grant carefully drafted for Wilberforce's presentation to Parliament two resolutions to be transmuted on acceptance into clauses of the bill which renewed the charter. The preamble urged, cautiously enough, the adoption of measures designed gradually to promote the "religious and moral improvement" of the inhabitants of India. Specifically, the East India Company was to appoint chaplains in India and on board the larger merchantmen for the resident and travelling Europeans. These clauses were passed in the Committee of the House and then by the House. As in the struggle for abolition the way was easy until interests were aroused. Emboldened by success Wilberforce then added an extra clause providing more definitely, but still cautiously, that the directors of the East India Company should be empowered and required to send out "fit and proper persons" to act as "school-masters, missionaries, or otherwise." This too was passed. The brotherhood, their abolition cause now in dark eclipse, were delighted with this compensating victory. "The hand of Providence was never more visible than in this East Indian affair," Wilberforce records in his journal for May 19 after he had "called at Grant's." "How properly is Grant affected."[12]

The rejoicing was too soon. "Like a giant roused from sleep, India House began to stir."[13] The directors, with reason enough, had no fancy to see their preserves invaded by Methodists and "enthusiasts." They held a special meeting and resolved to put a stop to such nonsense. "East Indian directors met," wrote Wilberforce, "and strongly reprobated my clauses."[14] Immediately they set in action all the forces which they were so well able to command. When the bill to renew the charter was read for the third time, with Wilberforce

[12]*Life of Wilberforce,* II, 25.   [13]R. Coupland, *Wilberforce,* p. 384.
[14]*Life of Wilberforce,* II, 26.

on hand to fight for his clauses, and Grant in the gallery watching the
unequal combat with "melancholy pleasure," East Indian puissance
was abundantly demonstrated. The "little tumult in the court of
proprietors"[15] had troubled the waters of Parliament, and the resolutions were borne away on the tide. Wilberforce protested vainly that
no rash or unfitting measures were premeditated, and argued fruit-
lessly that the intention was not "to break up by violence existing
institutions, and force our faith upon the natives of India; but gravely,
silently, and systematically to prepare the way for the gradual diffusion of religious truth."[16] He might just as well have been silent. The
power of commerce was against him; and commerce was too powerful
to be troubled even by Wilberforce. "The East India directors and
proprietors have triumphed," he wrote to Gisborne, "all my clauses
were last night struck out on the third reading of the Bill, and . . .
twenty millions of people . . . are left . . . to the providential protection
of—Brama."[17]

The defeat revealed how impracticable was Grant's first mission
scheme. Grant had hoped for a mission patronized by the Company
and the government. Wilberforce's resolutions did not venture nearly
so far; yet they had met a response crushingly adverse. His resolutions
failed "from the simple fact that there was then positively no missionary spirit in the nation." "The East India Charter Act of 1793 was
the true reply to the Calcutta-plan of 1787."[18]

MISSIONARY SOCIETIES

The Clapham Sect were not completely defeated. They had yet
more strings to their bows, and more men at their call. India was not
the only mission field that had attracted their attention. The colony at
Sierra Leone, of which Macaulay was now Governor, was itself in
part a missionary venture, freely admitting Methodist and Presbyterian missionaries, and was later to become the centre from which
missionaries were sent to the natives of the surrounding territories.
But the Clapham Sect had even wider interests. After the American
Revolution Australia had been selected as the dumping ground for
convicts sentenced to transportation. The first shipload were gathered

---

[15]*Ibid.*, p. 27.   [16] *Ibid.*, p. 26.
[17]*Ibid.*, p. 27.
[18]Charles Hole, *Early History of the C.M.S.*, p. 21.

in the fall of 1786, and by some chance Wilberforce learned that they were to be transported and left in a strange land without any offices of religion whatever. Wilberforce at once communicated with Henry Thornton, and the two hastened to Pitt. They succeeded in arranging for the appointment of a chaplain, and managed to secure a chaplain who would go. On October 22 Henry Thornton took this chaplain, the Rev. Richard Johnson, to Woolwich to be introduced to his hapless parishioners, and so to undertake the duty of carrying the gospel to Botany Bay.[19] The year 1787, therefore—the year in which Grant drafted his proposal for missionary enterprises in India and in which he began his own private mission in Gumalti, the first English mission to the natives of India—saw also the infancy of two other Clapham schemes: a Negro colony was sent to Sierra Leone and a chaplain was sent to Botany Bay. These three tributaries were destined to flow into one river greater than the originators had imagined.

An exterior agency was the uniting channel. In 1783 a few clergymen, of whom John Newton and Richard Cecil were the most distinguished, had formed the Eclectic Society to discuss matters of common interest to Evangelicals.[20] The Society gradually enlarged, took in a few laymen, and in time gathered its representatives from the Clapham group, with whom from the first it had been in close and sympathetic touch. In 1786 the Society, knowing of Wilberforce's move for a chaplain for the convicts, gave a meeting to a discussion on "What is the best method of planting and propagating the Gospel in Botany Bay?" Rev. Richard Johnson, the chaplain not yet departed for Botany Bay, was invited to the meeting, but did not manage to be present. Three years later when Grant's "Proposal" had come to England the Eclectics were again *au courant,* and called a meeting to discuss "What is the best method of propagating the Gospel in the East Indies?" In 1791 after the institution of the Sierra Leone Company the Eclectics became interested in that new field, and gathered to discuss "What is the best method of propagating the Gospel in Africa?" Melville Horne, the chaplain to Sierra Leone, was present at the meeting. After 1791, the Eclectic Society did not again discuss missions for five years.

[19] John Venn, *Life of Henry Venn,* pp. 439-40.
[20] J. H. Pratt, *Eclectic Notes,* p. 3. Unfortunately the notes of the Eclectic Society's discussions were not preserved until 1798.

Before the five years had passed the Baptist and London Missionary Societies had been formed, and the *Evangelical Magazine*[21] had
expressed the hope that Evangelical Dissenters and Methodists and
even "members of the Established Church of Evangelical sentiments"
might unite in a missionary society. In 1795 Simeon discussed at the
Rauceby Society (a society similar to the Eclectic) the question of
missions, and agreed to get in touch with Wilberforce and Grant about
the possibility of action. The idea of a separate missionary society for
the Church of England is said to have occurred here for the first time
but the effort seems to have been dropped.

In 1796 Simeon, now a member of the Eclectic Society and greatly
interested in the new undenominational London Missionary Society,
proposed an Eclectic discussion on the question, "With what propriety, and in what mode, can a mission be attempted to the heathen
from the Established Church?" The Eclectics were dubious about the
possibility of action. The majority were afraid of the opposition of the
bishops, and shrank from seeming to interfere with the Society for the
Propagation of the Gospel (S.P.G.), and the Society for Promoting
Christian Knowledge (S.P.C.K.). "Not more than two or three"
believed that anything could be accomplished within the Established
Church. But the two or three had been seized with a great idea, and
Basil Woodd, one of them, later declared that "this conversation
proved the foundation of the Church Missionary Society."[22]

To see the further progress we must go from the Eclectic Society
back to Clapham. If Clapham action inspired Eclectic thought,
Eclectic thought in turn stimulated Clapham action. In 1796, however, the Clapham Sect were chiefly occupied with another missionary
scheme. Robert Haldane of Scotland was now endeavouring to get
government sanction for another mission in India, a private endeavour
to be undertaken and financed by himself. Not surprisingly he met
with no more success than had Wilberforce and Grant three years
earlier. But the brotherhood had naturally been interested in the
attempt, had employed their influence on behalf of Haldane, and, as
usual, had gathered frequently for discussions and "Cabinet Councils"
on the matter. The following are some of the references in Wilberforce's diary for 1796 which seem to refer to Haldane's scheme:

[21]III, 12.   [22]Carus, *Memoirs of Simeon*, p. 111.

[Oct. 8.] "Very busy seeing Pitt and Dundas about . . . East India missions. . . ."

[Dec.] "10th. To Grant's to meet Haldane. . . ."

"22nd. . . . House—went home with Dundas and Pitt, and staid awhile discussing—Mission business in hand. 23rd. Breakfasted early with Dundas and Eliot on Mission business; Dundas complying and appointing us to dinner again, where Grant . . . sat long. . . ."

"26th. Grant, Eliot, and Babington at dinner—consultation on East India missions, and discussing all evening."

And, early in 1797, he records "A Cabinet council on the business. Henry Thornton, Grant, and myself, are the junto."[23] When Haldane's plan was finally laid aside the brotherhood turned their attention to the Eclectic proposals.

Simeon, of course, would have brought the Eclectic discussions to the Clapham council rooms. The first definite reference to Clapham response appears in Wilberforce's journal, which in July 1797 mentions a dinner at Henry Thornton's, "where Simeon and Grant to talk over the Mission scheme." Simeon seems to have persisted in his enthusiasm, for two days later Wilberforce wrote: "Simeon with us—his heart glowing with love of Christ. How full he is of love, and of desire to promote the spiritual benefit of others."[24] Again a little later the diary mentions another gathering at Thornton's "for Missionary meeting—Simeon—Charles Grant—Venn. Something, but not much, done—Simeon in earnest."[25] In 1797 also, to awaken missionary interest in his colleagues at India House, Grant laid on the table of

[23]*Life of Wilberforce*, II, 176, 185, 186, 193. In their account of this matter Wilberforce's sons were as unfair to Haldane as they continually were to most others with whom they had no sympathy. For a discussion of the plan see *ibid.*, p. 176-7, and *Memoirs of Robert Haldane and James Alexander Haldane*, p. 106-33. Wilberforce's sons later acknowledged, with no other explanation, that, through lack of knowledge, they had not done justice to Haldane.
[24]Carus, *Memoirs of Simeon*, p. 150.
[25]*Life of Wilberforce*, II, 251. The biographers inaccurately comment that this was "the first commencement" of a plan which "issued, in the year 1800, the Church Missionary Society for Africa and the East." "The first commencement" must be credited to the Eclectic Society; and, as succeeding pages will show, the Society was instituted not in 1800, but in 1799. The error arose in a curious way. Waiting for the patronage of the Archbishop of Canterbury (see p. 77), the Society did not hold an anniversary in 1800. The first anniversary being held in 1801, the fourth in 1804, and so on, the error became almost universal that the Society was founded in 1800. The Rev. Charles Hole in his exhaustive *Early History of the C.M.S.* (p. 97) points out this error, and shows that in the early years it even found its way into the C.M.S. reports. The error is repeated in Coupland's admirable *Wilberforce* (p. 378), and in W. L. Mathieson's *English Church Reform* (p. 15).

the Court of Directors his *Observations* published at first for private
circulation.

All these discussions, however, issued in no definite action, until
in 1799 the Eclectic Society—now including Simeon, John Venn,
Grant, and a close friend Josiah Pratt—was recalled to the question
by Venn, who on March 18 introduced another missionary discussion
by a prepared speech on, "What methods can we use more effectually
to promote the Knowledge of the Gospel among the Heathen?"[2]
Grant proposed the founding of a missionary seminary; but Simeon
advocated a missionary society, and with characteristic promptitude
set forth three questions, "What can we do? When shall we do it?
How shall we do it?"[27]

After vigorous debate it was decided to form a missionary society
forthwith. Venn laid down the dictum that the society must be conducted "on the church principle; but not on the High Church principle"[28]—thus distinguishing it respectively from the London Missionary Society, and the Society for the Propagation of the Gospel. Pratt
added the qualification that it must "be kept in Evangelical hands."[2]
Two weeks afterwards, on April 1, 1799, the eager group held another
meeting to draft the rules for the proposed society, and on April 12
at the Castle and Falcon Inn in Aldersgate Street—in the very room
where, four years earlier, the London Missionary Society had been
founded—they formally brought into being their long-projected missionary society. Neither Simeon nor Grant were present at that meeting. The only Clapham representatives were Charles Elliott and John
Venn.

The new society selected its officers with great care. Wilberforce
was requested to be President; but he did not wish to take that
position. He and Charles Grant were made Vice-Presidents. Later
James Stephen was also made a Vice-President. Henry Thornton, the
accustomed man of business, was made Treasurer; and John Venn
was appointed Chairman of the Committee—which included Josiah

---

[26]Pratt, *Eclectic Notes*, p. 96.
[27]Carus, *Simeon*, pp. 168-9. "How shall we do it? It is hopeless to wait for
missionaries. Send out Catechists. Plan two years ago. Mr. Wilberforce." These
are the Eclectic notes—evidently a reference to what Wilberforce had proposed
at Henry Thornton's in 1797. Pratt, *Eclectic Notes*, pp. 98-9.
[28]*Ibid.*, p. 98.
[29]Josiah and J. H. Pratt, *Memoir of the Rev. Josiah Pratt*, p. 471.

Pratt, Charles Elliott, and Thomas Babington. Simeon, of all the men the most likely, was not on the Committee. The reason probably was that in the days of slow travel it was essential for committee men to live in London. Zachary Macaulay was not in England in the month of the Society's formation. He returned later in the same year, in October visited the Committee to discuss African questions, and later became a member.[30]

Thus far the Society had not decided on its name, which might almost have been the "Clapham Missionary Society." The decision was soon made, and revealed clearly enough the Clapham concern for Sierra Leone and India. The name was, "Society for Missions to Africa and the East." The later name, "Church Missionary Society," was first used as a convenient abbreviation, and was not adopted officially till 1812. As early as 1805, however, Henry Martyn in his journal refers to it as the Church Missionary Society.

Next, John Venn and Simeon drafted a set of rules for the Society, and Venn wrote a prospectus: *An Account of a Society for Missions to Africa and the East.* No less important a duty was to secure if possible the approval of the church authorities. Grant, it will be remembered, had in 1792 interviewed the Bishop of London and the Archbishop of Canterbury about his earlier scheme for missions in India. Wilberforce, Grant, and Venn now interviewed the Archbishop to present a copy of the rules and of Venn's prospectus, and a special letter signed by Venn as Chairman of the Committee. The Archbishop responded with a caution indicative of the distrust with which so "enthusiastic" an undertaking as a missionary society was then regarded. In spite of repeated interviews he delayed more than a year before he committed himself to any reply; and even then he regretted that he "could not with propriety at once express his full concurrence and approbation," though he summoned up his courage and ventured magnificently to promise that he would "look on their proceedings with candour."[31]

---

[30]In 1801 the Committee is recorded as thanking him for a letter on the education of Africans. In the same year the Society consulted with Grant and decided to translate the Scriptures in Oriental languages. The voice of the Society was ever the voice of Clapham.

[31]Hole, *Early History of the C.M.S.*, p. 58. The Bishop of London, good old Dr. Porteus, went a step further and promised to ordain suitable men for missionary work.

Even this tepid commitment seemed to be more than some of the Society anticipated; and with the encouragement it generated they decided to proceed more boldly in their designs. The day afterward the Committee got in touch with Zachary Macaulay to inquire about the prospects of missionary endeavour in Sierra Leone.

The greatest difficulties were yet to come. There now appeared two problems: to open India to missionaries; and to obtain missionaries for India or anywhere else. The Society quickly learned that the idea of missionary service was almost foreign to contemporary Christian thought. Even among the "serious men" at Cambridge Simeon discovered that no one responded. "I see more and more," he said sadly, "*Who* it is that must thrust out labourers into His harvest."[32] After waiting until 1802 and finding no volunteers, the Society in some humiliation accepted two missionaries from Germany, bringing them for a preliminary residence at Clapham and later dispatching them to Africa.[33]

East India missions were still more difficult. No volunteers appeared until 1802, when Henry Martyn, "Simeon's spiritual son," offered himself for service. But the securing of the man only emphasized the remaining difficulty of getting him to India. William Carey and John Thomas, two Baptist missionaries, had arrived in India without the Company's licence on November 11, 1793, just a fortnight after John Shore had become Governor-General. With a sympathetic administration they found easy admittance, particularly as the Charter Act of 1793 making entrance into India without licence a high misdemeanour did not become law until February 1794. Thomas was fortunately a surgeon and found no difficulty in securing permanent residence. Carey avoided trouble by becoming an official in an indigo factory. With the passing of the Charter Act, however, the difficulties of entrance greatly increased. Even Charles Grant could not get passage on a Company's ship for a man with the avowed intention of preaching to the Indians.[34] And if the missionary did

[32]Eugene Stock, *History of the C.M.S.*, I, 74.
[33]In its first fifteen years the Society sent out twenty-four missionaries. Of these, seventeen were Germans. And of the remaining seven, who were English, only three were ordained.
[34]In 1813 Wilberforce wrote, "No missionaries have ever been suffered to go to India in the Company's ships—the only ships . . . which have sailed for India; they have therefore stolen out . . . circuitously and unlicensed . . . but it is due to the Government abroad to say that several of the missionaries, when

reach India he was liable to deportation on arrival. Grant, however, was not without recourse. If he could not send a missionary he promised to get an appointment for a chaplain in the Company's service. The Missionary Society "cheerfully acquiesced, as the appointment . . . might ultimately lead, under God, to considerable influence among the Heathen."[35] So in 1805, six years after the Missionary Society was formed, Henry Martyn, the first volunteer, departed for India as a chaplain to the East India Company. Henry Martyn, though counted one of the great missionaries, was never a missionary in the ordinary sense. He remained a chaplain to the East India Company at a salary of £1,200 a year. Yet he was a chaplain by necessity, a missionary by intent, and he performed really heroic missionary labours.

Meanwhile the Clapham Sect were pursuing other labours outside the circle of the Missionary Society. They alleviated their defeat in the charter struggle of 1793 by the appointment, in the same year, of John Shore as Governor-General of India. Wilberforce was present when Pitt and Dundas made their decision in favour of Shore, and Wilberforce and Grant combined to induce Shore to accept. The appointment was from their standpoint a fortunate one. Shore, indeed, was not able to do much to further their missionary schemes. He did build new churches, but he found the Europeans would not tolerate missions; to Wilberforce he wrote, "they needed first to Christianize themselves." In 1795 he reported officially that most regular chaplains were not "respectable characters." Yet he did accomplish something. Sir John Kaye said of him: "At a time when to be corrupt was to be like one's neighbours, he had preserved, in poverty and privation, the most inflexible integrity." And when he became Governor-General, "he resolved to make it be seen that the Christian religion was the religion of the State." Shore's influence did something to elevate the tone of official life.

Clapham strength was augmented also by the election, in 1794, of Charles Grant as Director of the East India Company. Before Grant had been a year in the directorship he succeeded in getting an official

---

there, have been kindly treated. It is the Court of Directors at home that is hostile, more than the Government in India." J. S. Harford, *Recollections of William Wilberforce*, p. 29.
[35]Stock, *History of the C.M.S.*, I, 82.

dispatch protesting against the profanation of the Sabbath; and two years later he secured an order for churches to be built. No move, however, was made in India and the order remained dormant for twenty years. Grant in particular used his influence to secure the appointment of suitable men as chaplains; and the men he selected: Claudius Buchanan, Henry Martyn, Thomas Thomason, David Corrie, and Daniel Wilson, left their mark permanently on Anglo-Indian life.

Of these men Claudius Buchanan, appointed in 1796, took the biggest part in the home labours of the Clapham Sect. While Buchanan was at Cambridge, a protégé of Henry Thornton and Simeon, Grant, after his arrival from India, visited Simeon to discuss with him the mission scheme. Simeon took Buchanan to the interview, and Buchanan was inspired by Grant to become a missionary in India. Because it was impossible for Buchanan to go as a missionary, he welcomed the opportunity which Grant provided to go as a chaplain in the Company's service.

From his earliest days in India Buchanan had a distinguished career, and he soon achieved an eminent place in Anglo-Indian society. He became greatly concerned for the evangelism of India, and, early in the nineteenth century, to stimulate greater interest among the English, he made use of a method similar to that which had won Clarkson to the cause of abolition. He provided large prizes in Oxford and Cambridge for essays on the civilization and moral improvement of India. Through this plan he attracted the interest of many students who afterward became eminent in Indian labours—including young Charles Grant, son of Charles Grant of Clapham, and Hugh Pearson, afterwards Buchanan's biographer. To supplement these efforts he wrote in 1805 a *Memoir of the Expediency of an Ecclesiastical Establishment for British India.*[36] The book was in its way a sensation, but all Buchanan's efforts, and the whole Christian movement in India, were soon negatived by untoward happenings in the Indian army.

In 1806 a serious mutiny occurred amongst the Sepoy soldiers at Vellore, and this at once gave the opponents of missions an opportunity; they ascribed the cause to the disturbing effects of missionary

---

[36]Lord Teignmouth wrote a review of the book in the *Christian Observer,* 1806.

propaganda. When the news reached England an even greater storm was aroused there. A member of the East India Company, named Thomas Twining, wrote a pamphlet urging the Court of Directors to expel all missionaries from India, and to stop all printing of the Scriptures in Indian languages. He expressed alarm, indeed horror, at the activities of the newly formed British and Foreign Bible Society, and of Buchanan himself. He warned the Society and "their patrons at Clapham and Leadenhall Street" that "religious innovation" was extremely dangerous to British interests in India, that British interests could be secured only by allowing the people to continue in their "prejudices and absurdities." A "war of pamphlets" ensued, in which a Bengal officer, Major Scott Waring, recommended a clean sweep of every English missionary, and personal recall of Buchanan as a culprit. The Court seemed in general but too well disposed to such proceedings. But the Clapham Sect had powerful influence in the East India Company, and Grant and Teignmouth with the support of their friends were able to block the scheme.

The "war of pamphlets" unsheathed many swords. Sydney Smith flourished his in the pages of the *Edinburgh Review,* in his bitter article on "consecrated cobblers." Wilberforce felt that Sydney Smith's article had done serious damage to their cause. Southey made what riposte he could in the first number of the *Quarterly.* But, before any rash measures were undertaken, Lord Teignmouth joined in the fray. His prestige as an ex-Governor-General, his wide knowledge, and his conspicuous moderation on all subjects, gave him impressive influence. His pamphlet, *Considerations on Communicating to the Natives of India the Knowledge of Christianity,* was a bit heavy—as were most of the others—but it was a crushing reply to the extravagances of his opponents. "It was said, at the time, and with undeniable truth, that if this pamphlet had appeared at the beginning of the controversy, no other need have been written. It was sensible, argumentative, conclusive; and it demolished the Waringites."[37]

Another phase of the struggle began in 1808 when Buchanan (not recalled but of his own volition) returned from India to join his comrades in their campaign. His return was as important to the popular side of missions as the arrival of Grant from India in 1790

[37]Kaye, *Christianity in India,* p. 155.

had been to the official side. He immediately changed the tactics of
the conflict. Instead of flinging pamphlets at his opponents he
preached sermons to his friends. Early in 1809 he preached
a sermon on "The Star in the East," which was said to have
"kept the minds of a large auditory in a state of most lively sensation
for an hour and twenty-five minutes."[38] At the annual meeting of the
Church Missionary Society in 1810, with Wilberforce in the chair,
supported by Babington, Grant, Simeon, and Macaulay, he preached
another stirring sermon on "The Light of the World," in which he
referred to the previous abolition of the slave trade, and urged that as
one victory had just been won for humanity in Africa, so another must
be won for Christianity in India. In 1811 he widened his audience
by the publication of his *Christian Researches in Asia,* which attracted
much attention, and further stimulated interest in the East.

The Charter of 1813

Back of all this enthusiasm, however, was the disquieting memory
of the 1793 defeat, and the knowledge that even if missionaries could
be sent to India they would find the door shut in their faces. The
"Saints" did not forget, but they were crusading with a purpose; they
were looking ahead. They knew that in 1793 the charter had been
renewed for a period of twenty years, and that in 1813 this period
would be ended. In 1813 they intended to be armed with such
strength that their purposes would not be lightly frustrated by a "little
tumult in the court of proprietors." The years of activity and publicity
were awakening the public interest upon which they were relying for
support; the missionary societies had organization and influence; and
above all, the "Saints" themselves had received a thorough schooling
in the art of public agitation and were determined to introduce into
the battle of the charter the methods which had been successful in
winning abolition.

Early in 1812 therefore they began to get into action. In February,
Wilberforce wrote that he was looking forward to the renewal of the
charter as to a great era when the friends of Christianity would wipe
away what he had long thought "next to the Slave Trade, the foulest
blot on the moral character of our country." He felt that the cause

[38]Hole, *Early History of the C.M.S.,* p. 185.

of "gospel light" for India was one for which it was "worth while being a public man," and was already "busily engaged in reading, thinking, consulting, and persuading." For, though he indulged a "humble hope" that better days were ahead for India, he was "but too well aware, that if the unbiassed judgment of the House of Commons were to decide the question, fatal indeed would be the issue."

He had no intention of leaving the question to the unbiased judgment of the House of Commons. He interviewed Perceval, the Prime Minister, he wrote to Gisborne calling on him to stir up the clergy, he composed an article for the *Christian Observer*. He was determined to leave no stone unturned to "call into action the whole force of the religious world." Susceptible as he naturally was to the rights of property he was now willing to "abolish the East India Company altogether" rather than not provide for India "a passage for the entrance of light, and truth, and moral improvement and happiness."[39]

Wilberforce was not labouring alone. "We are all at work," he wrote, "about the best mode of providing for the free course of religious instruction in India."[40] To make definite their plans Buchanan drafted a prospectus for the proposed episcopacy in India. He despatched a copy to Macaulay and Wilberforce, asking them to submit it also to Grant and Teignmouth for approval. Grant laid before the House of Commons his *Observations,* which made such an impression that the House ordered them to be printed. Macaulay undertook the arduous labour of preparing circulars to be broadcast throughout the country. Babington was set apart as the "chief conspirator" detailed to organize the hundreds of petitions for which the circulars would pave the way. Grant, Babington, and Wilberforce went in a deputation to the Prime Minister to commend their purpose to his approval. And the whole brotherhood consolidated all their efforts by almost daily consultations at Clapham.

Less than two pages of Wilberforce's diary include the following references to the campaign:

[1812] "March 7th. Writing to the Bishop of St. David's about East India Christianizing. Dined at Speaker's—sat next to George Holford and Leicester. Talked to former about East India mission, and Buchanan. Cunninghame of Lainshaw breakfasted with me, to talk about getting the General Assembly of Scotland to take up the cause of Christianizing India.[41] Dined at Lord Carrington's. . . . I told them Sabat's story, which they scarce believed, or about infanticide. . . . To town, calling at Bartlett's Buildings to inquire what done about East India Company's charter. Conference at Butterworth's till near five. Settled that the different sects should apply separately to Perceval, and to the chief members in the House of Commons, stating their deep interest—and also inform the minds of their people every where throughout the country."[42]

Yet despite the activity, and despite Wilberforce's politically arranged breakfast and dinner parties and his incessant interviewing, the "Saints" discovered that people were not so stirred about the benighted Indians as they had been about the enslaved Negroes. "I am sadly disappointed," Wilberforce confessed, "in finding even religious people so cold about East Indian Instruction." "I begin to despair," he added a few days later, "of much being gained for the Christian cause in the East India charter discussion."[42]

Though disappointed, the brotherhood did not permit any cessation of propaganda. In April 1812 they enlisted in their campaign the forces of their Missionary Society. They arranged a special general meeting, which attracted about four hundred gentlemen, including many members of Parliament, and which in its protracted course was addressed by a formidable succession of the Society's orators, including Babington, Stephen, Thornton, and Wilberforce. Wilberforce called the meeting a "grand assemblage," and added modestly, "I spoke with acceptance." It concluded with the Society pledged to exert itself to promote Christianity in India, and a committee appointed to seek interviews with His Majesty's ministers, and to use all possible means of obtaining a favourable outcome of their endeavour.

All these preliminaries had just been paving the way for the opening of the parliamentary battle in 1813. As the time drew near, therefore, the friends redoubled their efforts. They knew that the struggle would be difficult, because they were aware that a great many of the Anglo-Indians genuinely believed that the introduction

[41]The General Assembly afterwards sent to Parliament the first petition on the subject.   [42]*Life of Wilberforce*, IV, 14-15.

of Christianity would jeopardize British interests in India. But the Clapham Sect had their own Anglo-Indians, and were convinced that such fears were groundless; and, at whatever risk, they were determined to remove the bar against Christianity.

In January of 1813 Josiah Pratt, the first editor of the *Christian Observer,* made an important departure in the campaign by commencing another magazine, the *Missionary Register.* The *Register* was designed to promote interest in missionary endeavour and to publish reports of all missionary societies then active. Its work was very thoroughly done, and its pages are still mines of information about early missionary labour. In its day it was an influential magazine especially in Evangelical circles, and even in its first year by entering vigorously into the Charter struggle it helped much to win the battle.

Anxious to commence the battle in good time, Wilberforce brought the question before Parliament on February 19, 1813, by presenting a petition of the Scottish S.P.C.K., praying that the charter bill might make it legal to impart the teaching of Christianity in India. The Anglo-Indians "had hardened in the opinion that the licensing of missionaries should be reserved in the new charter as in the old for the Court of Directors of the Company." On March 22, on motion of Lord Castlereagh, who accepted the principles of the resolutions of 1793, the Commons went into Committee of the Whole House on the East India Company's affairs. Wilberforce, William Smith, and Stephen joined in the three hours' debate trying to win adequate consideration for their purposes.[43] But the result was not encouraging. The temper of the House was manifestly hostile. "The truth is," Wilberforce reported, "and a dreadful truth it is, that the opinions of . . . a vast majority of the House of Commons would be against any motion which the friends of religion might make. . . ." "But I trust," he added significantly, "it is very different in the body of our people; and petitions are to be promoted with a view to bring their sentiments and feelings to bear upon the opposite tenets and dispositions of the members of parliament."[44] "The public voice alone promises something," said Buchanan in similar strain, "If every city and town in

[43]R. Coupland, *Wilberforce,* 387. *Parliamentary Debates,* XXIV, 654-9; XXV, 227-56.
[44]*Life of Wilberforce,* IV, 102.

England and Scotland were to petition . . . the business would acquire a new complexion before the end of May."[45] The weapons which had killed the slave trade were the only ones which held any promise for this new fight. And the Clapham Sect turned from the disheartening prospect in Parliament to gather still more strength from public agitation.

"Not a day was lost," and Wilberforce commenced writing "a multitude of letters," urging his correspondents in turn to bestir themselves, and organize petitions to the House of Commons. To Hannah More he wrote a long letter about denying "religious or moral light" to the East Indians. "You will agree with me," he said, "that now the Slave Trade is abolished, this is by far the greatest of our national sins. . . . But all this is to lead you to stir up a petition in Bristol, and any other place." To another friend he wrote: "You petitioned in the case of the Slave Trade, and those petitions were eminently useful; so they would be now; and what is more, after having been talked of, their not coming would be highly injurious; so lose no time." "Can you venture," he asked a third friend, "to add your sanction to the opinion . . . that our East Indian Empire is safer under the protection of Brahma with all his obscenities and blood, than under that of God Almighty? . . . I am persuaded, my dear friend, that you will hereafter regret your inactivity."[46]

A constant stream of such letters from a public leader with the position and prestige of Wilberforce must have exercised no little influence in the country. But, though he persevered, "excessively busy stirring up petitions" for "the greatest object which men ever pursued," enthusiasm lagged, and "the spirit of petitioning" spread but slowly.[47]

Further deliberation followed "in council at Henry Thornton's," and additional methods of propaganda were adopted. A great public meeting was arranged for the city of London; and, it being "effective," others were arranged in different parts of the country. Large quantities of campaign literature were distributed, and it was supplemented by a series of vigorous letters which Buchanan wrote to the London *Times*.

The excitement outside was interrupted by a further reverse in Parliament. The House of Commons began the examination of witnesses, calling two former Governors-General, Warren Hastings and Lord Teignmouth.[48] Hastings refused to commit himself about the effect of admitting missionaries to India, but resorted to the ancient evasion of the slave trade that safety would be found in delay. Lord Teignmouth rendered some help; but he was given questions purposely phrased so as to limit the effectiveness of his replies. The total gains were dubious. Commons sentiment was visibly moving toward another defeat for the "Saints." In the urgency of the peril the Clapham Sect broke their cherished Sabbath rest, and for once gathered at Henry Thornton's for a "Cabinet Council" on a Sunday afternoon. They decided that to forestall disaster in the approaching examination in the House of Lords immediate action was necessary. Wilberforce was not at a loss for tactics. "You know enough of life," he told Hannah More, "to be aware that in parliamentary measures of importance, more is to be done out of the House than in it." Before Parliament reassembled Wilberforce had employed his gifts of diplomacy, and his friendship with such men as Lords Grenville and Wellesley to such a satisfactory conclusion that he was able to report an agreement that (for the moment) both in the Commons and the Lords "religion should be left out of the examination."[49]

But two months now remained to turn the scale, and the brotherhood girded their loins for the last battle. Wilberforce resumed his incessant interviewing. Interviewing was Wilberforce's forte. "All had access to him, and he could enter every where. He was the link between the most dissimilar allies. Bishops and Baptists found in him a common term." He even put off his Easter holidays. "I cannot spare the time now," he explained, "when it is so much needed for East Indian religion and seeing people on it." Grant, Teignmouth, and Buchanan supplemented Wilberforce's interviews with their pamphlets. And, as of old, "Cabinet Councils" at Clapham directed and co-ordinated their efforts. Wilberforce's diary has the typical comment: ". . . consulting . . . with Grant and Stephen, and looking over the list of the House of Commons, to see whom we severally ought to speak to . . . talked over the mode of proceeding in the question in cabinet council with Grant, Babington, Stephen, and Henry Thornton."[50]

[48]*Parliamentary Debates*, XXV. 415-47.   [49]*Life of Wilberforce*, IV, 109-12.
[50]*Ibid.*, IV, 113, 116-17.

It must, therefore, have been with much anticipation that the friends waited for the 1813 anniversary of the Missionary Society, which they forthwith converted into a timely mass-meeting for their campaign. John Venn was now ill, and William Dealtry, a like-minded clergyman whom the Clapham Sect would soon choose to be Venn's successor, was taking Venn's place, and was chosen to preach the anniversary sermon. Wilberforce, Grant, Thornton, Babington, Macaulay, and Simeon, were all there to hear and to judge. Dealtry exceeded their expectations. His sermon was such as to electrify the whole congregation. It was ordered to be printed *"instantly"* to add to the campaign literature. But Dealtry's sermon was not all. After-wards came the annual meeting, where doubtless the others delivered more of their glowing speeches. The results at any rate seemed to be satisfactory. "The whole Christian world seems stirred up," Simeon reported, "almost as you would expect it to be in the Millennium."[51]

With aroused public opinion in their favour the "Saints" mar-shalled their forces for a renewed struggle in Parliament. Even now the battle was hard fought. When the preliminary resolutions were introduced the enemy professed themselves willing to concede an episcopal establishment for the white residents in India, but were flatly unwilling to agree to the admission of missionaries for the natives.[52] The decisive debate came on June 22, 1813, and William Smith, Thornton, Wilberforce, and the two Charles Grants, senior and junior, all joined in advocacy of their cause.[53] Wilberforce in his earnestness rose once more to the level of some of his great anti-slavery speeches. The report in *Parliamentary Debates* is fortunately printed verbatim from a published copy. Some characteristic excerpts will suffice to show the ground of his appeal and the quality of his plea. He began by stating that there was only one remedy for the ills of India's suffering multitude.

That remedy, Sir, is Christianity, . . . for Christianity assumes her true character, no less than she performs her natural and proper office, when she takes under her protection those poor degraded beings, on whom

[51]Carus, *Memoirs of Simeon*, p. 364.
[52]*Parliamentary Debates*, XXVI, 529-63.
[53]*Ibid.*, pp. 827-73. In his speech Wilberforce used material from Grant's *Observations*, which he called a "Memoir written by a dear and most honoured friend." *Ibid.*, p. 842.

philosophy looks down with disdain, or perhaps with contemptuous con-
descension. On the very first promulgation of Christianity, it was declared
by its great Author, as "glad tidings to the poor"; and, ever faithful to
her character, Christianity still delights to instruct the ignorant, to
succour the needy, to comfort the sorrowful, to visit the forsaken. . . .

Animated, Sir, by this unfeigned spirit of friendship for the natives of
India, their religious and moral interests are undoubtedly our first concern; but the course we are recommending tends no less to promote
their temporal well-being, than their eternal welfare; for such is their
real condition, that we are prompted to endeavour to communicate to
them the benefits of Christian instruction, scarcely less by religious principle than by the feelings of common humanity. Not, Sir, that I would
pretend to conceal from the House, that the hope which, above all
others, chiefly gladdens my heart, is that of being instrumental in bringing them into the paths by which they may be led to everlasting felicity.
But still, were all considerations of a future state out of the question, I
hesitate not to affirm, that a regard for their temporal well-being would
alone furnish abundant motives for our endeavouring to diffuse among
them the blessings of Christian light and moral instruction. . . .

. . . the evils of Hindostan are family, fireside evils: they pervade the
whole mass of the population, and embitter the domestic cup, in almost
every family. Why need I, in this country, insist on the evils which arise
merely out of the institution of Caste itself; a system which, though,
strange to say, it has been complimented as a device of deep political
wisdom, must surely appear to every heart of true British temper to be a
system at war with truth and nature; a detestable expedient for keeping
the lower orders of the community bowed down in an abject state of
hopeless and irremediable vassalage. . . . Even where slavery has existed,
it has commonly been possible (though in the West Indies, alas! artificial
difficulties have been interposed) for individuals to burst their bonds,
and assert the privileges of their nature. But the more cruel shackles of
Caste are never to be shaken; as well might a dog, or any other of the
brute creation . . . aspire to the dignity and rights of man. I will not
think so injuriously of our opponents as not to be persuaded, that they
would indignantly spurn at the very idea of introducing such a system
into this country. And are not the natives of India, our fellow-subjects,
fairly intitled to all the benefits which we can safely impart to them? . . .
But, as I have already stated, our opponents should remember, that
Christianity, independently of its effects on a future state of existence,
has been acknowledged even by avowed sceptics, to be, beyond all other

institutions that ever existed, favourable to the temporal interests and happiness of man: and never was there a country where there is greater need than in India for the diffusion of its genial influence. . . .

Again in India we find prevalent that evil, I mean infanticide, against which we might have hoped that nature herself would have supplied adequate restraints, if we had not been taught by experience that for our deliverance even from this detestable crime we are indebted to Christianity. For it is not to philosophy, it is not to civilization; it is not to progress in refinement or in the arts and comforts of social life; it is not even to liberty herself that the world is indebted for this emancipation. The friends of Christianity may justly glory in the acknowledgment of one of its greatest enemies that infanticide was the incorrigible vice of all antiquity; and it is very striking that both in India and in China, where the light of Revelation has never penetrated, this detestable crime still asserts its superiority over nature itself, no less than over virtue. To this in India is added the destruction of the sick and aged, often by their nearest relatives. . . .

Another practice . . . [which was] . . . greatly discouraged, though not absolutely prohibited by the Mahometan government, and which in consequence had considerably declined, has increased since the country came under our dominion. Great pains were taken by the missionaries a few years ago to ascertain the number of widows which were annually burnt in a district thirty miles round Calcutta, and the House will be astonished to hear that in this comparatively small area 130 widows were burnt in six months. In the year 1803 within the same space the number amounted to 275, one of whom was a girl of eleven years of age. I ought to state that the utmost pains were taken to have the account correct; certain persons were employed purposely to watch and report the number of these horrible exhibitions; and the place, person, and other particulars were regularly certified. After hearing this you will not be surprised on being told that the whole number of these annual sacrifices of women who are often thus cruelly torn from their children at the very time when from the loss of their father they must be in the greatest need of the fostering care of the surviving parent, is estimated, I think, in the Bengal provinces, to be 10,000; the same number at which it was calculated many years ago. . . .

And now, Sir, I shall do little more than allude to another class of enormities, which by that very enormity, are in some measure shielded from the detestation they would otherwise incur: I allude to the various obscene and bloody rites of their idolatrous ceremonies, with all their unutterable abominations. . . . Indeed, to all who have made it their business to study the nature of idolatrous worship in general, I scarcely need remark, that in its superstitious rites, there has commonly been found to be a natural alliance between obscenity and cruelty; and of the Hindoo superstitions it may be truly affirmed, that they are scarcely less bloody than lascivious. . . . A gentleman of the highest integrity, and better qualified than almost any one else to form a correct judgment in this instance; I mean Dr. Carey, the missionary, has calculated, that, taking in all the various modes and forms of destruction connected with the worship at the temple of Jaggernaut in Orissa, the lives of 100,000 human beings are annually expended in the service of that single idol.

It has often been truly remarked, particularly I think by the historian of America, that the moral character of a people may commonly be known from the nature and attributes of the objects of its worship. On this principle, we might have anticipated the moral condition of the Hindoos, by ascertaining the character of their deities. If it was truly affirmed of the old pagan mythology, that scarcely a crime could be committed, the perpetrator of which might not plead in his justification, the precedent of one of the national gods; far more truly may it be said, that in the adventures of the countless rabble of Hindoo deities, you may find every possible variety of every practicable crime. Here also, more truly than of old, every vice has its patron as well as its example. Their divinities are absolute monsters of lust, injustice, wickedness and cruelty. In short, their religious system is one grand abomination. Not but that I know you may sometimes find, in the sacred books of the Hindoos, acknowledgments of the unity of the great Creator of all things; but just as, from a passage of the same sort in Cicero, it would be contrary alike to reason and experience to argue, that the common pagan mythology was not the religion of the bulk of mankind in the ancient world; so it is far more absurd and groundless, to contend that more or fewer of the 33,000,000 of Hindoo gods, with their several attributes and adventures, do not constitute the theology of the bulk of the natives of India. . . .

And now, Sir, I am persuaded, that in all who hear me, there can be but one common feeling of deep commiseration for the unhappy people whose sad state I have been describing to you; together with the most earnest wishes that we should commence, with prudence, but with zeal, our endeavours to communicate to those benighted regions, the genial life and warmth of our Christian principles and institutions, if it can be attempted without absolute ruin to our political interests in India. . . . For my own part . . . I should deem it almost morally impossible, that there could be any country in the state in which India is proved, but too clearly, now to be, which would not be likely to find Christianity the most powerful of all expedients for improving its morals, and promoting alike its temporal and eternal welfare.[54]

"Never," said his biographers, "did he speak with greater power." "He spoke three hours," said a hostile critic, "but nobody seemed fatigued: all indeed were pleased; some with the ingenious artifices of his manner, but most with the glowing language of his heart. Much as I differed from him in opinion, it was impossible not to be delighted with his eloquence. . . ."[55] Later, Sir John Kaye said more objectively of the speech, "It was a noble piece of special pleading, not exempt from exaggeration."[56]

The speech, however, does not explain the decision. Twenty years earlier Wilberforce had spoken in the same place for the same cause, and had been overwhelmingly defeated. But he now had on his side just what in his former attempt he had lacked: the militant enthusiasm of the country at large. The long agitation had served its purpose. The petitions which had been so diligently cultivated came pouring, according to plan, from all parts of the country, so that the final appeal was supported and supplemented by 837 petitions, bearing more than half a million signatures.[57] Such numbers, then wholly without precedent on such a subject, made an impression on Parliament which could not be mistaken, and of which Wilberforce made good use in his appeal. Owing to them more than to the oratory a favourable vote was won. "Blessed be God," Wilberforce wrote hastily to his wife, "we carried our question triumphantly about three, or later, this morning." "I heard afterwards," he said, "that many good men had been praying for us all night."[58]

Significant as this victory had been, one more battle remained to be fought. The debate had been only on the preliminary resolutions, and an opportunity to reverse the decision might occur in the passage of the bill itself. For the enemy "were not disposed to yield without another struggle." On July 12 Wilberforce wrote: "Our opponents mean to make their utmost exertions to defeat us. . . . They have

[54]*Ibid.*, pp. 831-72.   [55]*Life of Wilberforce*, IV, 125.
[56]Kaye, *Christianity in India*, p. 276.   [57]*Missionary Register*, 1813, p. 235.
[58]*Life of Wilberforce*, IV, 121, 120.

been working in private with more success than we had conceived possible. We must therefore meet exertion with exertion."[59] The "Saints" had suffered too many defeats not to be wary to the last. But this time they need not have been apprehensive. The second victory was secured on the final reading of the bill, and atoned for the first defeat twenty years before. The later scene was indeed greatly changed. On the first occasion Charles Grant had been sitting in the gallery, watching Wilberforce go down to defeat. Now not only was Grant with Wilberforce on the floor, but he had with him his son Charles, who gave some of the most brilliant speeches of the debate.[60] Thornton was on the floor, too, and Babington, and James Stephen, and, including these, nine members altogether from the ranks of the C.M.S. They were a valiant company, and they won a well-earned victory. "The East India Bill passed," wrote Wilberforce in his diary, "and the missionary, or rather the Christian, cause fought through, without division, to the last. We were often alarmed. . . . The petitions, of which a greater number than were ever known, have carried our question instrumentally, the good providence of God really." "To those who observe the signs of the times," he wrote to a friend, "the prospect is very encouraging. . . . I cannot but draw a favourable augury for the welfare of our country."[61]

Buchanan thought of a different feature. "Now we are all likely to be disgraced," he said. "Parliament has opened the door, and who is there to go in? From the church not one man."[62]

The Clapham Sect therefore did not cease their missionary labours with the passing of the 1813 charter. They failed indeed to achieve the desire which Grant had cherished since 1805, i.e., to make Brown or Buchanan Bishop of India. But they did find missionaries to go; and when Reginald Heber was appointed Bishop they had in him a close friend who ordained their candidates and furthered their plans. They also continued to labour for their Missionary Society, to attend anniversaries, to make speeches, and ever generously to follow their words with their financial support.

[59]Hole, *Early History of the C.M.S.*, p. 299.
[60]"It must have been a fine thing to have seen the two Charles Grants—father and son—fighting side by side on the floor of the House of Commons." Kaye, *Christianity in India*, p. 273.
[61]*Life of Wilberforce*, IV, 124-5.
[62]Pearson, *Memoirs of Buchanan*, II, 307-8.

But this chapter cannot accompany them further. In the 1813 battle they had won the central fight. They had not only secured an Episcopal establishment in India; they had secured the first grant for Indian education.[63] They had opened to India a door, through which all Christians of all the world could enter. The Clapham Sect had done this almost completely by themselves, with their own enthusiasm and their own resources. Even the struggle for abolition was not as exclusively theirs as was this one. In the whole long battle hardly a name is mentioned from without their little circle. It was their wide horizon of interest, their disregard of established prejudices and vested interests, their Missionary Society, their appeal to the religious fervour of the middle classes, their skill in parliamentary tactics and public agitation, their patient, concerted, and harmonious labours, their religious passion, their indomitable courage, and their untiring persistence, which achieved what would otherwise have been thought at once imprudent to attempt and impossible to attain.

Their labours in this endeavour as in others reveal their essential soundness and their far-seeing discernment. They did not exercise themselves excitedly for little things. They were governed by great purposes, and looked to great ends. They saw unmistakably while it was dim to other people that a nation dominant commercially and politically incurs obligations which should be measured only by its loftiest principles and its most sacred heritage. And they gave their best to ensure that these principles should be built into the structure of Anglo-Indian relations. Wilberforce knew that he was finishing only the first stage, when, after the 1813 victory, he wrote: "I am persuaded that we have . . . laid the foundation stone of the grandest edifice that ever was raised in Asia."[64]

[63]The bill provided for an annual grant of a lakh of rupees (£10,000) for promoting education among the natives. However, no real system of education was established till much later.

[64]*Correspondence of Wilberforce*, II, 271.

CHAPTER FIVE

People must be fit for freedom

THE CHURCH MISSIONARY SOCIETY in which the Clapham Sect had taken so much interest was, in common with all other contemporary missionary societies, indebted to a different society which has already been mentioned, the British and Foreign Bible Society. But an inquiry into the establishment of the British and Foreign Bible Society leads again to the plans and councils of the Clapham Sect. The Bible Society, however, is but one of a long series of efforts to promote education and circulate good literature. It will be well, as a preliminary, to consider some of the earlier endeavours.

The later years of the eighteenth century and the early years of the nineteenth witnessed a notable advance in popular education— an advance to which, in the early stages, the most significant contribution was made by the institution of the Sunday School. Sunday schools were not then a new idea. Luther had formed them in Germany; Cardinal Borromeo, in the seventeenth century, had formed them in Milan; John Wesley had organized one in his parish in Georgia; and numerous other leaders had made tentative experiments. But Robert Raikes, who opened his school in Sooty Alley in 1780, was the first to make the movement a practical success. In a few months Wesley was reporting, "I find these schools springing up wherever I go." Five years later the idea had so grown that a group of friends formed the first Sunday School Society to promote the organization of schools and to provide the necessary funds.[1] Within two years this association—of which one of the leading spirits was Henry Thornton, and two of the supporters were Granville Sharp and Hannah More—organized two hundred schools; and by that

[1]See *Plan of a Society Established in London for the Support and Encouragement of Sunday Schools.*

time, 1787, the total number of Sunday school scholars in England
was 250,000.[2]

The Sunday schools undertook as one of their primary obligations
to teach the hitherto illiterate masses to read. They were conducted
largely by Wesleyan societies, or by Evangelical clergymen, fired by
the Evangelical belief that "the free study of God's word was the
proudest heritage of Englishmen." "Purely religious motives" therefore stimulated a widespread increase in literacy, and brought, as
Green said, "the beginnings of popular education."[3]

But England at the time of Burke's *Reflections on the Revolution
in France* had small enthusiasm for popular education. Even "good
churchmen" looked askance at the idea, and referred darkly to the
happenings across the Channel. The leading bishop of the day,
Bishop Horsley, declared that there was "much ground for suspicion
that sedition and atheism were the real objects of some of these
institutions rather than religion."[4] The Scottish General Assembly
was moved to issue a "Pastoral Admonition" which inveighed against
the teachers of Sunday schools, and warned that there was good
reason to fear that their labours were "a cover for secret democracy
and liberty." It was said that the Pitt Cabinet seriously contemplated
a bill to suppress Sunday schools altogether. As late as 1819 Cheshire
magistrates desired Sunday schools to be forbidden.[5] When Mrs.
Hannah More commenced her work in Cheddar in 1789 she met
prolonged opposition. One farmer said that it was preordained that
servants should be ignorant, and that it was a shame to alter the
decrees of God. Another objected that he did not want his ploughmen
wiser than he himself; "he did not want saints but workmen." And
on the day when her first school opened another landowner exclaimed

[2]Henry Thompson, *Life of Hannah More,* p. 88.
[3]J. R. Green, *History of the English People,* IV, 274.
[4]W. L. Mathieson, *England in Transition,* p. 59. To Bishop Horsley's charge
Rowland Hill, who is said to have established the first Sunday school in London,
replied, "Respecting the little army we are about to raise to overthrow the King
and constitution, it should be considered that the children in these schools of
sedition are, on the average, only from six to twelve years of age; consequently
they will not be able to take the field at least ten years; and, half of these being
girls, unless we raise an army of Amazons, with a virago Joan at the head of
them, we shall be sadly short of soldiers to accomplish the design." *Ibid.*
Nevertheless these children made the next generation a different generation from
that of their fathers.
[5]J. L. and B. Hammond, *The Town Labourer,* p. 93.

with alarm that it was "all over with property; if property is not to rule what is to become of us?"[6]

Needless to say, those who originated the Sunday schools were not revolutionary, any more than were those who fought for abolition. But it is a commentary on their position that in venturing on these labours they were undertaking what contemporary right-wing critics considered as dangerous radicalism. Moreover, the critics were not entirely wrong. The Sunday schools in the beginning were often illiberal enough. Hannah More's scheme was as narrow as could well be imagined. The son of a farmer might be taught the "beneficial and appropriate knowledge for the boy of this class," but the children of day labourers must be given "no writing," nor any reading but the Bible, the catechism, and "such little tracts as may enable them to understand the Church service." Yet, though the immediate motive of many of the Sunday schools may have been partly to teach content-ment with the existing social order, the ultimate results were wider. The children were taught to be content but they were also taught to read, and literacy was the necessary prelude to democracy. In the long run "by giving to workers that . . . possibility of concerted action which only education can bestow" the Sunday schools were "unwit-tingly promoting the very revolution they wished to resist."[7]

The most noticeable Sunday school work in which any of the Clapham Sect engaged was that in the village of Cheddar in the Mendip Hills. In 1789 Wilberforce while on a visit to Mrs. Hannah More was disturbed by the poverty and brutality of the villagers. He induced Mrs. More to make some effort for their welfare, and promised the support of himself and Henry Thornton. The labours subsequently undertaken at Cheddar and in the neighbouring country included many schemes for moral and material improvement, but chief among them was the establishment of Sunday schools. In a short time Mrs. More and her sister had gathered upwards of five hundred children in their various schools, and they continued their organization until they had established schools over an area of seventy-five square miles, and could gather at their festivals as many as thirteen hundred children. This work was directed and largely

[6]Martha More, *Mendip Annals,* pp. 208, 210, 212.
[7]C. E. Raven, *Christian Socialism,* p. 15.

financed by Wilberforce and Thornton. For some years Thornton's support amounted to £600 annually.

Sunday school activity by the Sect, however, was not confined to Wilberforce and Thornton. Most of the individual labours are probably unrecorded, but Zachary Macaulay is mentioned as one of the earliest supporters of Sunday schools,[8] Babington was in his youth a Sunday school teacher,[9] and Grant introduced the Sunday school into Scotland, personally supported two schools for twenty years, and for a long time himself acted as teacher.[10]

The Clapham Sect were interested not only in Sunday schools; they were enthusiastic in the support of all movements for education. Wilberforce and his friends were the first to plan, between 1802 and 1804, an Anglican scheme of primary education, of which they seem to have been thinking as early as 1798; but their scheme was squeezed out between the other schemes which arose about that time. John Venn was one of the first clergymen to introduce parish schools. He boasted before his death that every child in Clapham parish could be taught to read gratuitously, that every family could be supplied with a Bible, and that every inhabitant could find accommodation to worship God.[11] At Clapham, indeed, there were maintained by private benevolence no fewer than six schools for poor children.[12] In addition, Henry Thornton supported schools at Southwark[13] and Wilberforce others at Sandgate and the "two towns adjoining."[14] Babington wrote a treatise on Christian education which had some little vogue. And in the colony at Sierra Leone Macaulay laboured to achieve universal education. He established there schools for children which reached an attendance of three hundred, and night schools for adults which attracted large numbers.[15] After returning to England he befriended and assisted Joseph Lancaster, but with equal liberality also gave his support, and the support of the *Christian Observer,* to

[8]*Christian Observer,* 1839, p. 800.

[9]*Ibid.,* 1838, p. 130.

[10]*DNB,* "Charles Grant."

[11]John Venn, *Annals,* p. 135. *Christian Observer,* 1815, p. 28.

[12]R. de M. Rudolf *et al., Clapham and the Clapham Sect,* p. 90.

[13]*Ibid.,* p. 109. His father John Thornton also gave munificently to education and founded a college in America even during the War of Independence.

[14]*Christian Observer,* 1838, p. 576.

[15]*Ibid.,* 1839, p. 762.

Andrew Bell.[16] Wilberforce also aided and supported both these men, and James Stephen supported Bell. Grant originated at Hailey-bury a college for the training of Indian civil servants. Macaulay was an eager advocate for London University, and, when it was estab-lished, sat on its first Council.

Many of these movements for secular education were as suspect as the Sunday schools had been. Pitt, who had been content to leave the country almost without education, wrote in 1802 that he was strongly persuaded that Lancaster's project if allowed to operate was likely to produce mischief, and that it was necessary to find a safe substitute. Davies Giddy, later President of the Royal Society, said in the House of Commons in 1807: "However specious in theory the project might be, of giving education to the labouring classes . . . it would teach them to despise their lot in life, . . . it would render them factious and refractory, . . . it would enable them to read seditious pamphlets, vicious books, and publications against Christian-ity; it would render them insolent to their superiors; and in a few years the result would be that the legislature would find it necessary to direct the strong arm of power towards them, and to furnish the executive magistrates with much more vigorous laws than were now in force."[17] Even Cobbett thought that the demand for popular education was "despicable cant and nonsense." Against such a spirit the early advocates of popular education made slow headway.

The Clapham Sect, however, in their enthusiasm for popular education had no hope for a civilization of ignorant citizens. Wilber-force expressed their opinion when in 1819, pleading in the House of Commons for education of the poor, he declared that "if people were destined to be free, they must be made fit to enjoy their freedom." Neither he nor any of the others foresaw what that freedom would mean, but in their constant support of education they builded better than they knew.

[16]*Ibid.*, p. 800. Lancaster's efforts gave rise to the Royal Lancastrian In-stitution, which in 1814 was succeeded by the British and Foreign School Society. Bell's effort gave rise in 1811 to the National Schools Society. Broadly speaking, the National Society was Church of England and the British and Foreign School Society was Non-Conformist, though many Churchmen such as Wilberforce and Macaulay supported both.
[17]*Parliamentary Debates*, IX, 798-9.

The eagerness of the Clapham Sect for education did not, however, make them insensitive to objections of their opponents that people who could read the Bible could also read seditious and subversive literature. The Sect were as little anxious as any Tory squire to see the popular appetite being fed with such nutriment. But they attacked the problem from a better angle. They put their faith not in the preservation of ignorance, but in the production of good literature to satisfy the demand which education would create. And in this, as in other labours, they were led into distant reaches which in the beginning they in no wise anticipated.

The first literary crusade of the company, however, had been undertaken for the benefit not of the poor but of the rich. In 1788 Hannah More had produced her first "methodical battery on vice and error" in her *Thoughts on the Manners of the Great*. The "great," she contended, set the standard. "To expect to reform the poor," she remarked, "while the opulent are corrupt, is to throw odours into the stream, while the springs are poisoned."[18] In 1790 she followed this publication with a second, *An Estimate of the Religion of the Fashionable World*. Both books were widely read. Seven large editions of the former were sold in a few months, and five editions of the latter in two years. And in consequence the "manners of the great" were said to have been "materially improved."[19]

Hannah More's efforts were followed by a much more powerful blast from Wilberforce himself. Soon after his conversion Wilberforce began to form the idea of delivering to the world his "religious manifesto"; and in August 1793 he "laid the first timbers" of his proposed treatise. But, save on holiday visits to Gisborne and Babington, he could find little time to work at it, and he used to read over the parts with the brotherhood to get their criticism and counsel. So he made slow progress, and did not have the book ready for the press till April 1797. Even then the publisher was not anxious to take it, for, though the wit and brilliance of Mrs. Hannah More might create sales, religious works in general had then but a poor audience. However, as Wilberforce intended to put his name to the book the publisher made a bold venture and issued an edition of 500 copies bearing

18Thompson, *Life of Hannah More*, p. 80.
19J. H. Overton, *The Evangelical Revival in the Eighteenth Century*, p. 127.

the formidable title, *A Practical View of the Prevailing Religious System of Professed Christians in the Higher and Middle Classes in This Country Contrasted with Real Christianity.* Strange to say the book became an immediate success. Within six months 7,500 copies had been sold. And the popularity "at that time without precedent" increased with the years. By 1826 fifteen editions had been issued in England and twenty-five in America, and translations had been made into French, Dutch, Italian, Spanish, and German.[20]

The brotherhood as they watched the first success were delighted. Thornton immediately sent a copy of the treatise to young Macaulay in Africa; Grant received from John Newton a letter in which he referred to the author as "an instrument of reviving and strengthening the sense of real religion where it already is, and of communicating it where it is not."[21] Even later and less prejudiced writers agreed that the influence of the work was great. Philip Anthony Brown says that it marked the beginning of the practical influence of Evangelicalism among the upper classes.[22]

The Clapham Sect did not end their labours with the production of literature for the fashionable world. They had also "strongly felt the need for literature suitable for circulation among the lower middle and labouring classes, and had given the matter much anxious consideration."[23] The lead was again taken by Mrs. Hannah More, who later explained what she attempted to do: ". . . as an appetite for reading had . . . been increasing among the inferior ranks in this country, it was judged expedient, at this critical period, to supply such wholesome aliment as might give a new direction to their taste, and abate their relish for those corrupt and inflammatory publications which the consequences of the French Revolution have been so fatally pouring in upon us."[24]

The first effort was the publication in 1792 of a pamphlet *Village Politics* by "Will Chip." Will Chip was a character created by Mrs. Hannah More, the real author, and his crisp and homely philosophy caught the fancy of the poorer classes, as the philosophy of the previous works had caught the fancy of the educated. The tract sold by

[20]*Life of Wilberforce*, II, 205.   [21]*Ibid.*, p. 201.
[22]P. A. Brown, *The French Revolution in English History*, p. 179.
[23]Viscountess Knutsford, *Zachary Macaulay*, p. 129.
[24]*The Works of Hannah More*, V, vii-viii.

thousands, and thousands more were purchased by the wealthy, and even by the government, and distributed gratis. Its success was a revelation of how powerful a weapon the cheap tract might be. Mrs. More, aided by her sister and some others, among whom Henry Thornton was a principal figure, thereupon decided to issue a regular series of similar tracts, every month "a tale, a ballad, and a tract for Sunday reading." These were stored in certain selected shops or repositories and so were called the "Cheap Repository Tracts."[25] As they were designed to supplant "the infidel and Jacobinical trash" then popular in England, they were sold at a penny apiece, some even at a halfpenny. Such a price could be maintained only by the support of a liberal subsidy; but Henry Thornton seems to have taken that obligation as his own.[26]

The use of the tract as a method of propaganda was not new to England at this period. Puritanism had "spawned pamphlets." The S.P.C.K., founded in 1698, had promoted the circulation of religious tracts and books. The Society for Diffusing Religious Knowledge among the Poor, formed in 1750, had united Anglicans and Non-Conformists in a similar endeavour. John Wesley had set the example for the Evangelical school by circulating tracts in multitudes. His journal of December 18, 1745, notes: "We had within a short time given many some thousands of little tracts among the common people. . . . And this day *An Earnest Exhortation to Serious Repentance* was given at every church door, in or near London, to every person who came out. . . . I doubt not but God gave a blessing therewith." In 1782 Wesley established the Society for the Distribution of Religious Tracts among the Poor. The Clapham Sect itself had had previous experience with the circulation of tracts, for the Society for the Reformation of Manners which Wilberforce had established in 1787 had undertaken as one of its duties the distribution of tracts, and so had been the precursor of Hannah More's endeavours. But all these efforts were spasmodic and ephemeral compared with the Cheap Repository Tracts.

The success of the venture continued to be unprecedented. Nearly two million tracts were sold in the first year. The finances consequently

[25]*Notes and Queries,* Third Series, VI, 242.   [26]*Ibid.,* pp. 242-3.

grew beyond Thornton's capacity; but, to maintain the publication, he organized an association, of which he remained the treasurer.

The Clapham Sect naturally hailed the scheme with pleasure, and assisted with pens and purses. Unfortunately there are no clear records of the venture, but Thornton apparently wrote tracts himself as well as provided money,[27] and John Venn lists three of the tracts as his productions.[28] Typical Clapham enthusiasm was also given to the distribution of the tracts. At that time pedlars largely supplied the literary needs of the country districts. Clapham was quick to realize the possibilities of the pedlar. In 1796 Mrs. More wrote to Macaulay, then in Africa, "Mr. Henry Thornton, and two or three others, have condescended to spend hours with the hawkers to learn the mysteries of their trade, and next month we hope to meet the hawkers on their own ground."[29]

With the sparkle and brilliance of Mrs. More, and the diligence of Thornton and his helpers, the tracts continued to be written and to be circulated until they were familiar in every part of England, and formed the "principal part of many an English cottager's library."[30] In 1798, however, the constant strain of production proved too much for the principal contributor, Mrs. Hannah More, and the series was brought to an end.

Its phenomenal success had revealed in an extraordinary way how eager and how wide a market was now ready for cheap religious literature; and that knowledge was in turn to lead to further experiments on which the Clapham Sect were once more to find their interests centred.

Just how much direct connection the Cheap Repository experiment had with the formation of the Religious Tract Society it seems now impossible to determine. Tradition has always confidently affirmed that the one gave birth to the other. The volume celebrating the first Jubilee of the Religious Tract Society maintains this point of view. And many writers, with how much knowledge one is not sure, have added their confirmation. Lady Knutsford says that the Society grew

[27]J. C. Colquhoun, *Wilberforce and His Friends*, p. 123.
[28]Venn, *Annals*, p. 140.
[29]Knutsford, *Zachary Macaulay*, p. 129.
[30]Thompson, *Life of Hannah More*, p. 150.

naturally "out of the great success which had attended upon the distribution of the Cheap Repository Tracts."[31] Balleine says that it "was founded to develop the work that Hannah More had begun";[32] and the *Encyclopaedia of Religion and Ethics* adds confirmation to this opinion.[33] One thing is certain; the amazing success of the Cheap Repository Tracts was not unknown to the men who, in 1799, one year after the Repository series had ended, followed with the idea of a Religious Tract Society.

The Clapham Sect, however, had no direct connection with the founding of the Religious Tract Society. At the time of its birth they were occupied with the formation of their Missionary Society, which came into being just one month later. Yet they must have been fully conversant with the proceedings of the Tract Society, for one of their neighbours and intimate friends, Joseph Hughes, Baptist minister of Battersea, was an eager supporter of the Society, and was elected Honorary Secretary.[34] And within a year they had within the Society's ranks a "member for Clapham," Zachary Macaulay, who forthwith took an active interest in the Society's work, became the means of providing thousands of Bibles for the French prisoners of war then in England, and in a few months was travelling on the Continent to gather data on the possibilities of expanding the work abroad.

Indirectly, Clapham gave a great deal to the Religious Tract Society, for Wilberforce's *Practical View* had converted Legh Richmond, who became the Society's most prolific writer. Richmond's works rivalled those of Hannah More in their popular appeal. He sold two million copies of one tract, *The Dairyman's Daughter,* and five million copies of his works during his lifetime. Moreover Wilberforce's influence did not end with Legh Richmond. The matter and style of his *Practical View* became "a guide and inspiration to many tract-writers," and "the influence of Wilberforce's direct and stirring appeals may be traced in many early publications of the Religious Tract Society."[35]

The Clapham company, therefore, would be watching with sympathy any further experiment in the circulation of tracts, and

---

[31]*Zachary Macaulay*, p. 236.
[32]*History of the Evangelical Party*, p. 166.   [33]See article, "Sects."
[34]S. G. Green, *Story of the Religious Tract Society*, p. 5.
[35]*Ibid.*, p. 3.

ience would be the more ready to lend their aid when in 1804 the Religious Tract Society began its greater development.[36]

While the Religious Tract Society was struggling to its feet the Clapham Sect were occupied with another scheme of a different nature. They were undertaking to establish not a series of isolated tracts, but a regular magazine, under their own control, and devoted to their own views and to the defence of their causes. They had long felt the need of such an auxiliary in their campaigns. In 1780 Wesley's *Arminian Magazine* had made a surprising reference to "the number of magazines which now swarm in the world."[37] But, however the scanty supply may have impressed the people of the times, the Clapham Sect, engaged in so many crusades, found that the number on which they could rely for satisfactory support was very small indeed. Of the more acceptable the *Monthly Review* was Whig in politics and Non-Conformist in religion; the *Critical Review* and the *British Critic* were dull and heavy and High Church; and the *Evangelical Magazine,* under mixed management, was weak in public, social, and literary material.

The friends therefore began to speculate about establishing a magazine in which their position would be more satisfactorily represented. They had been considering the possibility in 1798. On July 8 of that year Wilberforce reported that he and Babington went over to Thornton's "to talk over the matter of the Magazine and its editor." At that time indeed their ambition did not extend beyond the modest hope that the magazine might admit "a moderate degree of political and common intelligence." But their hope if modest was persistent. Thereafter Wilberforce was "constantly in communication about the project with Babington and Henry Thornton, and they also discussed the matter in all its bearing with other friends."[38] And Zachary Macaulay on his long walks to and from Clapham used to meditate on the potentialities of a periodical which "should counter-

---

[36]The Eclectic Society had been stirred by the success of Mrs. More's tracts, and had held a discussion on the possibility of establishing a tract society. Tentative beginnings were actually made, the Rev. Thomas Scott attempting to produce the literature. But the venture was not sustained, the Eclectics probably finding the Religious Tract Society a sufficient outlet for their purposes. J. H. Pratt, *Eclectic Notes,* pp. 12-15.

[37]*Arminian Magazine,* 1780, Preface.

[38]Knutsford, *Zachary Macaulay,* p. 250.

act the evils existing . . . in the religious world and at the same time
recommend religion to the consciences of the worldly."[39]

In 1799 the proposal had acquired such interest that Josiah Pratt
after the usual manner carrying Clapham projects to the Eclectic
Society, proposed there for discussion the question, "How far might a
periodical publication be rendered subservient to the interests of
religion?"[40] Unfortunately no notes of the discussion have been preserved. Toward the end of the same year, however, the Clapham Sect
decided to publish a *Prospectus,* which they commissioned John Venn
to prepare, and which made formal announcement of the intention to
produce such "an interesting review of religion, literature, and politics, as a clergyman may without scruple recommend to his parishioners, and a Christian safely introduce into his family."[41]

Following moves came slowly. A Governing Committee was
selected, which consisted of seven members, of whom six were Wilberforce, Macaulay, Venn, Grant, Thornton, and Josiah Pratt.[42] Of
these, Thornton provided the funds to establish the paper, and Pratt
was appointed Editor.[43] Next, the friends decided to make an impor-
ant departure from contemporary custom. Magazines were then
expensive. The cheapest published was the *British Critic* at half a
crown. But the Clapham Sect were wise enough to profit by past
experience, and in January 1802 they boldly introduced the *Christian
Observer* to the public at one shilling.[44]

Unfortunately it is not now possible to determine all the contributions to this paper of the Clapham Sect, though from references one gathers that they must have been many. Macaulay intended
before his death to make a list of the articles that the brotherhood had
written, but was prevented by illness from fulfilling his purpose.[45] All
the friends were hearty supporters of their magazine, and contributed
liberally to it. Before his death in 1815 Thornton published in it no
fewer than eighty-three articles.[46] But Macaulay, as ever, shouldered
the heaviest burden. After a few months Josiah Pratt resigned the

[39]*Ibid.,* p. 235.
[40]Pratt, *Eclectic Notes,* p. 93.
[41]Venn, *Annals,* p. 135; *Christian Observer,* preface to first volume.
[42]Pratt, *Eclectic Notes,* p. 94.
[43]Josiah and J. H. Pratt, *Memoir of the Rev. Josiah Pratt,* p. 11.
[44]Wilberforce's sons make another of their not infrequent errors when they
say (II, 309) that the *Christian Observer* was first published in January, 1800.
[45]*Christian Observer,* 1838, p. 405.
[46]Henry Morris, *Founders of the Bible Society,* p. 65.

editorship, and the Sect, calling one of their accustomed "Cabinet Councils," decided to pass the job on to Macaulay. Macaulay accepted it and for fourteen years added to all the other tasks that fell to him the laborious duties of an editor. He largely determined the policies of the *Observer,* wrote constantly for it himself, and persuaded others to write "whom no one else but he could have persuaded."[47]

In the fall of 1802 Wilberforce and Thornton each wrote an appeal to Mrs. Hannah More to use her pen in aid of the *Observer.* "My idea is," said Wilberforce, "that you should write some religious and moral novels, stories, tales, call 'em what you will. . . . The Cheap Repository tales, a little raised in their subjects, are the very things I want. . . ." Wilberforce thought that if he and Mrs. More worked together they could "greatly raise the character and increase the utility of the work." "The truth is," he confessed, "it is heavy. . . . If it be not enlivened it will sink. . . ."[48] In reply Mrs. More admitted that though the *Observer* was a "valuable miscellany," yet "it needed a little essential salt."

But despite occasional fears, the *Christian Observer* proved a lasting success and continued to be popular until long after the original founders had passed away. For a generation it was a stable institution in Evangelical circles.

Anyone who may think that a magazine in the hands of the Clapham Sect would be dull and unimportant would do well to read the following letter, written by Lord Byron, in no wise one of their admirers, after its review of his *Giaour*:

December 3, 1813

SIR:

I have just finished the perusal of an article in the *Christian Observer* on the "Giaour." You perhaps are unacquainted with the writer, and at all events I have no business to inquire. I only wish you would have the goodness to thank him very sincerely on my part for the pleasure (I do not say unmixed pleasure) which the perusal of a very able, and I believe just criticism has afforded me. Of course I cannot be an impartial witness of its justice, but it is something in its favour when the author criticized does not complain of its sentence. This is not affectation; if I felt angry I could not conceal it even from others, and contempt can

---

[47] J. H. Overton, *The English Church in the Nineteenth Century,* p. 71.
[48] *Life of Wilberforce,* III, 67-8.

only be bestowed on the weak, amongst whom the writer of this article
has certainly no place.

I shall merely add that this is the first notice I have for some years
taken of any public criticism, good or bad, in the way of either thanks
or defence, and I trust that yourself and the writer will not attribute
to any unworthy motive my deviating for once from my usual custom to
express myself obliged to him.

I have the honour to be very sincerely your most obedient humble
servant.

BIRON. [sic]

P.S. I cannot fold this without congratulating you on the acquisition of
a writer in your valuable journal whose style and powers are so far above
the generality of writers as the author of the remarks to which I have
alluded.[49]

It is important to remember that in 1802 the abolition of the
slave trade had not yet been achieved, the Missionary Society had
not properly got under way, the second struggle over the East India
charter had not yet commenced, the British and Foreign Bible Society
was not yet founded, and the long campaign for emancipation was
still far in the future. It may easily be seen, therefore, how important
it was for the Clapham Sect that thus early they forged for themselves
so powerful a weapon. Hereafter on the first of every month they had
the ear of a large section of the religious public of the middle class,
and thereby were enabled, as they could not otherwise have done, to
win a favourable hearing for their many causes.

The *Christian Observer* was hardly under way when the turn of
events attracted Clapham once more to the Religious Tract Society.

On December 7, 1802, the Committee of the Tract Society were
addressed by a visitor, the Rev. Thomas Charles, a Methodist minister
from Wales. Mr. Charles told the Committee of the distressing
scarcity of Bibles in Wales, and suggested that to supply the need
another society might be formed, similar to the Tract Society. His
earnestness and enthusiasm made a deep impression on the Committee,
and one of them, Mr. Hughes, the Baptist minister of Battersea,
exclaimed, "Surely a society might be formed for the purpose; and if
for Wales, why not for the Kingdom; why not for the whole world?"[50]

49 *Christian Observer*, 1813, p. 731.
50 William Canton, *History of the Bible Society*, I, 10.

The Committee were so taken with the idea that they followed up their meeting with a series of others[51] to explore the possibilities of such an endeavour. But they had not proceeded very far before they felt that the success of such an undertaking would require the aid of outside experience, and of other men whose rank and influence would gain the patronage that was necessary properly to establish the society.

"Their eyes very naturally turned towards the suburbs of Clapham."[52] And when, on February 8, 1803, they boldly resolved to make application to His Majesty for his patronage of the proposed society, they immediately decided that Mr. Hardcastle, who was a well-known business man and a resident of Clapham, together with Mr. Hughes, should visit Mr. Wilberforce "relative to the above application."[53] Actually they first approached Grant, and went with him to a breakfast at Wilberforce's, where they broached their scheme to Wilberforce himself.

Such a scheme was sure of a favourable reception at Clapham, for Clapham already had Bible societies of its own. John Thornton in his lifetime had given away immense quantities of Bibles and religious books in all parts of the world, and printed many at his own expense. He also, in 1780, at the time of the Gordon riots, was largely instrumental in establishing the earliest of the Bible societies, designed especially to serve soldiers and sailors. Before the British and Foreign Bible Society was founded, this society had circulated 30,000 Bibles. At its formation in 1780 it was called simply the Bible Society. But— because it confined its labours to soldiers and sailors—its name was changed, after the formation of the British and Foreign Bible Society, to the Naval and Military Bible Society. The first ship among whose crew this Society distributed the Scriptures was the *Royal George*, which had four hundred of the Society's Bibles on board, when on

[51]Unfortunately the only minutes of the Religious Tract Society the writer could discover in the archives at the London Bible House consisted of a few pages *copied* from the minutes of the R.T.S. Committee, and covering the meetings which led to the formation of the British and Foreign Bible Society. These minutes seemed to have been copied by Henry Morris in preparation for his booklet *A Memorable Room*. Morris's name is signed to them, and they are marked "Manuscripts from R.T.S. Minutes, 19 j '96." It is from these MSS that the following references to the Committee meetings are made. There is, of course, no way of determining if the minutes of all the meetings have been copied; but these seem to be all that later writers have been able to discover.
[52]Henry Morris, *Founders of the Bible Society*, p. 31.
[53]MSS, minutes, R.T.S.

August 29, 1792, it went down at Spithead, "with twice four hundred men."[54] Henry Thornton, following in his father's footsteps, became "a very Bible Society in himself," and spent as much as £2,000 a year in distributing Bibles. Moreover, the first Sunday School Society, in which Henry Thornton had so large an influence, made the distribution of Bibles and Testaments a regular part of its duties. Hannah More in her labours annually gave away about "two hundred Bibles, common prayer books, and Testaments." And for years Wilberforce had been distributing Bibles through his friends in the ministry.

A good reception at Clapham was therefore predicted for a central society, which should "combine . . . the scattered energies of all professing Christians; and so create a mighty instrument for the circulation of the truth."[55] And it is not surprising that a short while after the first appeal to him, Wilberforce should have been present at a meeting of the Committee of the Religious Tract Society (April 1803), nor that "chiefly at the suggestion of Mr. Wilberforce" the Committee should that morning, in true Clapham fashion, decide to make a preliminary survey to determine the actual scarcity of Bibles "in this and other countries," and so to gather accurate information on which to proceed.[56]

This meeting is important because the comment on it in the *Life* of Wilberforce has led many to think that the Bible Society was founded then, and chiefly by him. Wilberforce's personal account as recollected by his sons is as follows: "A few of us met together at Mr. Hardcastle's counting-house, . . . on so dark a morning that we discussed by candle-light, while we resolved upon the establishment of the Bible Society."[57] Even Coupland, presumably following this account, says: "The British and Foreign Bible Society was largely [Wilberforce's] creation."[58] But Wilberforce's sons exaggerated the part played by their father. The meeting referred to was one of a series (of which the minutes of thirty are preserved) extending over two years. The project had now been discussed for four months, and the Committee were disappointed with the meagre results of the meeting

[54]*Proceedings of the Naval and Military Bible Society*, 1875.
[55]*Life of Wilberforce*, III, 90-1.
[56]Morris, *Founders of the Bible Society*, p. 45. MSS, minutes, R.T.S., April 21, 1803.   [57]*Life of Wilberforce*, III, 91.
[58]*Wilberforce*, p. 376.

Wilberforce was for a long time unenthusiastic. Only gradually did he and his friends come to see how admirably this new society was suited to meet their ideas and to supplement their labours.

The Committee continued to hold meetings, and gradually to work towards a settled policy. Slowly it made progress. On January 10, 1804, after several less happy suggestions, it selected as the name of the society The British and Foreign Bible Society. Meanwhile by letter it was keeping in touch with Wilberforce, who suggested a public meeting to establish the Society. The Committee followed his suggestion and issued an announcement, signed by Granville Sharp and a number of others, calling a public meeting to mark its inauguration.[59]

At this meeting, on March 7, 1804, the British and Foreign Bible Society was formally established. Granville Sharp was in the chair. He was always averse to taking a place of distinction; for instance, though he attended the Committee on the Abolition of the Slave Trade for twenty years and was appointed Chairman, he never once acted as Chairman. But he became so interested in the Bible Society that he now agreed to take the chair. Clapham gathered its ranks to his support. Wilberforce was not present at the meeting but he expressed his approval of the project in a letter to some member of the committee who cannot now be identified. The letter was discovered only a few years ago in the archives of the British and Foreign Bible Society and was printed in the London *Times* of May 5, 1943:

PALACE YARD, WESTMINSTER,
March 7th

MY DEAR SIR,

I have seen your name subscribed to a printed paper calling a meeting this morning for ye truly important purpose of forming a Society for distributg Bibles. I presume you will attend, and being unable myself convenly to be present, I take the liberty of addressing you for the purpose of expressing my entire approbation of the plan, and my wish to concur in any measures which may tend to the promotion of the great object which is in the view of those gentlemen who so honourably to themselves have come forward on this occasion. Let me beg you to be so obliging as to give this assurance for me to any of my friends whom you may see

---

[59]MSS, minutes, R.T.S., Jan. 17, 1804; Jan. 26, 1804. Granville's Sharp's name was placed at the top of the list; all the others were set in alphabetical order.

at ye meeting and let me further request you to favour me with a
summary account of ye plan intended to be pursued, that I may be the
better prepared & enabled to cooperate in ye furtherance of ye common
object.

> I am with cordial Respect and Regard
> My dear Sir
> Your faithful friend
> (Signed) W. WILBERFORCE

From this time all uncertainty was ended. The Clapham Sect
unmistakably took the Society under its aegis. Wilberforce, Babington,
Grant, Macaulay, Sharp, and Stephen were all included in the
Committee appointed, Henry Thornton was selected for his accustomed job of Treasurer,[60] and of the three Secretaries chosen two
were those close friends of the Sect, Joseph Hughes and Josiah Pratt.
Charles Elliott later joined his friends on the Committee; and Sharp,
William Dealtry, and Gisborne were made Honorary Governors for
life. Pratt soon resigned and was succeeded by John Owen, who wrote
the history of the Society and whose daughter married one of the sons
of Wilberforce.

The Committee soon got into action and a general meeting of the
subscribers and friends of the Society was advertised for May 2, 1804.
Zachary Macaulay, "an active, judicious, and most useful Member
of the Committee" as Owen describes him, had solicited Lord Teignmouth—hitherto unconnected with the Society, although he had been
"among the earliest in the list of contributors"—to act as chairman.[61]
But Lord Teignmouth was ill, and for the second time Granville Sharp
performed the duties "with his characteristic urbanity and attention."
At the close Wilberforce "added much to the interest of the day" by
"a speech of equal animation and judgement." His oratory "produced
. . . a very sensible effect; and the meeting separated, with an increased conviction of the excellence of their cause, and a confirmed
resolution to unite with their zeal in the prosecution of its interests that
discretion which had been so opportunely and impressively recommended."[62]

[60] John Owen, *Origin of the Bible Society*, I, 63.
[61] *Ibid.*, p. 61.
[62] *Ibid.*, p. 62.

This meeting was designed to win public favour. To obtain further countenance the Committee now proceeded "to look out for such patronage as might shield their undertaking from the charge of insignificance, and stamp it with the recommendatory sanction of some high and honourable name."[63] After some consultation the Committee pronounced a "unanimous judgement" in favour of Lord Teignmouth as most "worthy to preside over the British and Foreign Bible Society." Shortly afterward Wilberforce and Grant were both elected to the office of Vice-President, and with a few others, these "together with the late Henry Thornton . . . filled up those stations, which . . . determined the character and fixed the respectability of the Institution."[64]

This chapter cannot follow farther the history and fortunes of the Society, and its continued associations with the Clapham Sect. The pages of Wilberforce's diary, the records of the other members, and the histories of the Society tell how constant were their labours, and how significant was the part Clapham played in stamping the Society with its broad and liberal principles.[65] It should be said, however, that Lord Teignmouth adopted the Bible Society as his special care and labour. Just as Wilberforce, Grant, and Stephen found their central interest in the fight against slavery, and Grant, Venn, and Simeon in the missionary movement, so Lord Teignmouth found his in the British and Foreign Bible Society. He made its cause his own. He worked for it with untiring zeal, defending it alike against active foes and injudicious friends, and retained his office of President till death, saying that he would be content to be forgotten as Governor-General of India, if only he might be remembered as President of the Bible Society.[66]

[63]*Ibid.*, p. 66.   [64]*Ibid.*, p. 71.
[65]An indication of their participation may be found in the list of chief speakers at the Bible Society's anniversaries. The speakers include:

1805	William Wilberforce		Henry Thornton
1806	Thomas Babington		Thomas Babington
1808	William Wilberforce	1813	William Dealtry
1809	William Wilberforce	1814	Henry Thornton
1810	William Wilberforce		Zachary Macaulay
1811	Thomas Babington		Charles Grant, Jr.
	Henry Thornton	1815	William Wilberforce
1812	William Wilberforce		William Dealtry
	Charles Grant		Robert Grant

At all these anniversaries Lord Teignmouth was in the chair. It is clear that Clapham interest did not end with the founding of the Society.
[66]In writing his memoir of Lord Teignmouth in 1834 Josiah Pratt said that "to enumerate his Lordship's services to this institution would be to write a history of the Society." *Christian Observer*, 1834, p. 273.

The Bible Society held a special interest for the Clapham Sect because it supplemented so well their other interests. It gave powerful support to the Sunday school movement; it aided the early missionaries to India by sending out large quantities of Bibles, and by providing translations into native languages; it followed up the Emancipation Act by sending out 100,000 copies of the New Testament with Psalms as an emancipation present to the freed Negroes; and it gave an impetus to the whole Evangelical movement by distributing in its first fifteen years a total of nearly two and a half million Bibles and New Testaments. Moreover, by the singleness of its aim it made possible a co-operation with other Christians, which, whenever possible, the Clapham Sect eagerly welcomed. One of its early anniversaries moved Wilberforce to write with enthusiasm of a "grand" sight, "five or six hundred people of all sects and parties, with one heart, and face, and tongue."[67] Such co-operation was unusual in that day. Owen relates how at the first meeting of the Bible Society he was so powerfully impressed by the sight of many denominations working together for a common religious purpose that he thought that the day marked "an important epoch in the religious history of mankind."[68] The Bible Society indeed—perhaps in part because it was so largely shaped by Clapham influence—had aims and methods equally congenial to their spirit. It was always recognized by them as not less "emphatically Claphamic" than the Missionary Society itself, and remained no less characteristically a Clapham cause.

The Bible Society was followed by one auxiliary society, in which the Clapham Sect were interested, and which therefore deserves brief mention.

Liberal as the Clapham Sect were, and eager as they were to work when possible with men of other faiths, they were always convinced Churchmen. And while they were willing to join with all Christians in circulating the Bible, they believed that to Anglicans the Book of Common Prayer should also be given. Simeon expressed their opinion: "The Bible first, the Prayer-Book next, and all other

---

[67]William Wilberforce's Anglo-Catholic sons are at pains to defend their father for having so agreed to unite with Dissenters, and admit only that he and his friends are "hardly to be blamed" for their "holy daring" which the "torpor of the Church" made necessary. *Life of Wilberforce*, III, 92.

[68]Owen, *Origin of the Bible Society*, I, 47.

books in subordination to these."[69] But none of their societies had specifically undertaken the circulation of the Prayer Book. So in 1812 Zachary Macaulay joined with some others in promoting the Prayer Book and Homily Society, a society modelled after the Bible Society, and devoted to the specific task of publishing and circulating "without note or comment" the Prayer Book and Homilies.[70]

Quite naturally the brotherhood joined earnestly in such a scheme. Lord Teignmouth, Wilberforce, Babington, and Grant all became Vice-Presidents; Henry Thornton was once more appointed Treasurer; and Charles Elliott worked with Macaulay on its Committee.[71] Macaulay, however, undertook the most arduous labours, and in 1825 "having rendered essential services to the Society" he was voted Honorary Governor for life.[72]

When it is recalled that most of the labours which the foregoing chapters have recounted, and still others yet to be mentioned, were carried on within the space of a few years, and that many of them were being undertaken simultaneously; when it is recalled that a space of twelve years, 1792-1804, saw the campaign for abolition, the organization of the Sierra Leone colony, the first East India charter struggle, the founding of the Missionary Society, the organization of the Cheap Repository Tracts, the institution of the *Christian Observer*, the founding of the British and Foreign Bible Society, the establishment on a wide scale of Sunday schools and other projects of popular education, and—as the next chapter will show—the undertaking of a multiplicity of philanthropic endeavours to relieve the poverty of the time; and when it is recalled that all these things were accomplished as the extra labours of a group of men already occupied by important duties of political, commercial, and professional life, and handicapped by the turmoil and reaction of one of the darkest and most troubled periods of their country's history, no further reminder is necessary that the Clapham Sect wrought a most unusual day's work in England. Just how unusual succeeding chapters must go on to show.

[69]G. W. E. Russell, *The Household of Faith*, p. 228.
[70]*Christian Observer*, 1839, p. 799.
[71]*Proceedings of the Prayer Book and Homily Society*, 1813. In 1814 Lord Teignmouth, Henry Thornton, Charles Simeon, and Zachary Macaulay had all paid the £10 10s. to become life members. *Ibid.*, 1814.
[72]*Ibid.*, 1825.

CHAPTER SIX

An industry in doing good

THE ACCOMPLISHMENTS listed at the end of the last chapter comprise a remarkable record for days of war and revolution, of fear and reaction, of external peril and internal suffering. Yet a good deal of the criticism of the Clapham Sect centres on these very achievements. Mr. Wilberforce, said William Hazlitt cynically, "carefully chooses his ground to fight the battles of loyalty, religion, and humanity, and it is such as is always safe and advantageous to himself."[1]

Hazlitt has had a long line of sneering descendants, not without representatives today, by whom the men who abolished slavery and wrought so many works of righteousness are recalled mainly to reflect not on the good deeds they did, but rather on the other deeds which they ought not to have left undone. Credited with keeping their eyes on misery in far places, Wilberforce and his company are often reproached with their social record at home. It will therefore be necessary, before taking up the story of their last crusade, to turn aside from the more characteristic Clapham enterprises and consider how far these reproaches may be justified.

At the outset it is well to recognize that the Clapham Sect were a group of wealthy men, who, though they were in many ways ahead of their times, were also unmistakably and inevitably of their times. It is useless to criticize them by the standards of twentieth-century socialism. They were part of an aristocratic society which had never thought of questioning the order which made some men rich and powerful and others poor and dependent. They never thought, save with horror, of any society in which these distinctions would be abolished. They accepted as part of the eternal fitness of things that they should live according to their station; and they maintained their

[1]*Spirit of the Age*, p. 220.

station with such zest, and heartiness, and magnificent hospitality, that their critics find therein ground for covert reproach. "In Egypt itself," jibed Thackeray, "there were not more savoury fleshpots than at Clapham."[2]

Further, the Clapham circle, for whom the savoury fleshpots formed such an accepted and unquestioned feature of their own lives, lent their powerful influence to the relentless policy of repression which for almost a generation ground down the poor in increasing misery, and which savagely persecuted persons with spirit enough to protest.

As early as 1795 Wilberforce gave Pitt support which perhaps was decisive in passing two severe measures of repression, the Treasonable Practices Act and the Seditious Meetings Act. And in 1815, during the years of hardship following the Battle of Waterloo, Wilberforce voted for the Corn Law which made the hungry poor still hungrier. Then he went on to support the further measures which were required to prevent the masses from revolting. In 1817 he defended the new Seditious Meetings Bill copied from the one of 1795 (though he urged that it run for three years only) and a number of other measures including the Habeas Corpus Suspension Bill, the passing of which ushered in the "last hundred days of English freedom."[3] Worse than all, in 1819 he defended "Peterloo."

On August 16, 1819, over 50,000 men, women, and children gathered in St. Peter's Field on the outskirts of Manchester to hear Henry Hunt, a radical politician, and other orators speak on parliamentary reform. Neither the speakers nor the crowd were armed nor bent on violence; but local magistrates, alarmed at the size of the meeting, ordered the Yeomanry to make their way through the crowd and arrest Hunt. When the soldiers were obstructed by the throng the magistrates in panic ordered a regiment of cavalry to charge. As a result eleven people were killed and several hundred were injured in what was afterward known as the "Massacre of Peterloo." More damaging than the magistrates' folly was the Government's uncritical defence of the deed. Ministers publicly thanked the magistrates for

[2]*The Newcomes*, chap. 11. Mrs. Oliphant likewise suggests that the "otherworldly" tenets of Clapham religion would not have been so incongruous in people who entered with less zest into the pleasures of this world. *Literary History of England*, III, 372-3.

[3]William Cobbett, *History of the Last Hundred Days of English Freedom*.

giving the order, arranged a hasty trial which railroaded Hunt to two years' imprisonment, and, when Parliament met in October, pleaded that repressive measures were necessary and passed the "Six Acts" which were designed to stifle reform by prohibiting unofficial meetings and taxing the Radical press out of existence. Wilberforce voted with the Government. He would not defend the magistrates: he declared that only those who could hope for good from civil war would fail to lament the tragedy. But he would not support a Parliamentary measure for an inquiry into the magistrates' conduct. He was convinced that England was nearer to civil war than it had been since 1646. He thought it necessary in the circumstances to support the "Six Acts," though he urged that they be enacted only as temporary measures.

Wilberforce's influence was a considerable factor in Parliament throughout these years. In 1817 the poet Southey said that "the weight with which his opinion comes to the public" was "far greater than that of any other individual."[4] Had Wilberforce and his "party of no-party men" set their faces against civil injustice as they set their faces against other injustices a different and happier chapter might have been written in English history.

To this indictment one must add that the philanthropy with which the Clapham Sect undertook to alleviate the distress against which they refused to allow a protest—especially that conducted for them by the unctuous More sisters—was frequently accompanied by a spirit of patronage, against which a people less degraded would have recoiled in just resentment. "They have so little common sense, and so little sensibility, that we are obliged to beat into their heads continually the good we are doing them" is the characteristic report from the More sisters at Mendip.[5]

The social record of the Clapham Sect is therefore not without its blemishes; but, as even a brief survey of their principal labours will show, the blemishes are not the whole of the record.

The Reformation of Manners

No activities of the Saints aroused more ridicule and contempt than those for the "reformation of manners"; and none are more open

---

[4] R. Coupland, *Wilberforce,* p. 409.
[5] Martha More, *Mendip Annals,* p. 67.

to criticism. But, though critics are prone to ignore it, even these labours had their necessity and their value.

"God Almighty has set before me," said Wilberforce in 1787, "two great objects, the suppression of the slave trade and the reformation of manners."[6] To achieve the latter object he began a campaign thoroughly representative of his time. Following a suggestion in Dr. Woodward's *History of the Society for the Reformation of Manners in the year 1692,* Wilberforce persuaded the King to issue a "Proclamation against Vice and Immorality." Then to ensure that the impetus did not end with the Proclamation he founded a Society for Giving Effect to His Majesty's Proclamation against Vice and Immorality[7] into which he entered with much earnestness and enthusiasm, and in which he was joined by Grant and Thornton.[8]

It was this society that aroused the wrath of both conservatives and radicals, and not without justification. Its persecution of a poor, inoffensive man named Thomas Williams, for instance, was a piece of pious cruelty for which there can be no defence.[9] Williams, who was himself a Christian and whose large family lived in abject poverty, was prosecuted for publishing Paine's *Age of Reason.* He repented and begged the Society not to bring him up for judgment. Nevertheless the Society stood "firm," as Wilberforce recorded in his diary, and proceeded to ruin the destitute family. But the frequent historical references to that act only show how the evils of the Society lived after it, while the good was readily forgotten. Some agency to do part of what the Proclamation Society aimed at was urgently needed. And, while it did much of its work blunderingly, and some of it odiously, it did make an effort to cope with certain evils in the presence of which most of its contemporary critics were smugly complacent.

The Proclamation Society, for one thing, waged a difficult battle against the besotted drunkenness of a period little changed since the time, not long before, when the Bishop of Salisbury had declared that "at any hour of the day . . . you may see some poor creatures mad

[6]*Life of Wilberforce,* I, 149.
[7]*Ibid.,* pp. 130-8.
[8]*Report of the . . . Society for Giving Effect to His Majesty's Proclamation,* 1799.
[9]There is an account of the Williams case in *Clio* by G. M. Trevelyan (pp. 112-13) ; but instead of the Proclamation Society Trevelyan puts in the name of the later Society for the Suppression of Vice, which did not start till 1802. There is also an account in *The Town Labourer* (pp. 242-3) by J. L. and B. Hammond, but the Hammonds are seldom fair to Wilberforce.

drunk . . . and committing outrages in the street, or lying dead asleep
upon bulks, or at the doors of empty houses."[10] The Society fought
vigorously to remedy such conditions. In their *History of Liquor
Licensing* Sidney and Beatrice Webb say it "set going a national movement," which produced a marked "lull" in crime, rioting, disorderly
conduct, and brutal amusements, and which became "an important
contributory cause of the remarkable advance in 'respectability' made
by the English working-man during the first two decades of the
nineteenth century."[11] In the record of the Society blemishes do not
appear on every page.

The Proclamation Society, however, received but lukewarm support, and in the early part of the nineteenth century was supplanted
by the Society for the Suppression of Vice.[12] In this society also the
Clapham Sect were much interested, Wilberforce scarcely less so than
in the earlier one. References to it are scattered through his diary.
Macaulay and Lord Teignmouth also joined in as active workers, the
latter at one time being President.[13] This society drew upon itself even
more ridicule than the former, and as with the former "unfortunately
. . . the attack has lived, while the defence has virtually perished."[14]
Joseph Hume, in Parliament, called it the "Society for Vice," and said
that apart from the stopping of indecent literature it had done hardly
a good thing.[15] A more formidable opponent, Sydney Smith, called
it "The Society for the Suppression of Vice among those with less
than £500 a year,"[16] and when the Society moved for the suppression
of bear-baiting, urged the objection that nothing had been done when
the aristocracy hunted foxes, and boiled lobsters alive. But, as Overton
remarks, it was "hardly an answer to those who were trying to check
the demoralizing effects of the illegal recreations of one class, to say
that the recreations of another class were cruel, though not illegal."[17]

[10]Sidney and Beatrice Webb, *History of Liquor Licensing*, p. 28.
[11]*Ibid.*, pp. 53, 82-4.
[12]Halévy (*England in 1815*, p. 395), says that the Proclamation Society was
reorganized as the Society for the Suppression of Vice. Actually the Proclamation
Society lived many years after the second society was formed. Moreover, the
prospectus for the later Society, *Proposal for Establishing a Society for the
Suppression of Vice* (1801), disclaimed "in the most explicit and ingenuous
manner every idea or wish to rival" the Proclamation Society.
[13]*Christian Observer*, 1839, p. 799.
[14]J. H. Overton, *The English Church in the Nineteenth Century*, p. 283.
[15]*Parliamentary Debates*, New series, VIII, 709. Hume was speaking on the
imprisonment of Mary Ann Carlile, who had been tried at the suit of the Society.
[16]*Edinburgh Review*, Jan. 1809.
[17]Overton, *The English Church in the Nineteenth Century*, p. 283.

Regardless of outside criticism the Clapham Sect continued through these societies, supplemented by much individual effort, to labour for the "reformation of manners." Their main efforts were directed to the abolition of duelling, of the lottery, and of brutal sports, and to the promotion of Sabbath Day observance.

Duelling was still prevalent at the end of the eighteenth century. For a considerable time gentlemen had been ceasing to wear swords because "iron of itself draws a man on"; yet the duel had by no means been abandoned. Pitt fought a duel with Tierney, Castlereagh with Canning, Wellington with Winchilsea. Daniel O'Connell killed his man in a duel. Wilberforce, Sharp, and Lord Teignmouth all received challenges, as Lord Shaftesbury did later. And the challenges were not idle. Wilberforce counted it a blessing that he was able to follow his conscience and refuse the duel without loss of public character. Fiery-tempered James Stephen confessed that "his strongest temptations were to duelling."[18]

Against duelling the Clapham Sect resolutely set their faces. Grant, on his second voyage to India in 1773, saw a fellow passenger killed in a duel and pressed the charge against the bellicose challenger till judicial action was taken in England. Sharp wrote a tract against duelling.[19] Wilberforce, appalled at Pitt's duel with Tierney, nearly precipitated a political crisis in an attempt to prevent it. Naturally even the Clapham Sect were able to make little immediate change in a custom so long established. But, if there were no achievements suitable for tabulation, Clapham influence did help to create the atmosphere which finally brought duelling into complete disrepute.

The lottery was another evil of the time. State lotteries were an accepted institution. But Clapham was uncompromisingly opposed to them. When Wilberforce on the night of the abolition triumph asked, "Well, Henry, what shall we abolish next?" Thornton in his sober fashion had immediately replied, "The lottery, I think."[20] He expressed a common opinion of the group. William Smith made a speech against lotteries as early as 1792; Wilberforce said that he spent twenty years fighting the lottery[21]; but Babington took the case against

[18]*Life of Wilberforce*, II, 93.
[19]*Remarks on the Opinions of Some of the Most Celebrated Writers on Crown Law, Respecting the Due Distinction between Manslaughter and Murder.*
[20]*Life of Wilberforce*, III, 298.
[21]*Correspondence of William Wilberforce*, II, 274.

lotteries as his especial charge in Parliament.[22] Once again the Clapham Sect achieved little visible result; but they helped to bring low contemporary standards into ultimate disrepute.

Still another evil was the brutality of popular sports. Bull-baiting and bear-baiting then combined with gin to make an English holiday. The animals were tortured in a manner cruel to the last degree, and sometimes were harried for days before being finally dispatched. Sir Richard Hill cited in the House of Commons a case where a troublesome bull had had its hoofs cut off, and was left to sustain and defend itself feebly upon its stumps.[23] To such cruelty the Clapham Sect were unalterably opposed; and they never lost their concern. In his last year in Parliament Wilberforce supported a bill for the prevention of cruelty to animals. But respectable society then thought that barbarous sports were a necessary outlet for the degraded passions of the lower classes, and, as ever, suspected that reformers had ulterior motives. In 1802 William Windham declared in the House of Commons that assaults on such amusements of the people "struck him in no other light than as the first step to a reform of the manners of the lower orders." He stated that if people were diverted from bear-baiting and such sports they would fall a prey to the Methodists and Jacobins, who would teach them to read—a serious peril, since it was among the "illiterate part of the people that Jacobinical doctrines had made the smallest progress." Courtenay supported Windham by saying that he had "proved incontrovertibly, that bull-baiting was the great support of the constitution in church and state"; and he joined in agreement with Windham that bull-baiting had saved England "from all the horrors of Jacobinism and fanaticism."[24]

Against such a temper neither the Clapham Sect nor their societies made much progress; but it is to their credit that they were opposed to the accepted sentiment of their time. They were a long way ahead of the opponents who derided them.

In addition to fighting such contemporary evils, the Clapham Sect laboured also to promote a more general observance of the Sabbath. In 1794 Wilberforce supported a bill for Sabbath observance. Later he gave up the idea of a bill, and promoted a voluntary association for

[22] *Christian Observer*, 1838, p. 127.
[23] *Parliamentary History*, XXXVI, 830.
[24] *Ibid.*, pp. 834, 842.

the same purpose.[25] He also made an attempt to obtain an act prohibiting Sunday newspapers, then coming into vogue. On one occasion he bought a copy of each of the nineteen Sunday papers then in circulation, read them through at one sitting, and condemned them all as "a collection of ribaldry and profaneness." To lessen the necessity for Sunday travelling, he persuaded Perceval, when Prime Minister, to abandon the custom of opening Parliament on Monday; and, to set an example to the nation, he induced Speaker Addington to hold his levees on Saturday instead of Sunday evenings. John Shore as Governor-General of India took the then unusual step of refusing to transact public business on Sunday. All the Clapham Sect followed the principle in private life, and reserved the Sabbath for rest and quiet in the Clapham homes. After the successive suicides of Whitbread, Romilly, and Castlereagh, Wilberforce expressed the opinion that if these had appreciated "the unspeakable benefit of the institution of the Lord's day," and, for one day in seven, had withdrawn their minds from the "ordinary trains of thought and passion" they might not have collapsed under the strain.

Critics of the present day find it only too easy to exhibit these and similar labours as an example of excessive Sabbatarianism. But it is wise to remember that only the uncompromising insistence that the Sabbath was a Holy Day first procured for industrial labourers relief from oppression *seven* days a week, and ensured working England the leisure which made popular education possible. "How many [of the lower classes]," asked Wilberforce, "would have remained unlettered, but for Sunday schools, which dependent [sic] on cessation of ordinary labour on sabbath."[26] The Sunday freed from labour was one of the first forward steps in modern social progress.

"Sabbatarianism" . . . gave England more than Sunday protection and the Saturday half-holiday. . . . The "Ministrations of the Sabbath" . . . inspired a thousand and one organizations for education and philanthropy. . . . They enabled working England to read and to think; they taught her how to propagate and to agitate. They brought the sobriety, the sense of solidarity, and the ability to organize, without which the Trade Union Movement, for instance, could never have been developed into a potent and self-disciplined force. . . . had Sunday been a day

[25]*Life of Wilberforce,* II, 271-2.
[26]*Ibid.,* II, 424.

devoted to carousal, or sport, or even to recreation, the vast body of social organizations, which became so marked a feature of nineteenth-century England, could never have been established.[27]

All the story of the Clapham attitude to the Sabbath is not told in jibes at gloomy "Puritanism."

To fight against popular though brutal sports, against state lotteries, against drunkenness, against sedition and blasphemy, and for a Sunday of rest and meditation, in short, to fight for the "reformation of manners" brought the Clapham Sect little glory, and much ridicule, and at times led them into extravagances and mistakes for which they must be gravely censured. Yet on the whole, even in these labours, they were inspired by high principles, and left their own and succeeding generations more deeply in their debt than has been commonly recognized.

CLAPHAM PHILANTHROPY

The Clapham Sect, however, did not confine their social concern to the "reformation of manners." They devoted themselves not only to the moral but also to the material well-being of the unfortunate classes about them. They laboured, as they would have put it, not only to "improve the manners" but also to "increase the comforts" of the poor.

Again, inevitably, they approached the problem from their own point of view. They belonged not to the Fabian Society, but to the eighteenth-century aristocracy. They saw poverty not as a problem to be solved, but as a situation calling for their sympathy. If men were victimized by a social system they would not assault the system, they would do their best to minister to the victims. They had their limitations; but within these limitations they laboured heroically.

Most of their labours were performed privately, or through small societies which are now remembered only from passing references or have perhaps vanished into complete oblivion. But sufficient evidence remains to indicate extraordinary exertions on behalf of people many of whom had few advocates of power and consequence. In 1796 Wilberforce helped to found the Society for Bettering the Condition of the Poor and later became its Vice-President. To obtain adequate information on which the Society could act Wilberforce

[27]J. W. Bready, *Shaftesbury,* pp. 394-5.

sent an elaborate questionnaire to a large circle of private friends.[28] Macaulay also laboured with Wilberforce in this Society. Southey's *Essays, Moral and Political* has a long and appreciative review of twenty years of the Society's work. Much good seems to have been accomplished by the thoughtful and wise measures taken to help labourers to self-support.[29] John Thornton was one of the chief movers in establishing the Society for the Relief of Persons Imprisoned for Small Debts. In five years it released 14,007 people—hapless folk who were imprisoned by the harsh debt laws of the time. (As late as 1824 the Lord Advocate said that "more than three quarters of the persons now imprisoned in Scotland are for small debts.") Wilberforce and Henry Thornton both became interested in this Society.[30] John Venn was a prime originator of the labours of the Society for Bettering the Condition of the Poor at Clapham.[31] Other organizations representative of the philanthropic interests of the "Saints" included the Society for the Reformation of Prison Discipline, the Indigent Blind Institution, the Foundling Hospital. With labours in such societies the "Saints" mixed all sorts of sporadic charities: to provide support for war widows, distressed sailors, "suffering Germans," "Spanish Patriots," French Protestants, Russian sufferers, Lascars, "foreigners in distress"; and for the "Refuge of the Destitute."

This list of societies and charitable endeavours is only very partial; but as a great many societies and schemes are mentioned only in passing reference in some biography, or just by name in a list in Wilberforce's diary, it would serve no useful purpose to pad the list. The details of these efforts are very hazy; but Macaulay, Thornton, Stephen, Babington, and Venn seemed to have been closely associated with Wilberforce in most of them, and very probably all of the Clapham Sect in some of them. It was said with truth of Wilberforce, Thornton, and Macaulay that it would scarcely be possible to mention a charity of their day which they had not at some time assisted, or to which they had not subscribed.

[28]*Life of Wilberforce,* II, 414-16.
[29]Halévy, *England in 1815,* p. 483; *Life of Wilberforce,* III, 43, *et passim;* Viscountess Knutsford, *Zachary Macaulay,* p. 242.
[30]*Parliamentary Debates,* New series, XI, 1171. *An Account of the Rise, Progress and Present State of the Society for the Discharge and Relief of Persons Imprisoned for Small Debts.*
[31]John Venn, *Annals,* p. 140. Clapham Vestry Minutes (MSS at Clapham).

The Clapham Sect did not rest content with such public and concerted activities. They also did much through individual efforts. Indeed they were philanthropists of a type not then familiar. They regarded the right use of money as one of the practical ways in which they could express their tremendous sense of personal responsibility. Wealthy themselves, they did not set high store by wealth. Some of them, from integrity and devotion to their chosen causes, deliberately put aside possibilities of greatly increased fortune. In India Lord Teignmouth and Grant both refused to enrich themselves by practices which then were considered conventional and even irreproachable. Zachary Macaulay, at one time worth £100,000, by his devotion to the Negro slaves virtually gave away all he had. He "sacrificed all that a man may lawfully sacrifice—health, fortune, repose, favour, and celebrity," and "died a poor man, though wealth was within his reach."[32] In consequence his son, Thomas Babington Macaulay, at a time when his parliamentary fame stood at its highest, was so reduced in circumstances that he had to sell the gold medals which he had gained at Cambridge. Wilberforce also by his generosity seriously depleted his family resources. In one year he gave away £3,000 more than he had earned.[33] And in the closing years of his life he had no house of his own, but lived with his different sons—even though he might at that time, says Sir George Stephen, have doubled his income by charging higher rents to his poor tenants.[34] Simeon "practiced boundless munificence."[35] John Thornton earned but to give away. His total givings were said to amount to more than £150,000.[36] William Cowper wrote of him that he had

> an industry in doing good,
> Restless as his who toils and sweats for food. . . .[37]

His son Henry emulated the worthy example by giving away two-thirds of his income.[38] Yet Henry had good company. "Others of the

---

[32]G. O. Trevelyan, *Life of Lord Macaulay*, I, 64.
[33]*Life of Wilberforce*, III, 4.   [34]*Antislavery Recollections*, p. 81.
[35]Lord Teignmouth, *Reminiscences of Many Years*, I, 57.
[36]R. de M. Rudolf, *et al.*, *Clapham and the Clapham Sect*, p. 105.
[37]"In Memory of the Late John Thornton," *Poetical Works*, p. 376.
[38]Before marriage Henry Thornton gave away six-sevenths of what he earned; after marriage two-thirds. In one year of distress he gave away £9,000. Here is a specimen of his spending:

1790	charity	£2,260	All other expenses	£1,543
1791	,,	£3,960	,,	£1,817
1792	,,	£7,508	,,	£1,616
1793	,,	£6,680	,,	£1,988

band of friends," says G. W. E. Russell, "even exceeded this proportion."[39]

The Clapham Sect, therefore, were not callous to the sufferings of the poor, nor insensible to the responsibilities of the rich. They were not touched with the prevalent lack of sympathy for the lower classes. They had a deep and genuine interest in the people whom the circumstances of their time were so cruelly oppressing. And yet, with what now seems inexcusable heartlessness, they supported the Seditious Meetings Bills, approved the suspension of habeas corpus, urged the government to still more stringent measures, and even defended Peterloo. Where lies the explanation?

CONSERVATIVE LIBERALS

It lies mainly in three sources. The first is the unreasoning fear created by the French Revolution. The Clapham Sect, especially in the slave trade conflict, had frequently suffered from that fear. But they themselves were more affected by it than they knew. Few Englishmen of their time escaped it—the liberals little more than the conservatives. Paris with its ferocious mobs, its guillotine set on high, and its streets drenched with human blood, had confronted civilization with something new and unknown, something "superhuman, immeasurable, incalculable."[40] To Englishmen it seemed that revolution took from men everything that gave them a civilization with dignity, culture, and continuity, and left them "like flies in a summer." The fear that revolution would spread to England was exaggerated; but it is easy to be wise after the event. At the time the peril seemed sufficiently real. The mobs of England were not like the mobs of France; but they were brutal enough and formidable enough to inspire alarm. Not long before in the Gordon riots of 1780 they had come near to burning down London. In the minds of the Clapham Sect, therefore, the thought of men gathering to concoct measures for a strike was always tinted with memories of the Terror. Industrial conspiracy seemed not far from revolution, and safety seemed to lie only in controlling at one stage what could not be controlled at another. Consequently while the Clapham Sect were genuinely concerned for miseries of the poor, they saw only infinite peril if the poor

[39]Russell, *The Household of Faith,* p. 227.
[40]Lord Rosebery, *Pitt,* p. 160.

themselves began in desperation to combine for their own deliverance.

Wilberforce cannot, then, be accused of hypocrisy—indeed he was never a hypocrite—when he said in 1795 that the sedition acts were only "temporary" sacrifices to preserve all liberties the longer, or when he urged on behalf of the Seditious Meetings Bill that "it is one of the peculiar excellencies of the British Constitution, to be able in times of popular commotion to strengthen the hands of the executive government, and afterwards, when the danger is past, to revert to our former state of liberty and freedom."[41]

The second and supporting explanation lies in the political economy which in the days of the Clapham Sect held unquestioned sway. Adam Smith, Ricardo, and Malthus had combined to teach that poverty was inevitable; that the increase of population outstripping the increase of the means of subsistence, left an inevitable fringe of society on the borderland of starvation; that there was an iron law of wages, allotting with scientific finality the total sum that could be left for labour; and that all interference with these scientific laws was unwise, and ultimately futile. Not only conservatives believed these things; radicals were not less convinced. As the Hammonds point out, the only difference was that the conservative believed in all kinds of privilege for himself, while the radical believed in privileges for no one, but naked, unrestrained competition for all. Both believed that wages and poverty were determined by natural law. Even Sir Francis Burdett declared that "no one gave less to the labourer than it was the interest of the labourer to receive";[42] and Francis Place argued against Shaftesbury's Ten-Hour Bill: "All legislative interference must be pernicious. Men must be left to themselves to make their own bargains; the law must compel the observance of compacts, the fulfilment of contracts. There it should end. So long as the supply of labour exceeds the demand for labour, the labourer will undersell his fellows, and produce poverty, misery, vice, and crime."[43]

The Clapham Sect were governed by the same convictions, and consequently, much as they sympathized with the starving crowds, they did not believe that "combinations" could bring any final relief

[41]Life of Wilberforce, II, 114; Coupland, Wilberforce, p. 421.
[42]J. L. and B. Hammond, The Town Labourer, p. 200.
[43]Graham Wallas, Life of Francis Place, p. 174.

any more than combinations could affect bad crops. They believed
that the condition of the labourer was determined by economics and
not by politics. And when they saw radicals agitating the people to
combine, they believed them only to be working for what in the long
run could not be attained by such methods, and only to be certain of
leading hapless and deluded sufferers to their own undoing.

To these explanations must be added a third. The Clapham Sect
looked at all problems from a single point of view. Their final question
always passed from material considerations to spiritual. They were
indeed concerned that the poor should be comfortable; but they were
more concerned that the poor should be pious. They were afraid that
clever agitators might make use of the resentment against unavoidable
poverty to undermine morality and religion, and were convinced that
the whole agitation stirring in the lower classes was thoroughly mater-
ialistic in tone and conducive to an anti-religious outlook. "I declare,"
said Wilberforce, "my greatest cause of difference with the democrats,
is their laying, and causing the people to lay, so great a stress on the
concerns of this world, as to occupy their whole minds and hearts, and
to leave a few scanty and lukewarm thoughts for the heavenly trea-
sure."[44] When Pitt by his Combination Acts so terribly ended the
early popular movements Wilberforce honestly thought he had ended
also a serious menace to the state and to religion, and expressed his
appreciation of Pitt's action in the striking phrase, "He stood between
the living and the dead, and the plague was staid."[45] With such conviction it is no wonder that the Clapham Sect dreaded the entire
agitation for reform and thought that sternest measures were most
merciful.

In all this the Clapham Sect reflected clearly the prevailing temper
of their time, and shared in its fear, its conservatism, and its cruelty.

What can be added of the Clapham Sect is that once they escaped
the bondage of this ill-favoured influence they were naturally liberal
in outlook and action. Their liberality, indeed, went far beyond their
pietistic concern to "improve the manners" and to "increase the comforts" of the poor. Wilberforce, for instance, the acknowledged leader
of the "Saints," introduced into Parliament as his maiden measure a

[44]*Life of Wilberforce,* V, 36.   [45]Lord Brougham, *Speeches,* II, 9.

bill for purifying county elections (1786), and he kept his reforming
temper through the years. In 1809 he supported Curwen's bill for
making the sale of parliamentary seats illegal. Even in the troubled
year of 1817 he declared himself still in favour of "moderate, gradual"
parliamentary reform; in 1822 he voted for Lord John Russell's
motion for reform; and in 1831—almost at the end of his life—in
spite of all the turmoil to which he was so adverse, he told his sons
that "on the whole" he would have been "favourable" to the Reform
Bill. His followers, like him, were for reform. William Smith said that
he attended every meeting on the subject for twenty-two years, and
he voted for reform to the end of his parliamentary career.[46] Henry
Thornton also supported parliamentary reform, and advocated the
unpopular income tax[47] and the Bank Restriction Act. Grant introduced into Parliament measures to prevent the prevalent bribery
used to obtain appointments in the East India Company, Stephen
forced the first movement for Chancery reform, and Granville Sharp
though never in Parliament, wrote vigorous tracts on parliamentary
reform. Trevelyan points out how Wilberforce retained his reforming
spirit through the years, while Pitt became "more and more the tool
of vested interests of every kind."[48] And that comparison might frequently be made between the Clapham Sect and their Tory associates.

The Clapham Sect also supported penal reform. Wilberforce was
utterly without the contemporary notion of the sanctity of law for its
own sake, and spoke scathingly about "our murderous laws," "our
bloody laws," and "the barbarous custom of hanging." As early as
1786 he carried through the Commons a small measure of penal
reform, and thereafter, "every time Romilly brought forward in the
Commons the abolition of the death penalty for an offence, Wilberforce intervened in the debate to support Romilly's proposal with his
influence."[49] In 1819 he presented a petition in the Commons against
the severity of the criminal code. He spoke with especial vehemence
against the stupid severity of the game laws, which he declared to be
"so opposite to every principle of personal liberty, so contrary to all
our notions of private right, so injurious and so arbitrary in their

[46]*DNB, s.v.*
[47]*Ibid., s.v.*
[48]G. M. Trevelyan, *British History in the Nineteenth Century*, p. 53.
[49]Halévy, *England in 1815*, p. 397.

operation that the sense of the greater part of mankind is in determined hostility to them."[50] And the attitude of Wilberforce was the attitude of the "Saints." Though, except for Fowell Buxton, they did not make penal reform a crusade of their own, they supported the others who did—Sir James Mackintosh, Jeremy Bentham, Romilly, and even Burdett.

The Clapham Sect fought for other progressive measures of the day. They advocated, for instance, the abolition of the press gang, the relief of "chimney boys," and the regulation of factory conditions. Granville Sharp, for instance, is said to have "moved all the powers of his age"[51] against the press gang. Wilberforce in 1802 joined with Sir Robert Peel in establishing the first Factory Act, but objected that the Act did not go far enough. In 1805 he took up the cause of the Yorkshire weavers. In 1818 he supported Peel in a further extension of the Factory Act. He lent his warm sympathy to the cause of the chimney boys. Sir James Mackintosh, himself a liberal, gave his judgment that though Wilberforce was by predilection a Tory, by action he must be judged "liberal and reforming."[52] And the description fits the leader scarcely better than it does the followers.[53]

Not less did the Clapham Sect show their essentially liberal spirit in their attitude to men of other faiths. On the one hand they were resolutely opposed to the oppression of any dissenting minorities and on different occasions gave them defence and protection;[54] and on the other hand they advocated emancipation for Roman Catholics. William Smith said in Parliament that "as a Protestant dissenter he pledged himself never to stand up in that House exclusively to obtain the removal of the laws operating against the dissenters, without coupling with it a motion for the restoration of their rights to the Roman Catholics, who were equally entitled to relief."[55] The others, staunch Churchmen though they were, naturally leaned to the liberal side. Wilberforce undoubtedly had a deeply grounded fear of

[50]Coupland, *Wilberforce*, p. 431.
[51]Sir James Stephen, *Essays in Ecclesiastical Biography*, II, 205.
[52]*Edinburgh Review*, 1838, p. 167.
[53]For a fine account of Wilberforce's social activities see Coupland, *Wilberforce*, pp. 426-35. What Coupland says of Wilberforce is largely true of the whole group. See also Halévy, *England in 1815*, pp. 395-7.
[54]Wilberforce received a public vote of thanks from the Methodists for his defence of their people.
[55]*Parliamentary Debates*, XLI, 361.

"popery." He warned his friends that Roman Catholic emancipation
could not settle the issue, that when emancipation came the Roman
Catholic church would not then be content merely to be on an equality
with "heretic teachers." Nevertheless, he wholeheartedly accepted the
principle of religious toleration, and gave his support to successive
measures against discrimination.

In 1797 Wilberforce carried through the Commons a bill to
enable Roman Catholics to serve in the militia. This bill was defeated in the Lords, but in 1807 he carried a similar bill through
Parliament. Both he and his friends grew more liberal with the years.
In 1805 Henry Thornton declared himself for outright emancipation
though Wilberforce and Babington had not then gone so far. In
1813, however, they joined with Thornton to fight for the admission
of Roman Catholics to Parliament. Wilberforce declared that the
elective franchise having been conceded to Catholics it would be
absurd and injurious to deny them seats in the House. In 1819 Wilberforce's diary shows him at Henry Grattan's house working with the
Whigs for a motion for Roman Catholic relief. When Grattan died in
the following year both Wilberforce and Grant voiced warm tributes in
the House of Commons. In 1821 Wilberforce made a strong speech in
support of Plunket's Roman Catholic Disability Removal Bill. He
reminded the House that Ireland was once called "The Mother of the
Saints" and "possessed more pure religion than any other country in
Europe," and he charged that England had not given to Ireland the
liberty which she cherished for herself. In the issue of emancipation,
again the attitude of the leader was the attitude of the group. Granville Sharp, indeed, differed from the rest; but Smith, Thornton,
Stephen, the Macaulays, the Grants, Dealtry, and Buxton all rallied
behind progressive measures toward Roman Catholic emancipation.
And the *Christian Observer* manfully supported them.

The reproach of conservatism, therefore, cannot be too lightly
thrown at the Clapham Sect. The men who in one of the most
reactionary periods of English history so far escaped the dominant
spirit that, in addition to their magnificent achievements in their
chosen fields—then thought revolutionary—they favoured parliamentary reform, penal reform, and the reform of the game and
criminal laws, fought for the first factory legislation, advocated

Roman Catholic emancipation, denounced state lotteries, opposed the press gang, supported the chimney sweep, and, against the accepted sentiment of the time, engaged in a multiplicity of enterprises to educate an illiterate populace—these men surely, although they had by no means cast off all the limitations of their age, cannot deservedly be classed as reactionaries.

Yet there are writers from the time of Cobbett and Hazlitt to the present day who have thus classed them. The Hammonds, for instance, rarely mention Wilberforce save to sneer at his conservatism and his piety. Certainly a picture sketched from references in their pages would be viciously untrue to the real Wilberforce.[56] But the Hammonds are not without clerical associates. Canon Raven, in his *Christian Socialism,* charges that Wilberforce "never realised that, while he was bringing liberty to negroes in the plantations, the white slaves of industry in mine and factory were being made the victims of a tyranny a thousandfold more cruel," and that Wilberforce "consistently opposed every single attempt to benefit the condition of the workers by legislation."[57] Had Canon Raven read a few copies of Zachary Macaulay's *Anti-Slavery Monthly Reporter* he would have rushed less thoughtlessly into his extravagant rhetoric that tyranny in factories was "a thousandfold more cruel" than tyranny on slave plantations. And had he read the *Life of Wilberforce* more carefully he would have found that Wilberforce did not "consistently oppose every single attempt" to benefit factory workers by legislation, but rather that he ardently supported the first attempt ever made to benefit them by legislation, and objected only, as we have seen, that the act did not go far enough. Canon Raven again makes a strange effort to contrast Evangelical conservatism with the social progressiveness of such men as Thomas Gisborne and Richard Oastler. But Gisborne was himself an ardent Evangelical. His social creed would have been

[56]The Hammonds are masterly economic historians, and their books are not only informative and illuminating, but are written in a style of unusual charm and a diction at times of classic dignity, and also with an infectious social passion. Nevertheless they seem quite incapable of understanding what religion meant to men like Wilberforce and Shaftesbury, and how much it was responsible for the dynamic of their lives. After reading their *Shaftesbury,* for instance, one is inevitably reminded of the reply to Southey concerning his *Life of Wesley,* "Sir! Thou hast nothing to draw with, and the well is deep." Bready's *Shaftesbury* is a much more penetrating interpretation of the dynamic of Shaftesbury's life.

[57]P. 12. This book is an excellent survey of the Christian socialist movement, but somewhat unfair to the preceding generation.

heartily endorsed by every one of his Clapham associates: "no man stands authorised in the sight of his Maker to enter into, or to continue in, any species of traffic or business, which is either in itself unjust and immoral, or which in any way tends on the whole to impair the happiness of the human race."[58] Oastler also was an Evangelical, and was led into his humanitarian labours by the door of the anti-slavery crusade—and from there went on to apply the same principles in other labours.[59]

One must remember, also, that the knowledge, and in no small part the development, of the hideous factory and mine conditions came late in Wilberforce's life. Wilberforce threw himself against the most titanic iniquity of his time. And to reproach him, and those who, with him, spent a lifetime of unwearied toil in exposing and exterminating one iniquity, for not also exposing and exterminating another is like reproaching Columbus for not also discovering Australia.

Canon Raven, moreover, repeats the common prejudice that the Evangelicals, of whom the Clapham Sect were the most conspicuous representatives, had a "contempt for this life" which led to the divorce of religion from life, and fostered the alliance between reformers and secularists.[60] It is, of course, easy to understand the aspects of Evangelical piety from which Canon Raven recoils. But on behalf of the Clapham Sect one must nevertheless urge that his judgment was wrong. After his conversion Wilberforce stated his conviction as to where his religion must lead him: "My walk, I am sensible, is a public one; my business is in the world, and I must mix in the assemblies of men, or quit the part which Providence seems to have assigned me."[61]

The Clapham Sect, the leading Evangelicals of their day, did not divorce religion from life. They linked religion to life. They linked it to hunted Negroes on the coast of Africa, on the high seas, and in the plantations of the West Indies. They linked it to standards of political conduct, to the corrupt manners of society, and to the debauched mobs of their time. They linked it to the wretches condemned by game laws, and oppressed in filthy prisons. They linked it to the ragged

---

[58]Gisborne, *Duties of Men,* p. 432.
[59]Alfred, *History of the Factory Movement,* I, 96.
[60]*Christian Socialism,* pp. 11-12.
[61]J. C. Colquhoun, *Wilberforce and His Friends,* p. 74.

children condemned otherwise to ignorance, and by philanthropic and benefit societies they linked it to the improvident and unfortunate poor. Their efforts were sometimes casual and their methods were often awry, but at every point at which they did touch life, it was their religion that led them to the contact. The religion may, indeed, have been otherworldly centred, but the circumference of its action embraced a weltering area of humanity, of which most contemporary religion was comfortably oblivious. Fairbairn judged more truly than Raven when he wrote: ". . . Evangelical piety . . . was the very reverse of *other*-worldly, intensely practical, brotherly, benevolent, beneficent, though somewhat prudential in the means it used to gain its most magnanimous ends. . . . He who speaks in its dispraise, either does not know it or feels no gratitude for good achieved."[62]

Neither the Clapham Sect nor the Evangelicals generally can be accounted responsible for whatever tendency there was to throw reformers into the camp of the secularists. The Evangelicals themselves were often the chief of the reformers and frequently established unexpected ties with men of progressive mind outside the Church. Wilberforce and his associates were drawn by common humanitarian interests into close connection with most of the leading secularists of their day. They found themselves fighting side by side with James Mill, Jeremy Bentham, Romilly, Fox, Hume, Brougham, Sheridan, and even Burdett. Lady Knutsford pointed out the amusing spectacle of these campaigners congratulating themselves in the abolition struggle on Sheridan's being their ally "whether drunk or sober."[63] In his penetrating analysis of English society of that period Halévy makes special point of this feature of the situation. "They [Wilberforce and his friends] were . . . on good terms with avowed Liberals, attached to no denomination, and with Free Thinkers who made no secret of their hostility to religion. It was enough, if their friends were animated by a sincere and practical zeal for the reformation of abuses, and the crusade against ignorance and vice. By a strange paradox men who were Protestant to the backbone, zealots for the dogma of justification by faith, were so devoted to philanthropy that on the common ground of good works they were reconciled with the most

[62]A. M. Fairbairn, *Catholicism: Roman and Anglican,* p. 292.
[63]*Zachary Macaulay,* p. 269.

lukewarm Christians, even with declared enemies of Christianity."[64]
Graham Wallas in his introduction to the English translation of
Halévy's work refers again to the same feature, and tells how he himself discovered, as soon as he became a practical politician, that there
was still a strong working alliance between Evangelical Christianity
and non-Christian radicalism.[65] Canon Raven should rather have
said that if reform was divorced from religion the Evangelicals were
least of all to blame.

The Clapham Sect of course did not find their primary interests in
what is narrowly known as "social reform." Their primary interests
lay in the abolition movement, the missionary movement, the Bible
societies, Sunday schools, and conservative philanthropy. But their
towering achievements in these fields render them such an obvious
mark for invidious criticism in other fields that they have not generally
received credit for being as liberal as they really were. They had the
unpropitious fate of being attacked in their lifetime by two masters
of English prose, and one master of sardonic wit,[66] whose brilliance
brought their worst failings into distorted focus and created an ill-
balanced tradition, which, even when true in detail, is untrue in
proportion. And the very permanence of their fame has kept them
ever since selected targets for ironic illustrations. That the whole
contemporary propertied class favoured coercive legislation and corn
laws can be recounted as illuminating economic record without any
alarms about religions or excursions into creeds; but that William
Wilberforce, the emancipator of the slaves, should vote for coercive
legislation or corn laws irresistibly invites a sparkling examination into
the narrowness of Evangelical piety.

A fair judgment of the Clapham Sect demands the balance of
three considerations:

1. Though they were unmistakably stamped with the mark of
their times, their general attitude was far more liberal than one would
infer from the stock references of their critics.

[64]*England in 1815*, p. 383. See also pp. 397, 509-11.
[65]*Ibid.*, pp. vi-vii.
[66]I.e., Cobbett, Hazlitt, and Sydney Smith. There have been some writers
who have been able to take a balanced view of their greatness and their imper-
fections, e.g. Sir James Stephen, the Trevelyans, and Professor Coupland, but the
predominant tradition is not so balanced.

2. Their central labours were of supreme significance to the world, and were accomplished in a spirit of disinterested devotion to high principles. It is but ungracious tribute hastily to present a patronizing approval of their anti-slavery labours, as a convenient stance from which to launch an oblique assault on some other action. The anti-slavery campaign was of a character unknown in the history of man-kind. Lecky says that it is one of the three or four perfectly virtuous labours in the history of nations. Previously there had been instances of men fighting nobly for deliverance of their fellows, who could appeal to them, from evils whose workings they could see. But there had been no precedent for this far rarer virtue, this passion for the deliverance of a strange race in a distant land, where the cries of the sufferers went unheard, and their wrongs were hidden from view. The men who gave their lives to that endeavour deserve as a conse-quence not a criticism more caustic, but a charity more liberal than usual. Seen in later perspective even the greatest among liberals always have strange blind spots. Though not without limitations few men deserve more than Wilberforce and his little brotherhood the grateful remembrance of mankind.

3. The Clapham Sect left an often unconsidered legacy to liberal movements. A later chapter will deal with this more fully. But here it is pertinent to say that a generation of persistent propaganda of humanitarian principles had many unpremeditated results. The senti-ments so nobly marshalled for the defeat of slavery did not confine themselves to the purpose for which they were invoked, nor expire when emancipation was achieved. They became manifest in a more sensitive humanitarianism which overflowed in many subsequent reforms, and helped other radicals to win other victories in the very areas which the Clapham Sect themselves left most alone.

CHAPTER SEVEN

The object is the extinction of slavery

"YOU HAVE CROSSED the Red Sea," came a cautious congratulation to Wilberforce after the abolition triumph of 1807, "but Pharaoh may follow your steps, and aim at some abridgement of the deliverance."[1] The Clapham Sect were fully alive to the peril. The immediate outlook was favourable. Not only England, but America and Denmark had abolished the slave trade; France, Spain, and Holland were withheld by the war from active trading; and only Portugal remained in the trade on any considerable scale.[2] The brotherhood began to lay plans for the consolidation of their victory.

Their first labours were directed towards Africa. On the same day which saw the end of the legal slave trade—January 1, 1808—Sierra Leone was to pass from the control of the Directors of the Company to the British Crown. The men of Clapham felt that—especially as the slave trade was about to cease—they ought not to abandon their original intention to make the colony a visible testimony in Africa that Negroes were capable of developing a Christian civilization.

Less than three weeks after the Abolition Bill had been passed they therefore gathered at a meeting in Freemasons' Hall, "for the purpose of concerting means for improving the opportunity presented by the abolition of the Slave Trade, for promoting innocent commerce and civilization in Africa."[3] The meeting adopted two series of resolutions (carefully prepared by Wilberforce beforehand) and formally established the African Institution, of which the main object was to promote civilization in Africa by providing "example to enlighten the minds of the natives, and instruction to enable them to direct their industry to proper objects."[4] The Institution, being launched in the high tide of abolition enthusiasm, secured wide support and dis-

[1] *Life of Wilberforce*, III, 360.
[2] *Christian Observer*, 1807, p. 680.
[3] *Ibid.*, p. 270.   [4] *Ibid.*, pp. 270-3, 679, 680.

tinguished patronage, the Duke of Gloucester becoming President. But the enthusiasm was naturally centred in the Clapham Sect. They had all rallied to the new cause. Lord Teignmouth, Babington, Grant, Sharp, Thornton, Clarkson, Macaulay, Stephen, Venn, Gisborne, William Smith, and Wilberforce were all on the first Committee (nominated by Wilberforce).[5] When the society was fully organized Wilberforce was a Vice-President; Babington, Clarkson, Grant, Macaulay, Sharp, Smith, and Stephen were Directors; Thornton was given his customary job as Treasurer;[6] and Macaulay, to whom as usual was assigned the real burden, was made Secretary. The *Christian Observer* said: "In the planning and formation of this Society, Mr. Macaulay, together with Mr. Wilberforce, Mr. Stephen, and some other leading abolitionists, took a principal share; but the chief labour, as in most other cases, fell upon Mr. Macaulay."[7]

The African Institution set to work in a large way, but was soon led to alter its original emphasis. For the slave trade did not cease with the official abolition. Most of the West Indian planters still believed that "buying was cheaper than breeding," and maintained a demand for slaves which encouraged a new business in illicit trading. Two years after the passing of the Abolition Bill smugglers "swarmed" on the African coast; and, under the cover of foreign flags, slave ships were brazenly fitted out in London and Liverpool, ostensibly to carry slaves to the Spaniards and Portuguese, actually to smuggle them to the British colonies. Stephen and Macaulay, who alone of all the members of the African Institution had local knowledge of the West Indies or of Africa, quickly realized how dangerous to the whole movement the illicit trading might become, and how impossible it was to promote civilization in Africa while slave traders continued to harry its coasts. Accordingly they concentrated their resources to meet the new peril, and transformed the African Institution actually into a large anti-slavery society.

Exploiting all the influence of the Institution the eager company laboured to make good the act of 1807. They obtained from the government the formation of a coast guard to intercept the African

---

[5]*Ibid.*, p. 271.
[6]*Ibid.*, 1808, p. 207.
[7]*Ibid.*, 1839, p. 796.

smugglers, the appointment of an investigating committee, and the establishment in Sierra Leone of a Court of Vice-Admiralty to expedite the processes of justice.[8] They succeeded in 1809 in getting an Order-in-Council giving the right of search against Portuguese vessels; in 1810 in obtaining a treaty by which Portugal forbade her subjects to carry on the trade in the parts of Africa that did not belong to her;[9] and in 1811 in winning their first decisive victory against the smugglers, by securing a law—drawn up substantially by James Stephen[10]—which made slave trading for British subjects a felony, punishable with transportation for fourteen years.

These concerted public labours were aided and supplemented by much direct personal influence. Wilberforce's diary shows him now urging "Yorke, First Lord of the Admiralty, to send out ships of war to Africa, and clear the coast by a thorough sweep"; now "supporting Mr. Barham's motion for the introducing free labour into the West Indies"; now working up an agitation to stop "the persecution of the missionaries, or rather the forbidding religion to the slaves in Trinidad and Demerara"; and now carefully outlining "subjects of action and deliberation for Abolitionists." But even Wilberforce's zeal did not satisfy his ardent associates, and when he became temporarily occupied with incidental duties Stephen wrote to him sharply that he must "resolutely *make* time to think and act on Abolition matters." Stephen and Macaulay of course were toiling as indefatigably as ever. "We are working like negroes," Stephen wrote, "for the negroes of Berbice, Sierra Leone, Trinidad, and Africa at large."[11]

Yet, despite the prestige of the African Institution, and the diligence of the Clapham warriors, the course of the battle was disheartening. It was so easy to capture slaves in Africa, so easy to smuggle them into the West Indies, and, in the "sealed book" of a large plantation, so difficult to prove that they had been smuggled, that the illicit trade grew to proportions scarcely less than those of the old legal trade. In 1810 Wilberforce wrote to Macaulay expressing his grief that the West Indians were "not accommodating themselves to the new system," and asking Macaulay what he thought of "firing

[8]*Ibid.*, 1808, pp. 338-9 (from Second Report of the African Institution).
[9]*Cambridge History of British Foreign Policy*, II, 235.
[10]George Stephen, *Antislavery Recollections*, pp. 9-10.
[11]*Life of Wilberforce*, III, 483, 486, 514, 546, 547.

a pamphlet at them."[12] It was not Macaulay, however, but Stephen who engineered the defeat of the smugglers, and prepared the way for the final emancipation.

Stephen devised a plan of establishing in the West Indies an official registry of all the slaves on each plantation. By that means he thought that he could provide against the continual addition of smuggled slaves. His comrades seized eagerly upon the idea, and determined, as a beginning, to have the scheme tried out in Trinidad. They pressed their plan with "many private interviews" and "urgent remonstrances" and succeeded in January, 1812, in getting Perceval, the Prime Minister, to issue an Order-in-Council, prepared by Stephen, authorizing an official registry of all slaves in Trinidad.[13]

Meanwhile the Sect, having taken counsel with Romilly and Brougham, had moved to press for an act of Parliament imposing a similar registration on all the West Indies. They resolved not to delay, and on January 6, 1812, at a consultation, "settled to proceed with Registry Bill this year." But they found that it was no easy task to prepare such a bill for Parliament, and still less easy to prepare Parliament for such a bill. The Government expressed fears about "interfering with the colonial legislature"; and, in a short time, Wilberforce had to inform Stephen of Perceval's judgment that "it would be more prudent to wait till another year in order to see how the engine should work in Trinidad, and rectify any errors, supply any defects, which experience should suggest."[14]

The next year (1813) was occupied with the East India Charter; but after that battle and a brief holiday the Clapham Sect took up again their old interest. Wilberforce left his country house and repaired to Stephen's to be present at a "meeting of the African Institution, to settle West Indian matters with Macaulay, Grant, and the interior council."[15]

However the Registry Bill might have fared, a new turn in world events shelved it altogether for a while. Napoleon at last was falling. In 1812 he had been defeated in Russia, in 1813 in Germany, and in 1814 in France. The dawning prospect of a general conference of

---

[12]*Ibid.*, p. 482.

[13]George Stephen, *Antislavery Recollections*, p. 25. Stephen was one of Perceval's closest personal friends.

[14]*Life of Wilberforce*, IV, 3, 19-20.   [15]*Ibid.*, p. 138.

the great powers suggested to the "Saints" a new possibility for an old plan. From the first they had been hoping for some international agreement to outlaw the slave trade; and, not without some valuable results, they had intermittently attempted to obtain action from other countries. In 1808 Wilberforce had written to Jefferson in America, and had advised Macaulay to have abolition pamphlets translated into Spanish. And in the same year when Spanish and Portuguese deputies came to England he had suggested to Macaulay and William Smith that it would be well "to get pretty well acquainted" with them with a view to having them "well impregnated with Abolitionism."[16] At the same time he kept a watchful eye on every action of his own country. To promote his cause he was ready to resort to "friendly violence" against the government; and he seemed able to make his power effective. In 1810, it has been mentioned, Clapham influence helped to win important concessions from Portugal, and in 1813 it also helped to win from Sweden a complete repudiation of the slave trade. "So strong a hold did Wilberforce have on the government that the slave trade sections of proposed treaties with foreign powers were submitted to him by Castlereagh for comment."[17]

There was now an opportunity to supplement the several gains by an international agreement to repudiate the trade. Wilberforce reproached himself for not "having foreseen this conjuncture, and been prepared with works in all the modern languages against the Slave Trade." He called the whole brotherhood into vigorous action. "We are much occupied," he wrote to Gisborne, "with the grand object of prevailing on all the great European powers to agree to a convention for the general Abolition of the Slave Trade." He judged that France would be favourable, and that Spain and Portugal would be "compelled into assent." With such prospect of success the brotherhood decided to concentrate on the new objective, and at a meeting of the African Institution Wilberforce, Stephen, Thornton, Macaulay, and William Smith joined in agreement "to give up the Register Bill for the present, and to push for a convention for the general Abolition —to present an address to the Crown, to negociate with the foreign powers, and to forward the measure by all means."

[16]*Ibid.*, III, 374, 384, 385.
[17]F. J. Klingberg, *The Anti-Slavery Movement in England,* p. 136.

The first means employed was a letter from Wilberforce to the Emperor Alexander of Russia, who was urged, in terms calculated to flatter and to appeal, to lend his powerful influence to the cause. This letter was followed by others to Talleyrand, the Archbishop of Rheims, Baron Humboldt, and Lafayette. Writing letters was not all. On the eve of peace a motion was passed in the House of Commons which enjoined the Cabinet to solicit from all the sovereigns of Europe the immediate abolition of the slave trade.

The Clapham Sect counted this as only the first step. They had no intention of trusting the matter to the decisions of cabinets and ambassadors. "We have some dark plots in our heads," wrote Henry Thornton, "for influencing the Allied Powers in favour of the abolition of the slave trade through this earth of ours, which earth three or four potentates . . . of whom Lord Castlereagh is one, seem to hold in their hands."[18] As Castlereagh, the British Ambassador, set out for Paris the Clapham Sect therefore proceeded with supplementary plans of their own. They had judged Castlereagh to be "a fish of the cold-blooded kind,"[19] and they determined that it would be wise to establish more direct connections at Paris, the better to apply their influence. They decided consequently to appoint their own ambassador, who should remain at Paris during the peace negotiations, to keep an eye on Castlereagh, to supply him with any needed information, and by whatever means possible to further their cause. Their choice fell on Macaulay, who was a fluent speaker of French and whose encyclopaedic knowledge and sleepless diligence admirably fitted him for the task.[20] Macaulay therefore set out for Paris as "Anti-Slavery Ambassador" of the Clapham Sect. He remained there for some time and kept tirelessly on the trail of Castlereagh.[21] But his mission was destined to failure. The French traders were so eager to grasp again the profits which the war had long withheld from them that Castlereagh could not have achieved much, whatever his desire. But Macaulay thought that Castlereagh had been indifferent to the cause; and, in

[18]J. C. Colquhoun, *Wilberforce and His Friends*, p. 327.
[19]*Life of Wilberforce*, IV, 175-7.
[20]In case Macaulay had any spare time in Paris he was commissioned as a secondary office to form a Bible Society there. A letter from Wilberforce to Lady Sparrow (May 3, 1814); MS in Wilberforce Museum at Hull.
[21]See letters from Macaulay to Castlereagh, in *Correspondence of Castlereagh*, 3rd series, II, 47-9.

anger and disappointment, he returned to his friends, who all assembled at Henry Thornton's house to welcome him and to hear the tale of his unsuccessful endeavours.

Consequently when Castlereagh returned in general triumph, bearing a treaty otherwise satisfactory, the Clapham Sect gave no echo to the national rejoicing. Contained in the treaty was an article pledging France to abolish the slave trade, but not until the end of five years when it would be well established again after the lull during the war. And so in the House of Commons, after the applause for Castlereagh had ceased, Wilberforce rose to protest that he could not join in the acclaim. "I cannot but conceive," he exclaimed, "that I behold in his hand the death-warrant of a multitude of innocent victims . . . whom I had fondly indulged the hope of having myself rescued from destruction."[22]

Foiled at Paris the persistent "Saints" now turned their eyes to the approaching Congress of Vienna, at which they hoped to retrieve their defeat by a general charter of abolition. An unexpected opportunity for preliminary politics occurred when the Emperor Alexander of Russia visited England, and expressed a desire to meet Wilberforce. But the Emperor proved more affable than helpful, and dodged the blame for the small gains at Paris by saying, "What could be done, when your own ambassador gave way?"[23]

The "Saints" grimly determined to make it less easy for Castlereagh to give way the next time. And they were at no loss what to do. They would send him to Vienna with a mandate so unmistakable that he would not be able to ignore it. They set to work, therefore, organizing another campaign to bring once more to their aid the force of public opinion. "Let the nation loudly and generally express its deep disappointment and regret," said Wilberforce, referring to the Paris treaty. "Our best hopes," he wrote again, "rest on the country's manifesting a general and strong feeling on the subject."[24] The crusader's call once more brought a response prompt and overwhelming. In thirty-four days, beginning June 27, 1814, there were sent to the House of Commons nearly eight hundred petitions bearing nearly one million signatures, a number at that time almost equal to one-tenth of the entire population of the country.[25] The whole nation was roused by the passionate crusade. "I was not aware," wrote Wellington in July on returning to England after his long absence, "of the degree of frenzy existing here about the slave trade."[26] "The whole nation is bent upon the subject," wrote Castlereagh, "I believe there is hardly a village that has not met and petitioned upon it: both Houses of Parliament are pledged to press it: and the Ministers must make it the basis of their policy."[27]

The ministers, being given the word of England, did make the abolition of the trade the basis of their policy. Wellington, now ambassador in Paris, and Castlereagh in Vienna fought stubbornly to obtain an international repudiation of the trade. The Clapham Sect determined again that they would do well themselves to keep in close touch with affairs, and make use of their own thorough knowledge. Wilberforce wrote to Macaulay:

You will concur with me that it may be well to furnish Lord Castlereagh with short notes like a lawyer's brief, of all the main propositions on which the case of Abolition rests, or rather I mean of all the facts. . . . I would abstain of course from any statements which might appear to him invidious. . . . A copy of this paper may then be made for the Duke of Wellington, and also for any other of the foreign ministers. Lord Castlereagh must also be provided with such a statement of the present condition of St. Domingo as will enable him to convince Talleyrand that the attempt to recover it by force will end in disgrace.[28] Stephen can best draw up the account I mean.[29]

The two toilers betook themselves anew to their labours. Stephen "furnished copious details," about St. Domingo and Macaulay amassed such a "vast body of convincing proofs" about the northwest coast of Africa that Wilberforce was delighted, and wrote to him, "I do not think a grain can be added to the weight with which your zeal, diligence, and method in preserving your papers, have loaded the scale in our favour." Even the Duke of Wellington—whom Macaulay sought out in a personal interview to fortify him in advance

[25]Klingberg, *The Anti-Slavery Movement in England*, p. 146.
[26]Elie Halévy, *England in 1815*, p. 400.
[27]*Correspondence of Castlereagh*, 3rd series, II, 73.
[28]The French were not only against abolition, but were contemplating a reconquest of St. Domingo from the Negroes and its return to the plantation system.   [29]*Life of Wilberforce*, IV, 209-10.

with the Clapham arguments—exclaimed in admiration that he could "not see how on earth" the French could escape the force of this evidence.[30]

In addition to providing the ambassadors with facts and arguments the Clapham Sect proceeded with their characteristic propaganda. Wilberforce was summoned to further interviews with the Emperor Alexander, and the King of Prussia also asked to talk with him. He corresponded diligently with prospective labourers in the cause: Cardinal Gonsalvi, Humboldt, Sismondi, Chateaubriand, and Madame de Staël. He prepared another printed letter to Talleyrand, which he distributed as a manifesto of the abolitionist party, and which Castlereagh, at his behest, put into the hands of all the sovereigns represented at Vienna. Clarkson meanwhile visited Paris and arranged for a reprint of his translated *History of Abolition*; he also prepared an Address for the representatives at Vienna. Macaulay kept in watchful contact with both Wellington and Castlereagh.[31]

Yet once more all the labour seemed to be in vain. The decision lay with France; and France was openly hostile. Abolitionists could not even get their letters in the French newspapers. For an ancient ghost had risen again. The Royalists remembered that of old abolition had been favoured by the revolutionaries; and now they did not trouble to draw nice distinctions. They still associated the freedom of the slaves with Jacobinism. "French Royalists," Lord Holland wrote to Wilberforce, "make no difference between you and me, or between me and Tom Paine."[32] Even worse, the French newspapers made it a point of national honour not be to persuaded by the English. Hence the total gain of all the plans, the petitions, the letters, and the toil, was a reluctant admission by France to prohibit French slaving north of Cape Formosa at the mouth of the Niger.

Even this small gain was ground for hope. The "Saints" remembered the days not so long before when the cause had seemed so hopeless in England. "Depend on it," Wilberforce reassured Macaulay, "we are gaining ground. God is with us."[33]

From what source help was to come the Saints little suspected.

[30]*Ibid.*, pp. 210-11.
[31]The *British Critic*, 1823, p. 316, refers to Wellington, Canning, *et al.* as "Agents of the African Institution."
[32]*Life of Wilberforce*, IV, 213.   [33]*Ibid.*, p. 218.

Napoleon suddenly returned from Elba, and, as a strategic bid for England's favour, proclaimed the immediate and total abolition of the French slave trade. Napoleon did not long remain in power to enforce his proclamation. But when British arms had restored Louis XVIII, British influence was too powerful to permit a repudiation of the policy once established. Castlereagh was able to report to Wilberforce in July 1815 an agreement for "the unqualified and total abolition of the Slave Trade throughout the dominions of France."[34]

This was not all that the Clapham Sect had hoped for. They had hoped for such an agreement not only with France but with all the slave-trading nations of Europe. Some gratification there was, of course, in the declaration by the eight powers (including Spain and Portugal who were still engaged in the trade) on February 8, 1815, condemning the trade and affirming their determination to abolish it as soon as possible. This declaration was annexed to the final act signed on June 9. To have won even so much was a memorable victory. And beyond peradventure the victory was due to the Clapham Sect.

. . . it is obvious that, without the unceasing efforts of Wilberforce and his friends, Castlereagh and his Government would have accomplished but little. Their goodwill cannot of course be doubted; but they needed a spur to make them sufficiently active when other matters were pressing on their attention. . . . it cannot be doubted . . . that, without the sustained and eager insistence of an organised public opinion in this country, the responsible statesmen would have allowed the iniquitous traffic to continue under the pretext that it was impossible to do otherwise.[35]

As this campaign was drawing to a close another was being revived by the "Saints." Before the defeat of Napoleon, it will be remembered, they had inaugurated a crusade to establish an official registry of slaves in the West Indies. At the prospect of international action on slave trading they had put aside their campaign for the Registry Bill. But they had not failed to keep in close touch with the colonies, and they had become increasingly aware that the illicit trade was thriving, not dying. They were at length convinced that

[34] *Ibid.*, p. 224.
[35] *Cambridge History of British Foreign Policy*, I, 499.

without some system of registration all the gains of the Abolition Act would be lost. On February 15, 1815, at the house of the President of the African Institution, Wilberforce, Babington, James Stephen, and his son James, who was henceforth to be a tower of strength to the abolitionists, met with some others, and, after a "long discussion," "resolved on pushing Registry Bill immediately."[36]

Wilberforce thereupon proceeded to sound the Government, which attempted to evade the question by saying that there was no actual proof of the alleged smuggling. But Wilberforce and his group knew that the lack of supervision made proof impossible, and they were attempting to introduce a measure which would at once establish the proof and make possible the prohibition. Stephen, who had been often provoked by similar vacillations of the Government, flared into anger at this excuse, and, to express his resentment, resigned his seat in the House of Commons. Once before when the Government was apathetic this "high-minded fanatic" had declared: "I would rather be on friendly terms with a man who had strangled my infant son than support an administration guilty of slackness in suppressing the slave trade." And in 1814 he had exclaimed, "If Lord Castlereagh does not keep to his pledges, may my God not spare me, if I spare the noble lord and his colleagues." But, though Stephen left the House of Commons, he allowed no slack to his anti-slavery labours, and within the next year he had written four pamphlets on the slave trade.[37] The "Saints" indeed determined to proceed with the Bill, and Wilberforce and Macaulay supplemented Stephen's pamphlets with others of their own. In July Wilberforce introduced the Bill to the Commons. But they were finally persuaded by Castlereagh that it would be wise to delay for a year, and make an effort to induce the colonies themselves to adopt the measure in their own legislatures. They consequently decided not to press the Bill until the next year.

As in their earlier campaign in 1800 they found that it was easier to drop an unpopular measure than to take it up again. The next session, 1816, brought three added obstacles to the Bill. There had come from Barbados news of a Negro insurrection, which though it had been but half-heartedly conducted, and was quickly suppressed

[36] *Life of Wilberforce*, IV, 243.
[37] Sir Leslie Stephen, *The Life of Sir James Fitzjames Stephen*, p. 22. *Life of Wilberforce*, IV, 249.

and horribly revenged, was none the less exploited to accuse the "Saints" of fomenting revolution by their propaganda. Then, to aggravate the situation, the West Indians in England, who understood no less than the Clapham Sect the possibilities of a Registry Bill, had organized a powerful opposition, and were alarming the country by their lurid propaganda. "I am assured," Wilberforce had written to Macaulay in 1815, "that they are mustering all their forces and all their natural allies against us, with the most assiduous diligence and systematic array. . . . Remember that we were challenged to prove in a committee the truth of our allegations, that slaves are smuggled, and also that the abuses we charge do really exist. Do consider about getting evidence from the West Indies against the next session." The West Indians even laid a voluntary tax upon every hogshead of sugar to raise funds to oppose the Registry Bill.[38] To complicate the matter the Spanish government—influenced not a little by Clapham pamphlets and propaganda—had at last moved to end the slave trade in its dominions, and the "Saints" feared that a defeat for them at home at such a time would injure their prestige abroad, and perhaps operate against them in the Spanish cabinet. "Depend upon it," Wilberforce wrote to Stephen, "the loud cry . . . that we were fomenting insurrections among the slaves, would operate powerfully against us in the Spanish Cabinet."[39] So Wilberforce held a consultation with Stephen, Macaulay, William Smith, and other abolition supporters, and decided that it would be well to quiet the home opposition by ceasing to press for the Registry Bill.

The next year, 1817, another obstacle arose to delay the bill still further. A period of severe depression was causing widespread distress in England, and, in the face of destitution among English workmen, Wilberforce hesitated to urge the plight of the Negroes. Early in the year he expressed his ideas in a letter to Macaulay:

I have for some time been unwillingly yielding to a secret suggestion that it would be better perhaps to lie upon our oars in the Registry Bill, and West Indian cause. When parliament meets, the whole nation, depend upon it, will be looking up for relief from its own burthens, and it would betray an ignorance of all tact to talk to them in such circumstances of the sufferings of the slaves in the West Indies. We should

[38]*Life of Wilberforce*, IV, 263-4, 304.   [39]*Ibid.*, p. 286.

specially guard against appearing to have a world of our own, and to have little sympathy with the sufferings of our countrymen.[40]

So the Saints dropped the Registry Bill, and in fact never took it up again in Parliament. But they finally achieved their purpose in an indirect way. During the years in which the Bill had not been brought into Parliament they had been exerting their personal influence to make the government urge upon the colonies the duty of themselves establishing a registry of slaves. And, as a nominal concession to the mother country, the colonial legislatures gradually passed registry acts of their own. In the colonies, of course, these acts remained quite innocuous. But in 1819 the Secretary for the Colonies adroitly achieved the whole purpose of the discarded Registry Bill. He introduced a measure establishing a register of colonial slaves in England.[41] Having admitted the principle the colonies could not escape this later measure. At last registries were compiled, and in this indirect manner, "after seven years of incessant labour and anxiety," especially on the part of Stephen and Macaulay, the Clapham Sect obtained the measure for which they had been so long contending. Wilberforce wrote joyfully to Macaulay, "No one has more right than you to be congratulated for no one has done or suffered so much as yourself in and for this great cause."[42]

The Move for Emancipation

The Registry Act came into force on January 1, 1820, and marked the beginning of the end. It "not only gave the finishing stroke to the Slave Trade Abolition and Felony Acts, but happily laid a foundation for those awful statistics of slavery which proved the battle-axe of Mr. Fowell Buxton in his many fearful contests for its total abolition."[43] An accurate registry involved investigation; and investigation revealed in horrible colours all the facts that had previously been suspected but could not be proved. The abolitionists became convinced that the evils of slavery which they had tried so

[40]*Ibid.*, p. 307.

[41]As early as 1815 Stephen had foreseen such a move, and wrote to Lord Bathurst: "Without a duplicate registry *here*, . . . and without public access to that registry, it would be worse than useless. . . ." Historical Manuscripts Commission, *Report on the Manuscripts of Earl Bathurst* (London, 1923), pp. 351–3; quoted in Klingberg, *The Anti-Slavery Movement in England*, p. 173.

[42]Knutsford, *Zachary Macaulay*, p. 315.

[43]George Stephen, *Antislavery Recollections*, pp. 18-19.

THE EXTINCTION OF SLAVERY

earnestly to eliminate were not incidental but inherent, and would not, and could not, be cured until slavery itself was abolished.

The Clapham Sect well knew that this conviction would involve them in a battle as stiff as any they had yet encountered. To abolish the property rights which the slaves represented was obviously a much more serious step than simply to prohibit the spoliation of Africa and the importation of new slaves. In the earlier campaign some of the planters themselves had become convinced that importation was no longer necessary, and that the planters would be just as well off by breeding their own slaves as by importing others from Africa. To set all the slaves free was a different matter. That would seem preposterous not alone to the West Indians but also to most Englishmen. Only a little earlier it would have seemed preposterous to most abolitionists. In 1807 during the debate on the Abolition Bill Wilberforce had said in the House of Commons:

He and those who thought with him made the distinction between the abolition of the trade and the emancipation of the slaves, and not only abstained from proposing the latter, but were ready to reject such a proposition when made by others. How much soever he looked forward with anxious expectation to the period when the negroes might with safety be liberated; he knew too well the effect which the long continuance of abject slavery produced upon the human mind, to think of their immediate emancipation; a measure, which, at the present moment, would be injurious to them, and ruinous to the colonies.[44]

Many of the slaves in the West Indies had come from wild and savage tribes, and were difficult to control and to work. Their owners, not without reason, believed that if these slaves were once free from compulsion they would retire to the mountains, where they would revert to their wild state, and, in their overwhelming numbers, become a peril to the tiny white population. In England, the Duke of Wellington expressed apprehension that emancipation might create the necessity of sending troops to exterminate the blacks. "Actual emancipation," said a later anti-slavery enthusiast, "was a grand concession to humanity which I firmly believe that the most sanguine abolitionist never contemplated in 1813."[45] But through their years of study the Clapham Sect had acquired a new faith in the Negroes, a

[44]*Parliamentary Debates,* 2nd series, IX, 143.
[45]George Stephen, *Antislavery Recollections,* p. 21.

faith that, while perhaps too sanguine, was, as subsequent events proved, not without knowledge of the Negro nature. And, whatever the perils of freedom, the Clapham Sect were now thoroughly convinced that slavery was too inherently wicked and unjust to be permitted under the protection of the British flag.

In 1821, therefore, the war-scarred veterans girded themselves for their last struggle, a struggle in which only a remnant of the initial company could now engage. The ranks had been broken. Henry Thornton, Granville Sharp, and John Venn had passed away. And, with the old ties breaking, the others had gradually moved from Clapham till at last only common interests and common labours, and the bonds of family and of long friendship, kept the aging group together. Even those who were left could no longer lead the battle as was their wont. Wilberforce, always in ill health, was now over sixty years of age and utterly unable to undertake the management of another parliamentary campaign.

Consultations were therefore held to select a successor on whom the mantle of Wilberforce might be laid. The choice fell on a young member of Parliament, Thomas Fowell Buxton. Buxton, like Wilberforce, was an Evangelical. His mother and his wife were both Quakers; and he was the brother-in-law of Elizabeth Fry. He, himself, was an ardent advocate of penal reform and a warm champion of the working classes. He was, indeed, a supporter of all good causes—his first public speech was at a meeting of the Norwich Auxiliary Bible Society. Obviously he was cut of Clapham cloth.

Wilberforce had long been watching Buxton. In 1816 when he had made a valiant speech on behalf of the poor weavers of Spitalfields Wilberforce had written him a letter almost prophetic. After expressing pleasure at the work for "the hungry and the naked" he continued: "It is partly a selfish feeling, for I anticipate the success of the efforts which I trust you will one day make in other instances, in an assembly in which I trust we shall be fellow-labourers." In 1817 when Buxton published his work on *Prison Discipline* Wilberforce wrote again: "I hope you will come soon into Parliament . . . and be able to contend in person, as well as with your pen, for the rights and happiness of the oppressed and friendless. I claim you as an ally in this blessed league."

On May 24, 1821, Wilberforce wrote to Buxton formally offering him the leadership of his "holy enterprise."[46] Buxton had long been interested in the anti-slavery movement, and the offer of succeeding Wilberforce was an honour tempting to a young man of thirty-five. Yet the responsibilities attached to that leadership were so serious that it was not until the autumn, after Wilberforce and Macaulay had gone to him for a personal interview, that he decided to throw in his lot with the older men and assume the leadership of "an alliance" that might "truly be termed holy."[47]

His successor secured, Wilberforce now began to outline the course of the campaign. In December, 1822, he wrote to Buxton: "My idea is, that a little before parliament meets, three or four of us should have a secret cabinet council, wherein we should deliberate and decide what course to pursue." Buxton, infected with the true Clapham spirit, replied that a "Congress on the subject" might be held early in January. Accordingly on the 8th of that month Buxton and Macaulay went to Wilberforce's house to discuss the plan of operations for the approaching season. Wilberforce proposed there a "serious talk of the interior Cabinet"; throughout this period there were "long and deep . . . deliberations, how best to shape those measures which were to change the structure of society throughout the western world."[48]

It was agreed that all hope of success lay in rousing once more a great public agitation. As far back as 1811 Stephen had said: ". . . we shall do nothing effectual to check colonial crimes till we blazen them to the English public, and arm ourselves with popular indignation."[49] Wilberforce had always relied on winning the moral sentiment of the people at large. In 1816 he had declared his belief that they would finally accord him victory: "I rely upon the religion of the people of this country—because the people of England are religious and moral, loving justice and hating iniquity, they consider the oppressed as their brethren whatever be their complexion. . . ."[50] Now in 1822 he wrote in his diary: "we must . . . call on all good men throughout the kingdom to join us in abolishing this wicked

[46]The rather long letter is quoted in full in Charles Buxton, *Memoirs of Buxton*, pp. 103-4.   [47]*Ibid.*, pp. 104-6.
[48]*Life of Wilberforce*, V, 157, 158, 160, 163.
[49]*Ibid.*, IV, 241.   [50]*Ibid.*, p. 291.

system, and striving to render the degraded race by degrees a free
peasantry."[51]

Among the English public the name of Wilberforce still carried a
magic that belonged to no other. Even before the "cabinet council,"
therefore, Wilberforce had decided to prepare the way for the campaign by publishing his slavery manifesto, as he had, years before,
published his religious manifesto. He had commenced the preparation
of the manifesto on the day on which Buxton and Macaulay called
on him, and thereafter kept working at it throughout the winter.
But writing was never his forte, and he now found it more difficult
than ever. He sighed for his "white Negroes" of the former days; at
one time Stephen thought of going to help him speed the drudgery
of research, but concluded that Wilberforce might better be allowed
to proceed at his own pace. Aided somewhat by the criticism of
William Smith, Wilberforce therefore laboured by himself; and early
in March 1823 published his *Appeal to the Religion, Justice, and
Humanity of the Inhabitants of the British Empire in Behalf of the
Negro Slaves in the West Indies.*

The *Appeal* achieved wide popularity and had an important influence, but naturally it was only a preliminary. The "Saints" would
not feel at home in any campaign without a society and a variety of
committees. They already had the African Institution, which in some
of their labours had done them much service. But for their present
purposes the African Institution was handicapped by the very advantages which aided its primary task. It was heavily weighted with high
patronage. In consequence it had grown increasingly conservative,
and was now entirely too conservative to be of much use in heading
a vigorous crusade. It had put a ban on publications, it disapproved of
public meetings, and it had a strong dislike for popular agitation. It
had served its purpose; but in the new campaign it promised to be
of but dubious assistance.

Zachary Macaulay, therefore, devised an institution nearer to
their heart's desire, the London Society for the Mitigation and
Gradual Abolition of Slavery throughout the British Dominions,
known more briefly as the London Anti-Slavery Society. This Society,
founded in 1823, showed that the survivors of the Clapham Sect were

[51]*Ibid.,* V, 158-9.

still active in anti-slavery labours. Its Vice-Presidents soon included Babington, Buxton, Clarkson, Smith, Stephen, and Wilberforce, while Zachary Macaulay, with his son Thomas Babington, served on the Committee.[52] Under this direction the Society began to organize publicity for the campaign. It circulated Wilberforce's *Appeal* and a pamphlet by Clarkson.[53] It requested Stephen to finish a work he had undertaken on the legal aspects of slavery, and thus secured the publication of the first volume of *Slavery Delineated*,[54] which for the next ten years was a handbook for all anti-slavery workers.

Thomas Clarkson, now 63 years of age, not only wrote his pamphlet but volunteered once again to join his old companions in the active work of the campaign. Immediately he was sent on a long journey to gather information for the Anti-Slavery Society and to organize local committees for its support. Concerning this journey he later wrote: "I travelled through the whole Kingdom in 1823 to rouse the people of England in our great cause. . . . I succeeded in forming nearly 200 Committees and the result was some hundred petitions to Parliament. . . . I travelled about 3,000 miles, and was absent from home nearly a year."[55]

Shortly came the opportunity to commence the campaign in Parliament. The Quakers, ever in the vanguard, had prepared a petition praying Parliament to take measures to redeem the slaves.[56] With the object of sounding the House and estimating prospects Wilberforce made an address on March 19, 1823, and presented the petition. He did not make a very propitious beginning. "Fatigue rather stupified me," he reported, "and I forgot the most important points." In addition Canning, then leader of the House, outgeneraled him and sidetracked the question without discussion. Wilberforce, who

[52]*Report of the Committee of the Society for the Mitigation and Gradual Abolition of Slavery throughout the British Dominions,* 1824.

[53]*Ibid.;* see also *Anti-Slavery Monthly Reporter,* I, 128.

[54]The first volume, published in 1824, dealt with the legal aspects of slavery and established what the abolitionists were now urging: the inhumanity of the *system* apart from the variable character of the owners. The second volume, published in 1830, dealt with slavery not as it theoretically appeared in legal statutes but as it actually was in West Indian plantations. Macaulay referred to the work as "Stephen's mighty book which marks the hand of a giant." However, Stephen could see in West Indians, "evil, only evil and that continually." W. L. Mathieson calls Stephen "the most learned, bitter and extreme of anti-slavery pamphleteers." *British Slavery and Its Abolition,* p. 227.

[55]E. L. Griggs, *Thomas Clarkson: The Friend of Slaves,* p. 162.

[56]*Parliamentary Debates,* New series, VIII, 624-30.

had been expecting a debate and preparing topics for reply, was quite confused. "Never almost in my life was I so vexed by a parliamentary proceeding. I felt as if God had forsaken me, whom just before I had invoked. . . ."[57]

Despite the initial reverse the war had at least been declared. After Wilberforce had finished Buxton rose for his maiden effort as leader, and gave notice that he would shortly submit a motion about the state of slavery in the British colonies.

On May 15, 1823, Buxton moved a resolution declaring slavery "repugnant to the principles of the British constitution, and of the Christian religion." In his speech he stated explicitly the new goal of the party. "The object at which we aim is the extinction of slavery—nothing less than the extinction of slavery—in nothing less than the whole of the British dominions:—not, however, the rapid termination of that state—not the sudden emancipation of the negro—but such preparatory steps, such measures of precaution, as, by slow degrees, and in a course of years, first fitting and qualifying the slaves for the enjoyment of freedom, shall gently conduct us to the annihilation of slavery."[58]

This statement might be considered reasonably temperate: but Canning judged it necessary to qualify still further the definition of the goal. Progress must be attended by "a fair and equitable consideration of the interests of private property."[59] Canning was a moderate abolitionist; he desired to be on the side of the angels, but he was extremely sensitive to the wishes of his West Indian friends. Now he effectively took the wind out of Buxton's sails. He cleverly introduced a series of resolutions providing immediately for a number of local and specific reforms of West Indian slavery in matters relating to the method of sale, Sunday labour, and the punishment of females. These resolutions offered prospect of immediate gain which the abolitionists had not anticipated and yet involved the temporary reversal of the drive for emancipation. Wilberforce, who had been selected to answer Canning, was again nonplussed. On the spur of the moment he decided to compromise and thus make sure of Canning's concessions. "I thank God," he wrote to his son later, "I

---

[57] *Life of Wilberforce*, V, 171.
[58] *Parliamentary Debates*, New series, IX, 265.
[59] *Ibid.*, p. 286.

judged rightly that it would not be wise to press for more on that night."[60]

While progress was slowly made in Parliament parallel labours were conducted without. "Cabinet councils" at Wilberforce's became the order of the day. The "conspirators" gathered for consultations of the "interior Cabinet," and busy labourers crowded Wilberforce's breakfast table until he was reminded of the "old bustle" of the abolition days.[61] In fact the old campaign routine again returned. There were letters to be written, interviews to be arranged, campaign literature to be distributed. Macaulay compiled from official colonial records a picture of *Negro Slavery* (1823), in colours of "horrid brilliancy" such as only Macaulay could have so accurately and terribly drawn. For the rest of the campaign, this book, combined with Stephen's *Slavery Delineated*, was the source of material for anti-slavery orators. There were, too, public meetings to be planned, speeches to be delivered. In 1824 at the first anniversary of the new Anti-Slavery Society, William Smith, Wilberforce, and Buxton spoke, and T. B. Macaulay gave his first anti-slavery address, "probably the happiest half-hour of Zachary Macaulay's life."[62] Once more also came the old business of "stirring up petitions." But the "Saints" had served a long apprenticeship in agitation, and they had helped to prepare a responsive public. "The country take up our cause surprisingly," Wilberforce noted in April 1823, "the petitions, considering the little effort, very numerous."[63]

The even tenor of the movement was abruptly disturbed by untoward events in the West Indies. The planters, angered at some minor regulations which Bathurst, the Colonial Secretary, had despatched to them, indulged in such ungoverned language that the slaves, overhearing, thought that an order for emancipation must have arrived, and that the masters were defying it. A mild insurrection resulted, in which little damage was done and no white person was killed. But all the repressed fury of the owners was vented on the

---

[60]*Life of Wilberforce*, V, 178.   [61]*Ibid.*, p. 180.

[62]Zachary, however, "took it in his own sad way," and commented on it to his son afterwards only to chide him for having folded his arms in the presence of royalty—the Duke of Gloucester had been in the chair. *Proceedings of the First Anniversary Meeting of the London Anti-Slavery Society*, 1824. G. O. Trevelyan, *Life of Lord Macaulay*, I, 110-12.

[63]*Life of Wilberforce*, V, 177.

poor slaves. Troops were sent against them and killed large numbers
of the hapless crowds; numbers more were court-martialled and
executed; and five were sentenced to the ghastly torture of one
thousand lashes apiece.

The first reports that reached England came from the planters.
The distorted accounts laid the responsibility for the whole trouble on
the abolitionists in England, and for a while brought the emancipation
movement into bad repute. But the truth gradually became known.
It was revealed that the planters had not only murdered slaves, but,
admitting hearsay evidence and actually conniving at perjury, their
court had sentenced to death a Methodist missionary named Smith, a
really noble gentleman, who had in many ways been in sympathy
with the Negroes, but who had done much to keep them in restraint.
Smith was not executed, but he soon died in his prison which, with
malice aforethought, was kept by his jailers in a condition in which
no human being could long survive. Smith's death dealt slavery a
blow from which it never recovered. Before it, for all the hopes of
the "Saints," the agitation had not taken hold of the country as a
whole. But Brougham brought the case to Parliament in a speech of
tremendous power, and outside Parliament "filled the sails of the
abolitionist movement with the great winds of popular agitation."[64]

The Clapham Sect were outraged at the tragedy. "Had I happened for instance to correspond with Smith," Wilberforce said,
"that alone would have hanged him."[65] Wilberforce had just suffered
a severe illness and was in weaker condition than ever. But he was
eager to get to Parliament to raise his voice in condemnation of the
deed. "I very much wish," he wrote to Stephen in June 1824, "if my
voice should be strong enough, to bear my testimony against the scan-
dalous injustice exercised upon poor Smith."[66] On June 11, the day
of the adjourned debate on his case in Parliament, he "went to

[64]G. M. Trevelyan, *British History in the Nineteenth Century*, p. 253. There
are good accounts of the Smith case in Harriet Martineau, *A History of the Thirty
Years' Peace*, I, 465; Mathieson, *British Slavery and Its Abolition*, pp. 141-6;
Klingberg, *The Anti-Slavery Movement in England*, pp. 219-23; R. Coupland,
Wilberforce, pp. 487-90; *Parliamentary Debates*, New series, XI, 961-99
(Brougham's speech).

[65]*Life of Wilberforce*, V, 222. In 1825 another Methodist missionary, Mr.
Shrewsbury from Barbados, was threatened with hanging, and in danger of his
life, it being urged that among other iniquities he had actually corresponded with
Mr. Buxton.

[66]*Ibid.*, p. 222.

Stephen's to be quiet for three or four hours" in preparation, and then proceeded to the House.

Wilberforce delivered his speech in the course of a long debate. At first he made a scathing indictment of the legal proceedings by which Smith had been condemned. "The speech [of the judge in the Smith trial] in which the evidence was summed up, was really worthy of any grand inquisitor that had ever exercised his office in that tribunal of oppression and cruelty." Yet Wilberforce judged the incident not by itself alone but by its significance.

The subject we are now considering is of no small importance, inasmuch as it involves a question of the rights and happiness of a British subject, and, still more, the administration of justice in the West-India colonies. But there is another point of view in which the question is to be regarded, in which it will assume far more importance, and excite a still deeper interest. Let it be remembered, that this House, about a year ago, declared its determination to ameliorate the condition of the slaves in the West Indies; and, more especially, by a course of religious instruction, gradually to prepare them for the safe participation in those civil privileges which are enjoyed by their fellow-subjects in this country. We know but too well, that a contrary spirit prevails very generally in the West Indies. It was not against Mr. Smith only, and the particular body of religionists with which he was connected, that the resentment of the colonial population was pointed; it was against all who were endeavouring, by religious instruction, to raise the condition of that degraded class whom we have taken under our protection. In Demerara, on the late occasion, all the missionaries were at first seized and imprisoned; and all of them, without exception, had been vilified and calumniated for a course of years in the Guiana newspaper. . . .

In Demerara, it was meant, by Mr. Smith's condemnation, to deter other missionaries from attempting the conversion of the slaves, and, by the terrors of his example, to frighten away those whose Christian zeal might otherwise prompt them to devote themselves to the service of this long injured body of their fellow-creatures. We ourselves, therefore, are upon our trial, and by our decision on the present question men will judge of the leanings of our opinion, whether, from the influence of the West-Indian proprietors in this country, and even in this House, we are not in some measure under the influence of the same prejudices which prevail in all their force in the colonies of Guiana. . . .

Let us not, then, be contented, as some respectable authorities appear to be, with expressing our sentiments on the shameful proceedings of the court-martial in a fugitive sentence which will possess no authority, and will be soon forgotten. Let us not be satisfied with coldly expressing, as our individual opinions in our speeches, that there were circumstances in the trial which are to be regretted; but let us do justice to the character of a deeply-injured man, by solemnly recording our judgment in the language proposed by the motion of my learned friend. Let us thereby manifest our determination to shield the meritorious, but unprotected missionary, from the malice of his prejudiced oppressors, however bigoted and powerful. Let us shew the sense we entertain of the value of such services, and prove, that, whatever may be the principles and feelings which habitual familiarity with the administration of a system of slavery may produce in the colonies, we in this House at least have the disposition and judgment and feelings which justice and humanity, and the spirit of the British constitution, ensure from the members of the House of Commons."[67]

Wilberforce sat down thoroughly disappointed with his own effort; and in truth he had not made one of his best speeches. "I quite forgot my topics," he lamented, "and made sad work of it."[68] Yet he rejoiced that he had had an opportunity of adding his protest to the inquiry. "I have delivered my soul," he said.[69]

It was well that he had "delivered his soul." That speech was the last he ever made in Parliament. Ten days later he was seized with another attack of illness, which left him so impaired in strength that, after anxious consultations with the brotherhood, he made the "very painful" decision to retire from public life. Accordingly, following the technical Parliamentary method for retiring from the House of Commons, he requested Buxton in February 1825 to apply on his behalf for the Chiltern Hundreds—"the first place," he said, "that I ever asked for myself"—and, amid sorrowful regrets of the "Saints," took his departure from Parliament. William Smith said that their "guiding spirit" would be gone. And Buxton recalled the inscription which the Carthaginians placed upon the tomb of Hannibal, "We vehemently desired him in the day of battle."[70]

Though Wilberforce had retired from Parliament, the end of the

[67] *Parliamentary Debates*, New series, XI, 1269-76.
[68] *Life of Wilberforce*, V, 222.
[69] G. W. E. Russell, *History of the Evangelical Movement*, p. 39.
[70] *Life of Wilberforce*, V, 228-30, 233-4, 238-9.

Clapham Sect was not yet. Stephen and Macaulay were labouring as prodigiously as ever for emancipation. Stephen acted as solicitor for the Anti-Slavery Society, and followed up his *Slavery Delineated* with an address to the electors of England, entitled *England Enslaved by Her Own Slave Colonies* (1826). Macaulay supplied information for Clarkson and still had much to do with the organization of the campaign, and he pursued his labour with all the old Clapham thoroughness. In September 1825 he wrote to Babington that he had just finished his analysis of the parliamentary papers of the last session. He followed this by outlining the anti-slavery plans for the next session. Brougham, he said, was to get an Order-in-Council relating to Trinidad extended to all the colonies; Dr. Lushington (eminent lawyer and warm supporter of Buxton) was to prevent the deportation of the free people of colour from the islands; Mackintosh was to defend Haiti; Buxton was to present a new plan for emancipation, and to expose the slave trade and slavery in Mauritius. As ever, a systematic agitation was to be maintained in England.

We are to prepare forthwith a pithy address ready to be printed in every newspaper in the kingdom the moment the Dissolution is announced, rousing the electors to require pledges. We are forthwith to prepare our correspondents everywhere for petitioning on the meeting of Parliament, and a Meeting will be held in London about a month before to give the tone and the example. The Speeches will furnish argument to the country; the Resolutions models. Wherever it may be prudent to do so, public meetings will be held in the large towns, and reports of the speeches put in the provincial papers.[71]

The following undated letter from Stephen to Macaulay is an illustration of the extraordinary devices to which the brotherhood would resort to further their causes. "I send you some Abolition puffs which I think may be useful, and some of which perhaps the newspapers will take without payment. But pray take care to have them copied in different hands, and sent by unknown messengers. I think if they were dropped in the boxes of newspapers they might be inserted; if published in the Times the rest would copy them."[72]

Macaulay added to these labours a more individual task of his own. He had been contributing articles on slavery to the *Christian*

[71]Knutsford, *Zachary Macaulay*, p. 431.
[72]*Ibid.*, pp. 430-1.

Observer, but in 1825 he made a new venture. He founded the *Anti-Slavery Monthly Reporter*, a small paper which was published usually twice a month, and ran from June 1825 to July 1836, a total of 113 issues.[73] Macaulay himself was its "sole and most prolific parent."[74] The issues were compiled and written with both painstaking thoroughness and stark realism. Through the last years of the emancipation struggle they maintained a never failing supply of constantly up-to-date material about the workings of the slave trade, which proved an invaluable source for all anti-slavery workers, and had a powerful influence both on the public and on the government. They represented a labour possible only to a man with encyclopaedic knowledge of colonial slavery, with fluent pen, and with extraordinary powers of application. The anti-slavery campaign witnessed many instances of titanic drudgery; but certainly none to surpass the sustained production of the *Anti-Slavery Reporter*.

Wilberforce, too, was still a power in the campaign. After his retirement from Parliament he was unable to engage actively in public labour, but his influence counted for much. As late as 1830 he heard from Brougham in Yorkshire, "The election turned very much on Slavery; your name was in every mouth, and your health the most enthusiastically received."[75] Moreover, although he had intended never to come into the public eye again his interest in emancipation was too great to allow him to fulfil his intention. In December 1826 his old friends pressed him to come to London for the annual meeting of the Anti-Slavery Society. "Above all," Macaulay wrote to him, "we feel the loss of you. Heart-stirring occasions are in prospect, when I should have delighted to see you engaged *cominus ense*." Wilberforce was reluctant to take any prominent part—"It seems," he wrote to Babington, "like wishing to retain the reins, when I can no longer hold them." To Stephen he expressed himself in similar vein, but his companions would have no refusal, and when the meeting was called Wilberforce was in the chair.[76] Again in a critical year, 1830, the

---

[73] The complete series is in the library of the Anti-Slavery and Aborigines Protection Society.

[74] This was Hannah More's description. It is probable, however, that Zachary Macaulay at times did have some assistance in his work. *Christian Observer*, 1839, p. 803.

[75] *Life of Wilberforce*, V, 318.

[76] *Ibid.*, V, 262-3.

friends appealed to Wilberforce to lend his aid by appearing once more at the annual meeting of the Anti-Slavery Society. A large audience gathered, as "all the old friends of the cause" assembled around Wilberforce. The venerable Clarkson moved that "the great leader in our cause" should take the chair; and Wilberforce responded with a tribute to his old "friend and fellow-labourer," and a reminiscence of the early days when they were beginning their campaign.

At this meeting the younger and more radical abolitionists, headed by George Stephen, broke away from the parent society and formed the Agency Committee—so called because it organized paid agents to lecture throughout England. The Agency Committee promoted perhaps the first publicity campaign in the modern manner. They furnished notes and materials for their lecturers, and gave them minute instructions, even for such details as handling interruptions in meetings. They placarded London with billboards, indeed "kept a little army of bill-stickers" who moved around and covered up the posters of their enemies. They posted lists of candidates in the parliamentary elections, marked "Anti," "Doubtful," and "Recommended with perfect confidence." (A specimen of a list is in the British Museum under "Colonial Slavery," Gladstone's name being among those labelled "Anti.") On one occasion they surprised friends and opponents alike by a demonstration of extraordinary thoroughness. They had complete arrangements for the call of a mass meeting all laid away for an emergency. At a strategic moment they set their well-oiled machinery in motion and summoned as by magic a great mass meeting at Exeter Hall, in which sixty-six members of Parliament appeared on the platform and agreed to vote as directed. Whatever one may think of their method one must agree that it was for such a time an extraordinary development of public agitation. Daniel O'Connell said to young George Stephen, "I have served a long apprenticeship to agitation, my young friend, but you are my master."[77] It is significant that the young insurgents won the favour of the older Clapham men. James Stephen was with them from the start and Wilberforce and Macaulay both added their approval.

The end was drawing near. In 1832 James Stephen died, his last public act being to preside at the annual meeting of the Anti-Slavery

[77]George Stephen, *Antislavery Recollections,* pp. 136 ff.

Society. Macaulay was now the only active worker of the group. He was toiling on with an industry that never flagged. In 1832 his daughter wrote: "Papa is extremely busy from 3 A.M. till 12 P.M. about this West Indian Committee. Mr. Buxton comes to see him every day."[78] Wilberforce, too weak to labour, kept in touch with his old friend and cheered him on in his work. "I congratulate you," he wrote Macaulay on New Year's Day, 1833, "on having entered on the year which I trust will be distinguished by your seeing at last the mortal stroke given to the accursed Slave Trade, and the emancipation of the West Indian slaves at length accomplished."[79]

The prospect, which now actually seemed to be dawning, of seeing the final end of the fifty years' campaign against slavery, so stirred Wilberforce that, though two years earlier he had "resolved never more to speak in public" he consented again to be present at an abolition meeting at Maidstone. On April 12, 1833, he came out of his retirement, and, twelve weeks before his death, went to the platform for what proved to be his last word in public. "It was an affecting sight," said his sons. His tiny crooked frame, almost buried beneath his cloak, seemed smaller and frailer than ever. "I had not thought," he said, "to appear again in public; but it shall never be said that William Wilberforce is silent while the slaves require his help."[80] As he proceeded with his speech the fire of his lifelong devotion burst, as of old, into flame. Something of the earlier spirit seemed again to take possession of the feeble body, and his voice was "restored again to some of that clarion character which had aroused slumbering parliaments."[81] Then, by a strange coincidence, as he was concluding his address a gleam of sunshine suddenly lit up the hall, as another gleam had lit up the House of Commons forty-two years before when Pitt was finishing his first great speech on slavery. And Wilberforce, catching the gleam and weaving it into his speech as Pitt had done on that distant morning, exclaimed that this "light from heaven" was their "earnest of success."[82]

The "earnest of success" was not false. In May 1833 Lord Stanley, the new Colonial Secretary, introduced the resolutions, prepared

---

[78]Knutsford, *Zachary Macaulay*, p. 466.
[79]*Life of Wilberforce*, V, 352.
[80]H. M. Wheeler, *The Slaves' Champion*, p. 97.   [81]*Ibid.*
[82]*Life of Wilberforce*, V, 354.

in collaboration with the younger James Stephen (in the Colonial Office), on which the bill for abolition was to be based. They were passed after six days. On July 25 the bill passed its second reading with a majority that made its final passage secure. By its terms all existing slaves were to be emancipated in a year's time, and were then to serve an apprenticeship to their former masters of seven years. On the masters was bestowed a gift of twenty million pounds. "Thank God," said Wilberforce, on the 25th, "that I should have lived to witness a day in which England is willing to give twenty millions sterling for the Abolition of Slavery."[83]

Meanwhile Zachary Macaulay had been taken very ill, and, though he afterwards recovered, he was too sick to take notice when the goal of his life was achieved. Wilberforce, who had made a temporary improvement, expected to be able to see the full consummation. But he was older than Macaulay, and, in a sudden relapse, on July 29, 1833, he died, almost in the moment of victory.

"It is a singular fact," said Buxton afterwards, "that on the very night on which we successfully engaged in the House of Commons, in passing the clause of the Act of Emancipation—one of the most important clauses ever enacted, . . . the spirit of our friend left the world. The day which saw the termination of his labours saw also the termination of his life."[84]

As the conversion of Wilberforce marks the genesis of the Clapham Sect, so his death marks at once the achievement of its greatest purpose, and its final dissolution.

[83] *Ibid.*, p. 370.
[84] Wheeler, *The Slaves' Champion*, p. 97.

CHAPTER EIGHT

The world has taken the credit to itself

THE PASSING of the Emancipation Act and the death of Wilberforce marked the end of the Clapham Sect. The original ranks had been gradually thinning, and the few survivors had reached almost the end of their labours. Zachary Macaulay and Thomas Clarkson, indeed, were to live for a few years more, but the campaigns were over. The old gatherings, the "Cabinet Councils," the eager planning and disciplined labours, the passionate crusades, could be no more. Nearly fifty years had passed since the labours had begun, and even Macaulay, the youngest of the band, was now an old man.

Granville Sharp had been the oldest. He was born in 1735. Hannah More, if she must be counted as one of the "great men," was born in 1745. Then came Charles Grant in 1746; John Shore and Charles Elliott in 1751; William Smith in 1756; James Stephen, Thomas Babington, and Thomas Gisborne in 1758; Charles Simeon, John Venn, and Wilberforce in 1759; Clarkson and Henry Thornton in 1760; and finally Macaulay, in 1768.

The first break in the circle had come in 1813 in the midst of the great fight over the East India Charter. John Venn and Granville Sharp had died within a few weeks of each other. Sharp had always been a little separated from the others. His knowledge and industry had made him a useful ally, and his uncommonly winsome spirit endeared him to all. But he was "rather the confidant and counsellor . . . than the comrade-in-arms,"[1] and, while by his busy pen he lent aid to many Clapham enterprises, he probably took little part in the parliamentary manoeuvres. Venn, nearer in age to the others, was an unquestioned member of the inner circle. He "prompted the deeper meditations, partook the counsels, and stimulated the efforts"[2] of all.

[1]R. Coupland, *Wilberforce*, p. 249.
[2]Sir James Stephen, *Essays in Ecclesiastical Biography*, II, 223.

Two years later, in 1815, another break came, when Henry Thornton, gracious host, died of tuberculosis. Claudius Buchanan caught cold at his funeral and died a few weeks later. Then in 1823, at the very beginning of the emancipation struggle, the circle was further narrowed by the passing of Grant; and in 1832, at the end of the struggle, two more gaps were created by the deaths of James Stephen and his Clapham friend Charles Elliott. In 1833, the year of triumph, Wilberforce passed away, to be followed in the same year by Hannah More, in 1834 by Lord Teignmouth, in 1835 by William Smith, in 1836 by Simeon, in 1837 by Babington, and in 1838 by Macaulay. Thomas Clarkson was the last survivor. In 1840 he was present at a great anti-slavery convention, and he lived until 1846.

Nearly a century elapsed before any memorial of the Clapham Sect was established in Clapham; but in 1919 a tablet was built into the south wall of Clapham parish church with this inscription:

LET US PRAISE GOD

For the memory and example of all the faithful departed who have worshipped in this Church, and especially for the under named Servants of Christ sometime called

"THE CLAPHAM SECT"

who in the latter part of the XVIIIth and early part of the XIXth Centuries laboured so abundantly for the increase of National Righteousness and the Conversion of the Heathen, and rested not until the curse of slavery was swept away from all parts of the British Dominions—

Charles Grant	John Thornton
Zachary Macaulay	Henry Venn
Granville Sharp	(Curate of Clapham)
John Shore	John Venn
(Lord Teignmouth)	(Rector of Clapham)
James Stephen	William Wilberforce
Henry Thornton	

"O God, we have heard with our ears, and our fathers have declared unto us, the noble works that Thou didst in their days, and in the old time before them."

The tablet, of course, bears the names only of those who had belonged to the Clapham parish church.

The hurry of their campaigns has admitted no opportunity to tell of the home life of these folk of the "sanctified villa"[3] of Clapham. The impression left by past chapters may be that in Clapham home life was all but submerged in ceaseless activities, endless engagements, and innumerable visitors. Even when Wilberforce had a house at Kensington Gore he was sometimes unable to be there from Monday morning till Saturday night. But the whole life of the Clapham Sect was not comprised in their many crusades. In spite of multifarious interests they centred their lives around their homes. None of them forgot either family or brotherhood, nor failed to provide seasons for both. In 1805 Wilberforce writes in his diary: "A residence near London would withdraw me from company, and give me more time. Yet I dread the separation which my leaving Broomfield would make from my chief friends, the Thorntons, Teignmouths, Stephens, Venn, Macaulay, with whom I now live like a brother."[4]

The home life of the group was happy and healthy to a rare degree. Their homes, indeed, could not quite escape the shadow of the brotherhood, and were deliberately used to perpetuate the "Clapham system." A letter from Henry Thornton to Charles Grant in 1793 encloses the following typical paragraph: "On the whole, I am in hopes some good may come out of our Clapham system. Wilberforce is a candle that should not be hid under a bushel. The influence of his conversation is, I think, great and striking. I am surprised to find how much religion everybody seems to have when they get into our house. They all seem to submit, and to acknowledge the advantage of a religious life, and we are not at all queer or guilty of carrying things too far."[5] But it is only a travesty which represents the men of Clapham as being made stern and gloomy by an austere religion. They were stern with themselves, and carried on their inner struggles with the earnestness of saints. But stern inward dealings with their own shortcomings did not make them sour with others. Those who knew them best emphasize an unusual happiness as a striking feature of

[3] Tom Ingoldsby, quoted in London *Times,* Jan. 31, 1879.
[4] *Life of Wilberforce,* III, 235.
[5] Henry Morris, *Life of Grant,* p. 200.

their family life. The Reverend William Knight, author of *The Missionary Secretariat of Henry Venn*, said that in the Clapham rectory was a "sunny cheerfulness" to be found in few family circles. John Colquhoun, who had been associate and friend of the entire group, has left us the following pleasant picture, which only an intimate could have drawn, of the group at Thornton's villa:

The sheltered garden behind, with its arbeil trees and elms and Scotch firs, as it lay so still, with its close shaven lawn, looked gay on a May afternoon, when groups of young and old seated themselves under the shade of the trees, or were scattered over the grounds. Matrons of households were there, who had strolled in to enjoy a social meeting; and their children busied themselves in sports with a youthful glee, which was cheered, not checked, by the presence of their elders. For neighbourly hospitality and easy friendship were features of that family life. Presently, streaming from adjoining villas or crossing the common, appeared others who, like Henry Thornton, had spent an occupied day in town, and now resorted to this well-known garden to gather up their families and enjoy a pleasant hour. Hannah More is there, with her sparkling talk . . . and the long-faced, blue-eyed Scotsman [Grant], with his fixed, calm look, unchanged as an aloe tree, known as the Indian Director, one of the kings of Leadenhall Street; and the gentle Thane, Lord Teignmouth, whose easy talk flowed on, like a southern brook, with a sort of drowsy murmur; and Macaulay stands by listening, silent, with hanging eyebrows; and Babington, in blue coat, dropping weighty words with husky voice; and young listeners . . . the young Grants, and young Stephen. . . .

. . . But whilst these things are talked of in the shade, and the knot of wise men draw close together, in darts the member for Yorkshire [Wilberforce] from the green fields to the south, like a sunbeam into a shady room, and the faces of the old brighten, and the children clap their hands with joy. He joins the group of elders, catches up a thread of their talk, dashes off a bright remark, pours a ray of happy illumination, and for a few moments seems as wise, as thoughtful, and as constant as themselves. But this dream will not last and these watchful young eyes know it. They remember that he is as restless as they are, as fond of fun and movement. So, on the first youthful challenge, away flies the volatile statesman. A bunch of flowers, a ball, is thrown in sport, and away dash, in joyous rivalry, the children and the philanthropist. Law and statesmanship forgotten, he is the gayest child of them all.

But presently, when the group has broken up, and the friends have gone to their houses, the circle under Henry Thornton's roof gathers for its evening talk. In the Oval Library, which Pitt planned, niched and fringed all round with books, looking out on the pleasant lawn, they meet for their more sustained conversation. In this easy intercourse even the shy Gisborne opens himself. At times the talk is interspersed with reading, the books chosen by the host . . . or he and Gisborne read by turns one of Wilberforce's brilliant orations. Or they vary their summer evenings by strolling through the fresh green fields into the wilder shrubbery which encloses Mr. Wilberforce's demesne; Broomfield, not like Battersea Rise, with trim parterres and close mown lawn, but unkempt—a picture of stray genius and irregular thoughts. As they pass near the windows that look out on the north, and admire the old elms that shade the slopes to the stream, the kindly host hears their voices, and runs out with his welcome. So they are led into that charmed circle, and find there the portly dean [Milner] with his stentorian voice, and the eager Stephen. . . . Another evening the party cross the common, and drop into the villa of the Teignmouths, or spend a pleasant hour in Robert Thornton's decorated grounds. . . . On Sunday they take their place in the old church, with the Wilberforces' and Macaulays' and Stephens' pews close to their own, and in the front gallery the Teignmouths; and they listen to the wise discourses of Venn; another Sunday they sit enchanted under the preaching of Gisborne.[6]

In the Clapham mansions, says Sir G. O. Trevelyan, "there was plenty of freedom, and good fellowship, and reasonable enjoyment for young and old alike. . . . There can have been little that was narrow and nothing vulgar in a training which produced Samuel Wilberforce, and Sir James Stephen, and Charles and Robert Grant, and Lord Macaulay."[7]

Emphasis on family life was only natural. It was a feature of

[6]*Wilberforce and His Friends*, pp. 305-8.
[7]G. O. Trevelyan, *Life of Lord Macaulay*, I, 62. Robert Grant was the author of two famous hymns, "O Worship the King" and "Saviour When in Dust to Thee." Among other famous Clapham children, Charlotte Elliott, daughter of Charles Elliott, wrote "Just as I am without One Plea," and "My God and Father While I Stray," and Henry Venn, son of John Venn, is remembered as the great Church Missionary Society secretary. Florence Nightingale was a grand-daughter of William Smith. G. O. Trevelyan justly observes, "Hobson and Brian Newcome are not fair specimens of the effect of Clapham influences upon the second generation" (*ibid.*).

Evangelical religion; and the Clapham Sect were ardent Evangelicals, whose religion was the central spring of all their lives. They were what Wilberforce called "true Christians" who knew what it was to practise "saintliness in daily life," and by whom the minutest details of action were "considered with reference to Eternity." They were in fact the chief lay representatives of the Evangelical religion of their day, the admitted lay leaders of that small party which, "amid an almost universal deadness," "kept alive the flame of spiritual religion" in the Church of England.[8]

Being Evangelicals they were without the exclusiveness of the High Church party. They were willing to take lightly all sectarian differences, and welcomed labour with men who held in the main the same views and fought for the same objects as themselves. They rejoiced especially that men of different denominations could join together in common Christian causes and, whenever possible, they made religious enterprises unsectarian. The Bible Society is a striking instance. William Jay of Bath said that he once heard Wilberforce say, "Though I am an Episcopalian by birth, I yet feel such a oneness and sympathy with the cause of God at large, that nothing would be more delightful than my communing once a year with every church that holds the Head, even Christ."[9] Even when co-operation was impossible the members of the group still maintained their friendly attitude. When they founded the *Christian Observer* they forthwith announced their determination "to admit nothing harsh or intemperate toward any sect of Christians."[10] They knew indeed that a great measure of their support lay outside the Established Church; that "without the aid of non-conformist sympathy, and money, and oratory, and organization, their operations would have been doomed to certain failure"; and they were ever generous in acknowledgment. On the whole, like other Evangelicals, they "encouraged an . . . undenominational temper."[11]

[8]G. W. E. Russell, *The Household of Faith,* p. 234.
[9]W. J. Jenkins, *William Wilberforce,* p. 192. Wilberforce went through three stages in his attitudes to other faiths. At first he was inclined to be narrow. Then as he laboured in his great causes with men of other faiths he grew tolerant in spirit. But in his later years when his sons became High Church, and when they were ministers themselves, he began to grow more cautious in his attitude towards Dissenters.
[10]"Prospectus" printed in *Christian Observer,* 1802.
[11]R. W. Dale, *The Old Evangelicalism and the New,* p. 17.

Yet they were thoroughly Anglican.[12] The Clapham Sect "was never consciously a sect, and its members would have protested vehemently if they had known that the word was to be applied to them." Granville Sharp, for instance, could easily "have demonstrated by a series of pamphlets the entire orthodoxy of every member."[13] They were convinced of the superiority of the Established Church, and believed that Dissent thrived only when Anglicans were neglectful.

They were by no means, however, as is sometimes represented, the dominant party of the Established Church. They were a minority, largely suspected and disliked, and in the higher church circles faced with coldness or "frank hostility." As late as 1810 the C.M.S. contained no names of peers or bishops, and many of the clergy refused to let its missionaries preach in their churches. Even when the Clapham Sect had won the fight to establish a bishop in India, the bishop appointed was opposed to them and would not ordain their candidates. The Society could not get its men ordained till after the appointment of Bishop Heber who, long before, had been won by Wilberforce's personal charm. When Granville Sharp died the vicar of Fulham would not permit a funeral sermon to be preached for him in Fulham church, because Sharp had helped the British and Foreign Bible Society.[14] Venn's brother-in-law was offered the mastership of Jesus College—then in the gift of the Bishop of Ely—on the condition that he would resign his connection with the Bible Society.[15] In 1815 and 1816 the bishops of Lincoln, Chester, Carlisle, and Ely all found occasion to oppose the Bible Society in their pastoral charges. Henry Martyn, for all his distinction, was barred from every church in Cornwall save his brother-in-law's. Simeon was black-balled from the S.P.C.K., and John Venn was refused admittance to Trinity College, Cambridge, because they were Evangelicals. And when the carriage of the Bishop of London took Hannah More to visit Venn at Clapham, it had to put her down at a public house a mile away because it would not do for a bishop's carriage to be seen at an Evangelical rectory. In fact the Evangelical party, "whatever else it may have been was the very reverse of dominant."[16] It was by

[12]William Smith was a Unitarian.
[13]E. C. P. Lascelles, *Granville Sharp*, p. 127.
[14]*Christian Observer*, 1813, p. 544.   [15]John Venn, *Annals*, p. 141
[16]W. E. Gladstone, *Gleanings of Past Years*, VII, 215.

no means negligible. Halévy says that "never in the history of Anglicanism had any party exercised so profound an influence."[17] But it
exercised that influence outside the pale of ecclesiastical favour.

In Parliament, too, the Clapham Sect were in a minority. The
whole of Wilberforce's following, including a much wider circle than
the Clapham Sect itself, never numbered more than twenty or thirty.
The influence they exercised was again because of the intensity of their
passion. They carried into their political life the same standards that
governed them elsewhere. Henry Thornton began his parliamentary
career by refusing to pay the bribe of one guinea a vote that was then
a matter of course. And his attitude was the considered attitude of
the group. Even Babington with less prestige than Wilberforce or
Thornton remained in Parliament for twenty years without bribery.[18]
The whole group presented to the House of Commons of their day
the impressive spectacle of men who put principle before party or
profit, "who looked to the facts of the case and not to the wishes of
the minister, and who before going into the lobby required to be
obliged with a reason instead of with a job."[19] Nominally they may
have been Tory, as were Wilberforce and Stephen, or Whig, as were
Babington and Smith; actually they were independent. To advance
their causes and to uphold their principles they would support any
government, or with equal resolution oppose any government—even
though their action might deal a painful blow to their party and
their friends. Wilberforce's diary has this typical comment (1807):
". . . Babington, and I, and Grant, and Henry Thornton too, all
settle down into trying the new ministry, and treating them as their
measures shall deserve."[20] It was said that the only times Pitt could not
sleep were at the time of the naval mutiny at the Nore and at the
first serious opposition of Wilberforce. Later it was charged that
Wilberforce's speech in support of the censure of Lord Melville
concerning the finances of the Admiralty contributed to Pitt's death.[21]
When Wilberforce retired from leadership of the anti-slavery party he
impressed on his successor "the importance of keeping this great cause

---

[17] Elie Halévy, *England in 1815*, pp. 383-4.
[18] Colquhoun, *Wilberforce and His Friends*, p. 216.
[19] G. O. Trevelyan, *Life of Lord Macaulay*, I, 70.
[20] *Life of Wilberforce*, III, 308.
[21] *Ibid.*, II, 71; III, 223.

in possession of its old honourable distinction of being one in which all party differences were extinguished."[22]

In consequence the "Saints" gained a unique moral ascendency over the House of Commons.

Confidence and respect, and, (what in the House of Commons is their unvarying accompaniment,) power, were gradually, and to a great extent involuntarily, accorded to this group of members. They were not addicted to crotchets, nor to the obtrusive and unseasonable assertion of conscientious scruples. The occasions on which they made proof of independence and impartiality were such as justified, and dignified, their temporary renunciation of party ties. They interfered with decisive effect in the debates on the great scandals of Lord Melville and the Duke of York, and in more than one financial or commercial controversy that deeply concerned the national interests. . . .

Where moral questions were concerned they became a sort of barometer by which doubtful men came to their decisions. ". . . they commanded the ear of the House, and exerted on its proceedings an influence, the secret of which those who have studied the Parliamentary history of the period find it only too easy to understand."[23] And they left an impression on the House of Commons which did not end with their passing. Sir G. O. Trevelyan gave his opinion that among the most permanent of their legacies is "their undoubted share in the improvement of our political integrity."[24]

The Clapham Sect showed Parliament something else almost as surprising as their own incorruptible rectitude. They showed that there was a sturdy, substantial section of the middle classes equally incorruptible—a reliable, decisive body that could be led neither by unlimited liquor nor unstinted gold to betray their allegiance to the men in whose causes they believed. Yorkshire, the constituency of Wilberforce, contained 16,000 freeholders, at a time when 400 borough members were returned by 90,000 electors all told. Yet Wilberforce was never defeated in Yorkshire, and could have been returned as member for the rest of his life. In 1807 his opponents spent £200,000 to defeat him, while Wilberforce's campaign costs—

[22]Viscountess Knutsford, *Zachary Macaulay*, p. 262.
[23]G. O. Trevelyan, *Life of Lord Macaulay*, I, 70.
[24]*Ibid.*, 71. "The 'Saints' were . . . laughed at and lampooned, but they had begun perhaps the most powerful movement in domestic and foreign policy in the nineteenth century." C. K. Webster, *The Foreign Policy of Castlereagh*, p. 22.

bringing voters to the polls was then a heavy expense—were £28,000. "The hold of Wilberforce and the anti-slavery movement on the solid middle class in town and country was a thing entirely beautiful— English of the best, and something new in the world."[25] Prime ministers and parties came and went, but the Clapham members were returned unfailingly to their seats. Not only Wilberforce but Grant, Stephen, Thornton, and Babington, all ended their parliamentary careers without a single defeat in an election. Their very presence in the House of Commons, even in the *ancien régime,* even before the Reform Bill, even in the time of rotten boroughs, demonstrated not only the idealism, but also the independence and the power of the middle classes.

The Clapham Sect were, indeed, in a unique position, and were able to perform a unique service to their day. Outside Parliament Clapham influence was able to ward off from worthy causes the weapons of contempt and indifference. Little as his Evangelical piety was liked by ecclesiastics, or by most of the aristocracy, Wilberforce was one of the most popular men in England. He was the favourite of the most fashionable of hostesses, and the celebrity sought out by the most distinguished visitors from foreign countries. No society was so distinguished that his presence did not bring to it an added brilliance. And his fellow workers, if they had less sparkling gifts, were yet men of power and reputation. A society founded, a cause advocated, by a few penniless clergymen and a few unknown enthusiasts might make but halting progress; but the countenance of Wilberforce, of a Director of the East India Company, and of an ex-Governor-General of India—to mention no others—brought new possibilities. By its favour the Clapham Sect could lift struggling causes to influence and income.

Within Parliament the Clapham Sect provided a link between the Dissenters and the government. The middle classes, the stronghold of the Sect, were also the stronghold of Dissent. The Clapham Sect could not have won their battles without the Dissenters; but the Dissenters could have achieved little without the Clapham Sect. Their fervour would have dissipated in fruitless strivings of little groups without capable leadership or adequate representation. The

[25]G. M. Trevelyan, *British History in the Nineteenth Century,* p. 54.

Clapham Sect provided leadership to which Dissenters gave willing allegiance, and were thus able to gather the scattered enthusiasms that might have trickled away in unharnessed streams, and to direct them into one mightly current, of which the combined power could be applied to the practical machinery of reform.

In fact Evangelicalism [in the Abolition campaign] played here a rôle similar to that which it has played in all the humanitarian movements of modern England. It constituted a link, effected a transition between Anglicanism and Dissent, between the governing classes and the general public, as represented by the great middle class. It prevented the formation of a reactionary group and won the support of the gentry and nobility, sometimes even of a member of the Royal Family, for a movement initiated by shopkeepers and preachers. And the action of the party was decisive in securing from Parliament the legislation which embodied the dictates of the national conscience.[26]

By this advantage the Clapham Sect were able to achieve what otherwise would have been impossible. For against them were arrayed the most powerful vested interests, the strongest forces of the time. ". . . Wilberforce's militant piety, like that of all the Clapham sect, impinged upon several vested commercial interests within the empire; it importuned and shadowed contemporary statesmen; it intruded itself into international relations."[27] And these interests were supported by professional and upper class opinion. "The bar were all against us,"[28] said Wilberforce in the early years of his campaign. And in 1832 he complained that the clergymen also had given but hesitating support. The clergy, indeed, were too conscious of certain features in their own situation. One abolitionist said that, with a single exception, the whole Episcopal bench, though their hearts were favourable, were afraid to support a principle that encroached on the rights of property, fearing that "if the slaves went, tithes would soon follow them."[29] Corruption and privilege were then so deeply rooted in church and state that perhaps Lord St. Vincent was expressing the secret feeling of most propertied people when, in 1833, he warned the House of Lords against setting up what was right against what was

[26]Halévy, *England in 1815*, p. 400.
[27]C. E. Fryer, *American Historical Review*, XXIX, July, 1924, 766-7.
[28]*Life of Wilberforce*, I, 293.
[29]George Stephen, *Antislavery Recollections*, p. 179.

established. "The whole fabric of society," he declared, "would go to pieces if the wedge of abstract right were once entered into any part of it."[30] In such an atmosphere the Clapham Sect might have been but voices crying in the wilderness; but, because they had as their support the religious fervour of the middle classes they were able to uproot the most deeply entrenched institutions of their time.

The importance of their campaigns and their victories cannot now be easily estimated. "Part of their work was so thoroughly done," says Sir G. O. Trevelyan, "that the world, as its wont is, has long ago taken the credit of that work to itself."[31] But, although most of their names are already fading from memory, the influence of their labours is written large in subsequent history. Because of the Clapham Sect England's policies and England's actions became more humane and more enlightened. Indeed, Clapham influence extended beyond England. "Politics . . . in that microcosm, were rather cosmopolitan than national."[32] Spain, Portugal, France, Holland, Sweden, Russia, and, at the international conferences, still other countries, were led by pressure from Clapham to actions they would not otherwise have taken. No peace negotiation, no council of the period, escaped the influence of the Clapham Sect. Amiens, Paris, Vienna, Aix-la-Chapelle, and Verona were all bombarded by Clapham letters and Clapham pamphlets; and sometimes persuaded by speeches and documents carefully planned by Clapham "Cabinet Councils," and painstakingly drafted by Clapham labourers. Castlereagh and Wellington were scarcely more ambassadors for England than for Clapham. It is unquestionable that Clapham passion and persistence and industry achieved what otherwise would have been unachieved. "For we know by our experience in other matters, that evil does not die of its own accord; but that things are what they are, and the consequences will be what they will be."[33]

The significance of the Clapham Sect is further revealed by a recognition of their singular timeliness. The slave trade was stopped before the economic expansion of European nations had well begun, and before slavery on a large scale was introduced into the home of

[30]*Parliamentary Debates*, 3rd series, XVIII, 261.
[31]*Life of Lord Macaulay*, I, 71.
[32]Sir James Stephen, *Essays in Ecclesiastical Biography*, II, 217.
[33]G. M. Trevelyan in the London *Times*, July 29, 1933.

the slaves. "It is terrible to reflect," says Dean Inge, "what might have happened if slavery had not been abolished before the partition of Africa among the Great Powers. The whole of the Dark Continent might have become a gigantic slave farm, with consequences to the social and economic condition of Europe itself which cannot be calculated."[34] Professor G. M. Trevelyan expresses the same opinion, saying that such a consequence might have "destroyed and corrupted Europe itself." He gives his judgment in a memorable picture:

On the last night of slavery, the negroes in our West Indian islands went up on to the hill-tops to watch the sun rise, bringing them freedom as its first rays struck the waters. But far away in the forests of Central Africa, in the heart of darkness yet unexplored, none understood or regarded the day. Yet it was the dark continent which was most deeply affected of all. Before its exploitation by Europe had well begun, the most powerful of the nations that were to control its destiny had decided that slavery should not be the relation of the black man to the white.[35]

What alterations in the course of world history had been made by the abolition of slavery before the plantation system had taken hold of Africa no one now can more than faintly estimate; but that the alteration did come in time is due more to the Clapham Sect than to any other single group.

In India too the influence of the Clapham Sect was not less timely. Had the old principle of isolation and exploitation continued, the relations between England and India would have been disastrous. They "would have hardened into soulless exploitation on the one side and on the other into servile fear and hate." That these relations did not develop is due partly of course to Edmund Burke's "imaginative grasp of the moral obligations of Empire," and to Pitt's statesmanship. But Burke and Pitt would have asked little more than the act of 1793. The Clapham Sect went further. ". . . they . . . planted in the public conscience of their countrymen not merely a sensitiveness to wrong, but a positive sense of obligation towards the backward peoples of the world. And in so far as the conduct of British Governments towards the native races in their charge was to be inspired throughout the coming century by the ideals of trusteeship, the honour of creating that tradition lay with them."[36]

[34]*England*, p. 111.
[35]G. M. Trevelyan, *British History in the Nineteenth Century*, pp. 254-5.
[36]Coupland, *Wilberforce*, p. 382.

They did more than create the tradition; they made possible the means for preserving it. For they opened India to missionaries, and the missionaries were to prove the best informed, and the most insistent opponents of political and commercial oppression. ". . . it was the influence of the missionaries which was to establish the principle that, in the backward regions of the world, it was the duty of the British power to prevent the ruthless exploitation of primitive peoples, and to lead them gently into civilised ways of life."[37]

Add to these achievements of the Clapham Sect what they did for England, through their support of popular education, and for peoples of all the earth, through the spread of religious literature—including hundreds of thousands of Bibles and Testaments—by societies which their influence helped to prestige and prosperity, and it can be appreciated that their tiny group left a real impression on world history.[38]

The Clapham Sect made another, and less suspected contribution to the England of later days. They have been reproached for their social attitudes; and, if by some writers rather unfairly, not without certain real justification. But, on a longer view, the reproach loses its effect. Temporarily they did support repressive policies and injure the cause of the labourer. But perhaps no people in England were doing more than they to make it impossible for such policies to survive. They gave all their gifts and their energies to the cultivation of humanitarian sentiment. At a time when the doctrine was not trite and commonplace, but novel and dangerous, they valiantly preached the brotherhood of man, the fundamental rights of man, and the shame of permitting for the benefit of commerce what was inherently degrading to humanity itself. They did not, it is true, grasp the full implications of such a doctrine. They were occupied with the immediate and terrible inferences for slavery. But it was of real importance to have proclaimed the doctrine; other reformers were soon pressing applications of a widely different nature. When, for example, Joseph Hume was arguing in Parliament for the abolition of the impressment

[37]Ramsay Muir, *A Short History of the British Commonwealth,* II, 223.

[38]After the publication of Stephen's article on "The Clapham Sect" T. B. Macaulay wrote to one of his sisters: "The truth is that from that little knot of men emanated all the Bible Societies, and almost all the Missionary Societies, in the world. The whole organisation of the Evangelical party was their work. The share which they had in providing means for the education of the people was great. They were really the destroyers of the slave-trade and of slavery." G. O. Trevelyan, *Life of Lord Macaulay,* I, 68.

of seamen he referred to the anti-slavery principle of "the great advantages which voluntary service of every kind had over coerced service."[39]

From the very beginning, indeed, many people apprehended the potential significance of anti-slavery principles and strenuously pointed out their ultimate consequences. Past chapters have indicated how persistently the Clapham Sect were accused of sowing the seeds of social disorder. In 1824 a certain Mr. Richardson, a strong admirer of Wilberforce, felt constrained to publish a serious warning. He pointed out how Wilberforce and his friends had been urging such questions as, "Are we not all of one father?" But, he objected,

Little do these zealous . . . advocates for Negro Emancipation dream that they are industriously sowing the seeds of anarchy and wild impatience of *all government,* and breaking down the pale of ORDER. These inflammatory appeals of Mr. Wilberforce and his friends, are equally CRUEL, *unchristian and unpolitic; cruel to the lower orders of society* in engendering and cherishing a spirit of dissatisfaction with their sphere and lot in life, which cannot and ought not to be elevated; unchristian in striking at the root of every gospel precept of *subordination* which commands all men to be satisfied with the station and sphere in which they were born.[40]

The truth is that, from their standpoint, the conservatives had good reason to be apprehensive. The doctrine of universal brotherhood has implications to which men will not forever be blind; and though the Clapham Sect were not awake to all of these implications they nevertheless preached the doctrine, and so helped to create the atmosphere in which other reforms were achieved. "The historian of the movement which produced the factory acts must not forget the many tributaries which swelled the main stream. But the source of the river was the piety and Christian sentiment of the Evangelicals."[41]

Another service was even more direct. They taught a methodology of agitation. In 1807 General Gascoyne said bitterly that the abolitionists had resorted to "every measure that invention or artifice could devise to create a popular clamour."[42] Their political conduct is one

[39]*Parliamentary Debates,* New series, XI, 1172.
[40]J. M. Richardson, *Anti-Slavery Emancipation,* pp. 12-13.
[41]J. E. Rattenbury, *Wesley's Legacy to the World,* p. 247 (quoting Halévy).
[42]*Parliamentary Debates,* VIII, 718.

of the most significant features in their history. Even in the years of Pitt's repression, even in the years following Waterloo and leading up to Peterloo, even at a time when all agitation was suspect and agitation to force the hand of the government was counted treason—all the while the Clapham Sect, by virtue of their causes, were conducting the most persistent, systematic, and widespread agitation that England had ever seen. They were developing a strategy of organization and propaganda which was a new and effective feature in English politics. They exploited all the known methods of moving the masses, all the expedients of the politician, all the tricks of the party campaign. And, out of their varied experiences and their different needs, they added new methods cleverly adapted to English conditions. Klingberg says that the later emancipation campaign was "a first instance of an appeal to public opinion by means of all the modern agencies of publicity; lecture, pamphlet, newspaper, and bill board. It is the first example of the open participation of women in a contest."[43] All these developments were originated, if not directly by the Clapham Sect, at least by men whom the Clapham Sect directly inspired. The Clapham Sect also developed the use of the anniversary, with its mass meetings, its well-planned oratory, and, later, its collections, and its provision for the attendance of women. They developed, too, and demonstrated by numerous examples, a strategy for preparing petitions, and bringing them at critical moments to bear on Parliament.

They gave expert teaching, in fact, in two things: first, how to create public opinion; and then how to bring the pressure of that opinion against the government. And thus, by the trend of their policy and the contagious example of their method, they quite outbalanced the conservatism of some of their individual actions. Sir G. O. Trevelyan well said of them:

By the zeal, the munificence, the laborious activity with which they pursued their religious and semi-religious enterprises, they did more to teach the world how to get rid of existing institutions than by their votes and speeches at Westminster they contributed to preserve them. With their May meetings, and African Institutions, and Anti-slavery Reporters, and their subscriptions of tens of thousands of pounds, and their petitions bristling with hundreds of thousands of signatures, and all the machinery

[43]F. J. Klingberg, *The Anti-Slavery Movement in England,* Preface.

for informing opinion and bringing it to bear on ministers and legislators which they did so much to perfect and even to invent, they can be regarded as nothing short of the pioneers and fuglemen of that system of popular agitation which forms a leading feature in our internal history during the past half-century. At an epoch when the Cabinet which they supported was so averse to manifestations of political sentiment that a Reformer who spoke his mind in England was seldom long out of prison, and in Scotland ran a very serious risk of transportation, Toryism sat oddly enough on men who spent their days in the committee-room and their evenings on the platform, and each of whom belonged to more Associations combined for the purpose of influencing Parliament than he could count on the fingers of both his hands.[44]

In 1838 Richard Cobden urged that the campaign against the Corn Laws would be irresistible "if agitated in the same manner that the question of slavery has been."[45] "In fact," says Halévy, "the revolutionaries at the very time when they charged the Tory evangelicalism of Wilberforce with assisting the oppression of the people by drugging its just anger to sleep, borrowed from the popular evangelicalism of the sects its methods of organization, its trifling subscriptions, its open-air meetings, and its paid service of itinerant preachers, sent from town to town to spread the new doctrine."[46] G. M. Trevelyan well states the pattern for the future which the "systematic propaganda" against slavery established:

Its methods became the model for the conduct of hundreds and even thousands of other movements—political, humanitarian, social educational—which have been and still are the chief arteries of the life-blood of modern Britain, where every man or woman with a little money, or a little public spirit, is constantly joining Leagues, Unions or Committees formed to agitate some question, or to finance some object, local or national. In the eighteenth century this was not so. The habits engendered by the anti-slavery movement were a main cause of the change.[47]

In short, while occupied mainly with objects of a missionary character, and inspired almost wholly by motives of a pietistic origin, the Clapham Sect, by the principles they evoked and the methods they developed, indirectly rendered to English social movements an outstanding service—a service which they themselves did not foresee,

[44]*Life of Lord Macaulay*, I, 67-9.
[45]John Morley, *Life of Richard Cobden*, p. 126.
[46]*History of the English People, 1815-1830*, p. 13.
[47]G. M. Trevelyan, *British History in the Nineteenth Century*, pp. 51-2.

which is still least suspected by those whom it has most benefited, but which nevertheless justifies the conclusion that they were indeed among the "pioneers and fuglemen" of English social progress.

If the Clapham Sect prepared the way for much of the agitation and many of the humanitarian victories of the following years, they left singularly little through lineal descent. The second generation of the "Confederation of the Common" were men of great pith and moment, and some of them, such as Sir James Stephen and Robert Grant, were scarcely less devoted labourers for their fathers' causes than the fathers themselves had been. But certainly the "Sect" passed completely with the death of the original company. In 1845 the younger James Stephen wrote sadly, "No 'Clapham Sect' nowadays."[48] There was indeed no "Clapham Sect"; and England was the poorer.

In the generation succeeding the Clapham Sect, religious fervour flowed into three main channels. The wide section of Wilberforce's following demonstrated the soundness of the earlier humanitarian movement by marching under a new leader in a new campaign. Slavery having been abolished, the time had come to take the next field. Hence in the year of Wilberforce's death, Lord Shaftesbury, "the Wilberforce of the whites,"[49] commenced his campaign for the unfortunate "factory-slaves," a campaign which was to issue in a virtual transformation of factory life. Under Wilberforce and Shaftesbury the Evangelicals left to England a legacy of extraordinary social achievements. Shaftesbury, however, shared one defect of his earlier brethren. He had even less love than Wilberforce had for the idea of democracy. He gained for the labourer in England more than any other single man of his century; but he voted against the Reform Bills of 1832 and 1867, and was hostile to trade unions and the genuine movements of the working class such as Chartism. He won democratic victories in an aristocratic temper.

The democratic temper found an outlet in another movement with wider sympathies—the Christian Socialism of Maurice and Kingsley. This movement, in a manner, supplemented the deficiencies of Shaftesbury's; and the two rendered real service to English social progress. Unfortunately religion took yet another attitude to social reform.

[48]*The Right Honourable Sir James Stephen: Letters*, p. 87.
[49]G. M. Trevelyan, *British History in the Nineteenth Century*, p. 55.

The Tractarians swung into alarmed reaction against all "Liberalism," and simply repudiated the social obligations of the church. Pusey lamented that the emancipation of the slaves had meant the expenditure of £20,000,000 "for an opinion." Hurrell Froude could feel no love for the "niggers" because they "concentrated in themselves all the whiggery, dissent, cant, and abomination that had been ranged on their side."[50] Newman, who said in later life that he "had never considered social questions in their relation to faith,"[51] paid attention to men who freed the slaves and fought for the birthright of the children in the mills, chiefly to pour scorn on them for forgetting "the prophetical office of the church."[52] The Tractarians, in fact, repudiated rather than challenged the new materialism, and diverted the attention of the church from social iniquities to lost mysteries of the past. "When the cry of the oppressed was ringing in men's ears and when Christians might have listened to the prophets of social righteousness or to the victims of social evil, fifty years were wasted in lawsuits over 'regeneration' and ritual, vestments and incense, and the precise meaning of sixteenth century rubrics."[53]

It is not to impugn the genuine contributions which the Tractarians made to English religion to say that for them to have obtained their later influence in this earlier period would have been a dark and incalculable tragedy in English history. Had the Tractarian spirit—as at first manifested—been dominant in the days of Wilberforce it would inevitably have blocked the abolition of the slave trade and the emancipation of the slaves, and have frowned upon the attempt to institute the Church Missionary Society and to evangelize India. It would have rendered impossible joint Christian enterprises such as the Religious Tract Society and the British and Foreign Bible Society. Had Wilberforce, for instance, swung to High Church sentiment instead of to Evangelical there would have resulted a different and less happy nineteenth century with different and less worthy ideals. When so much was done that reaction could not undo, when so many victories were achieved, and the way so opened for many more, then the time was ripe for the Tractarians to render their own

[50]H. L. Stewart, *A Century of Anglo-Catholicism*, pp. 9-10.
[51]C. E. Raven, *Christian Socialism*, p. 21.
[52]Stewart, *A Century of Anglo-Catholicism*, p. 11.
[53]Raven, *Christian Socialism*, p. 20.

services to England. But it would have been disastrous had they come at the time of, and in the place of, the Clapham Sect.

The Clapham Sect, in short, seem to have been raised providentially for their particular duties in their particular time. Their combined gifts and advantages, and their fervour and perseverance, enabled them to render services, religious, social, and political, that were at once cardinally important and critically opportune. Had their influence been lacking there seems no ground for believing that any other influence of the time could have accomplished their work. Without them there would have been at least a crippled and delayed growth of the principles and traditions that most worthily distinguish their nation's history.

But the Clapham Sect did more than just perform their own labours, more even than bequeath a method to others; they also caught the imagination and kindled the inspiration of others. In 1807, after the abolition of the Slave Trade, Sir James Mackintosh, in a grateful tribute to Wilberforce, said, "Who knows whether the greater part of the benefit that he has conferred on the world . . . may not be the encouraging example that the exertions of virtue may be crowned by such splendid success? . . . hundreds and thousands will be animated by Mr. Wilberforce's example . . . to attack all forms of corruption and cruelty that scourge mankind."[54]

The Clapham Sect, in fact, did a great deal to change the atmosphere of the nation. Professor G. M. Trevelyan traces the origin of Victorian optimism in significant part to the anti-slavery triumph. "Mankind had been successfully lifted on to a higher plane by the energy of good men and the world breathed a more kindly air."[55] Good had won such dazzling victories over such grim foes that multitudes of men were moved to a new faith in humanity, and a new confidence that almost any further victory might be possible. And that faith and confidence heartened the crusaders of the following generation. There was a fitting symbolism in the gleam of sunshine that lit up the last public words of Wilberforce. He and his faithful band had fought a weary battle under lowering skies. But at eventide there was light. They left England with an "earnest of success," and an awakened hope that days still brighter were to come.

[54]*Life of Wilberforce*, III, 302-3.   [55]London *Times*, July 29, 1933.

Appendix

THE NAME "The Clapham Sect" was made popular by Sir James Stephen (son of James Stephen) in his famous essay under that title. The essay was published in the *Edinburgh Review,* 1844, and was republished in *Essays in Ecclesiastical Biography.* Its opening paragraph suggests that its title was taken from an earlier article in the *Edinburgh Review,* an article which had been subsequently published in a separate collection. The paragraph begins as follows:

In one of those collections of Essays which have recently been detached from the main body of this Journal [the Edinburgh Review] . . . , there occur certain pleasant allusions, already rendered obscure by the lapse of time, to a religious sect or society, which, as it appears, was flourishing in this realm in the reign of George III. What subtle theories, what clouds of learned dust, might have been raised by future Binghams, and by Du Pins yet unborn, to determine what was *The Patent Christianity,* and what *The Clapham Sect* of the nineteenth century, had not a fair and a noble author appeared to dispel, or at least to mitigate, the darkness. . . .[1]

Further to make explicit his reference Stephen adds that his essay will endeavour to supplement individual biographies that have appeared, and thus make intelligible to future generations the allusions of his "facetious colleague," who, he indicates in a footnote, is the Rev. Sydney Smith.

From these grounds later writers have, without question, accepted "The Clapham Sect" as a phrase which Sydney Smith created. Many writers state without qualification that Smith coined the name, and

[1] *Edinburgh Review,* LXXX, July-October, 1844, 251. There are some minor changes in the republished essay; e.g., "our facetious colleague" is rendered "the facetious Journalist." The authors to whom Stephen refers are Mary Milner and Lord Teignmouth, whose books, *The Life of Isaac Milner* and *The Life of Lord Teignmouth,* Stephen's article is supposed to review.

some add specifically that he did so in the *Edinburgh Review*. But the present writer has discovered with surprise that within the entire scope of the bibliography of this thesis there is no reference to a page in Sydney Smith's works in which the phrase may be found. And he himself has been unable to find it.

Many similar phrases can be discovered. In the collection of Smith's *Works* published in 1839—the collection to which Stephen's essay evidently refers—there are numerous oblique thrusts at Clapham. Smith refers, for instance, to the *Christian Observer* as "the organ of a great political religious party (*Works,* p. 138);[2] to Mrs. Hannah More as belonging to "a trumpery faction" (p. 168); to Wilberforce as "the head of the Clapham Church" (p. 567); and makes other similar allusions (see pp. 113, 116n., 137, 167, 433, 562, 623). But he makes still more pointed references—and one which Stephen seems to be quoting—not in the *Edinburgh Review* articles but in *The Letters of Peter Plymley*:

Is not Mr. Wilberforce at the head of the church of Clapham? (p. 576).

William Wilberforce, Esq., and the patent Christians of Clapham (p. 584).

That patent Christianity which has been for some time manufacturing at Clapham (p. 596).
[The phrase "patent Christianity" is the one which in the opening paragraph of his essay Stephen uses in conjunction with *"The Clapham Sect."*]

A Methodistical chancellor of the true Clapham breed (p. 624).

But, after the most careful search, the writer has been unable to discover any place where Smith used that one phrase "The Clapham Sect." Indeed he feels confident that the phrase is not in any of Smith's published works.[3]

Two possibilities are open. The first is that Sydney Smith may have used the phrase only in speech, or in some article undiscovered, or not extant.

---

[2] The references for this appendix are given to the one-volume edition of Smith's *Works,* published first in 1839, and republished in 1869. *The Letters of Peter Plymley* are included.

[3] The writer is confirmed in this opinion by finding, on inquiry, that the reference is not known to Professors G. M. Trevelyan and Reginald Coupland, nor to the President of the Clapham Antiquarian Society, the Rev. T. C. Dale.

This possibility seems to be precluded by the explicit reference to articles republished from the *Edinburgh Review,* from which, relying upon memory, Stephen may have failed to disassociate similar phrases in *The Letters of Peter Plymley.*

The second possibility is that Stephen's opening paragraph has been misread. The meaning may be simply that from Smith's various references to Clapham, "future Binghams and Du Pins yet unborn" might be moved to spin subtle theories about "The Clapham Sect" of the eighteenth century. It may be, therefore, that the nickname had its birth in Stephen's own phrase.

This possibility seems to be supported by a later phrase in the essay which speaks of "that sect to which, having first given a name, we would now build up a monument."[4] There is, indeed, a still later phrase which speaks of "that confederacy, which, when pent up within the narrow limits of Clapham, jocose men invidiously called a 'Sect.' "[5] But this last phrase does not create insuperable difficulty. For, though the specific phrase "The Clapham Sect," may not have been used, men, both jocose and serious, had referred to the Clapham group as a "Sect." Brougham, for instance, in his *Historical Sketches,* speaks of Wilberforce as "the head, indeed the founder, of a powerful religious sect."[6]

All that can now be said is that neither of the two italicized phrases of Stephen, *"Patent Christianity"* and *"The Clapham Sect,"* can be found in the articles to which Stephen refers—Sydney Smith's contributions to the *Edinburgh Review,* but that the former phrase can be found in *The Letters of Peter Plymley.*

The most reasonable conclusion therefore is that, contrary to accepted theory, the phrase "Clapham Sect" was coined not by Sydney Smith but by Sir James Stephen.

[4]*Edinburgh Review,* LXXX, July-October, 1844, 269.
[5]*Ibid.,* p. 307.
[6]Lord Brougham, *Historical Sketches,* p. 346.

Bibliography

I. THE GENERAL SETTING

Historical

BROUGHAM, HENRY, LORD. *Speeches.* 4 vols. Edinburgh, 1838.

BROWN, P. A. *The French Revolution in English History.* Edited by J. L. Hammond. London, 1918.

BURKE, EDMUND. *Reflections on the Revolution in France.* London, 1790.

The Cambridge History of British Foreign Policy, 1783–1919. Vol. I, *1783–1815*; vol. II, *1815–1866.* Cambridge.

The Cambridge Modern History. Vol. VI, *The Eighteenth Century*; vol. IX, *Napoleon.* Cambridge.

CARLYLE, THOMAS. *The French Revolution: A History.* 3 vols. London, 1837.

DYKES, EVA BEATRICE. *The Negro in English Romantic Thought: or, A Study of Sympathy for the Oppressed.* Washington, 1942.

GREAT BRITAIN, PARLIAMENT. *Parliamentary Debates* (from 1803).

―――― *Parliamentary History of England from the Earliest Period to the Year 1803.* London, Hansard.

GREEN, JOHN RICHARD. *History of the English People.* 4 vols. London, 1880.

HALÉVY, ELIE. *History of the English People in 1815.* Translated by E. I. Watkin and D. A. Barker. London, 1924.

―――― *A History of the English People, 1815–1830.* Translated by E. I. Watkin. London, 1926.

HOOD, EDWIN PAXTON. *Vignettes of the Great Revival of the Eighteenth Century.* London, 1881.

INGE, WILLIAM RALPH. *England.* London, 1926.

KYDD, SAMUEL. *A Sketch of the Growth of Public Opinion: Its Influence on the Constitution and Government.* London, 1888.

LECKY, W. E. H. *A History of England in the Eighteenth Century.* 8 vols. London, 1878–1890.

―――― *History of European Morals from Augustus to Charlemagne.* 2 vols. London, 1877.

MARTINEAU, HARRIET. *A History of the Thirty Years' Peace, 1816–1846.* 4 vols. London, 1877–78.

MATHIESON, WILLIAM LAW. *England in Transition, 1789–1832: A Study of Movements.* London, 1920.

MAY, SIR THOMAS ERSKINE. *The Constitutional History of England since the Accession of George III.* London, 1912.

MUIR, RAMSAY. *A History of Liverpool.* London, 1907.

—— *A Short History of the British Commonwealth.* 2 vols. London, 1922.

PENNINGTON, ARTHUR R. *Recollections of Persons and Events.* London, 1895.

PHILIPS, C. H. *The East India Company, 1784–1834.* Manchester, 1940.

STEPHEN, LESLIE. *History of English Thought in the Eighteenth Century.* 2 vols. London, 1876.

SWINNY, S. H. *The Humanitarianism of the Eighteenth Century, and Its Results, in Western Races and the World.* London, 1922.

TELFORD, J. *A Sect That Moved the World.* London, 1907.

TREVELYAN, G. M. *British History in the Nineteenth Century.* London, 1922.

WEBSTER, C. K. *The Foreign Policy of Castlereagh, 1815–1822.* London, 1925.

Social and Economic

ALFRED, *pseud.* (SAMUEL KYDD). *The History of the Factory Movement, from the Year 1802 to the Enactment of the Ten Hours' Bill in 1847.* 2 vols. London, 1857.

ALCOCK, THOMAS. *Observations on the Defects of the Poor Laws, and on the Causes and Consequence of the Great Increase and Burden of the Poor.* London, 1752.

BAXTER, G. R. W. *The Book of the Bastiles: or, The History of the Working of the New Poor Law.* London, 1841.

BEER, MAX. *A History of British Socialism.* 2 vols. London, 1919, 1920.

BOOTH, WILLIAM. *In Darkest England and the Way Out.* London, 1890.

BURKE, EDMUND. *Thoughts on the Cause of the Present Discontents.* London, 1775.

COBBETT, WILLIAM. *A History of the Last Hundred Days of English Freedom.* Introduction by J. L. Hammond. London, 1921.

COLE, G. D. H. *A Short History of the British Working Class Movement.* 3 vols. London, 1927.

EDEN, SIR FREDERIC MORTON. *The State of the Poor: or, An History of the Labouring Classes in England, from the Conquest to the Present Period.* 3 vols. London, 1828.

EVELYN, JOHN. *Co-operation: An Address to the Labouring Classes, on the Plans to be Pursued and the Errors to be Avoided in Conducting Trade Unions.* London, 1830.

FIELDEN, JOHN. *The Curse of the Factory System.* London, 1836.

GAMMAGE, R. G. *The History of the Chartist Movement, from Its Commencement Down to the Present Time.* London, 1854.

GIBBINS, H. DE B. *English Social Reformers.* London, 1892.

GORE, CHARLES. *Christ and Society.* London, 1928.

HAMMOND, J. L. AND B. *The Skilled Labourer, 1760–1832.* London, 1919.

—— *The Town Labourer, 1760–1832: The New Civilisation.* London, 1917.

—— *The Village Labourer, 1760–1832: A Study in the Government of England before the Reform Bill.* London, 1919.

HANWAY, JONAS. *An Earnest Appeal for Mercy to the Children of the Poor.* London, 1766.

HOVELL, MARK, edited and completed by T. F. TOUT. *The Chartist Movement.* Manchester, 1918.

HOWARD, JOHN. *The State of the Prisons in England and Wales.* 2 pts. Warrington, 1777–1780.

INGE, WILLIAM R. *The Social Teaching of the Church.* London, 1930.

JEVONS, W. S. *The State in Relation to Labour.* London, 1894.

JOHNSON, THOMAS. *The History of the Working Classes in Scotland.* Glasgow, 1921.

KAY, JAMES PHILLIPS. *The Moral and Physical Condition of the Working Classes Employed in the Cotton Manufacture in Manchester.* London, 1832.

KIRKUP, THOMAS. *A History of Socialism.* London, 1913.

LINDSAY, A. D. *Christianity and Economics.* London, 1933.

MARSHALL, DOROTHY. *The English Poor in the Eighteenth Century.* London, 1926.

MORISON, J. COTTER. *The Service of Man: An Essay toward the Religion of the Future.* London, 1903.

NIEBUHR, R. *Moral Man and Immoral Society: A Study in Ethics and Politics.* New York, 1932.

PALEY, WILLIAM. *Reasons for Contentment; Addressed to the Labouring Part of the British Public.* London, 1793.

PORRITT, EDWARD. *The Unreformed House of Commons: Parliamentary Representation before 1832.* Cambridge, 1903.

RATTENBURY, J. ERNEST. *John Wesley and Social Service.* London, 1912.

RAVEN, CHARLES E. *Christian Socialism.* London, 1920.

TAWNEY, R. H. *Religion and the Rise of Capitalism.* London, 1926.

THORNTON, HENRY. *An Enquiry into the Nature and Effects of the Paper Credit of Great Britain.* Edited by F. A. von Hayek. London, 1939.

WADE, JOHN. *The Black Book: An Exposition of Abuses in Church and State.* London, 1835.

—— *History of the Middle and Working Classes.* London, 1833.

WARNER, WELLMAN J. *The Wesleyan Movement in the Industrial Revolution.* London, 1930.

WEBB, SIDNEY. *Socialism in England.* London, 1890.

WEBB, SIDNEY AND BEATRICE. *English Poor Law Policy.* London, 1910.

—— *The History of Liquor Licensing in England, Principally from 1700 to 1830.* London, 1903.

—— *Industrial Democracy.* London, 1897.

YOUNG, ARTHUR. *An Enquiry into the State of the Public Mind amongst the Lower Classes . . . in a letter to W. Wilberforce.* London, 1798.

Religious and Cultural

BALLEINE, G. R. *A History of the Evangelical Party in the Church of England.* London, 1908.

CARPENTER, S. C. *Church and People, 1789–1889: A History of the Church of England from William Wilberforce to "Lux mundi."* London, 1933.

CHAPMAN, E. M. *English Literature in Account with Religion, 1800–1900.* London, 1910.

COLE, G. D. H. *Politics and Literature.* London, 1929.

CORNISH, FRANCIS WARRE. *The English Church in the Nineteenth Century.* 2 vols. London, 1910.

COWPER, WILLIAM. *Poetical Works.* London, 1889.

DALE, R. W. *The Old Evangelicalism and the New.* London, 1889.

Encyclopaedia of Religion and Ethics.

FAIRBAIRN, A. M. *Catholicism: Roman and Anglican.* London, 1899.

FROUDE, J. A. "The Revival of Romanism"; in *Short Studies on Great Subjects,* vol. IV. London, 1907.

GLADSTONE, W. E. *Gleanings of Past Years, 1843–78.* 7 vols. London, 1879.

HAZLITT, WILLIAM. *The Spirit of the Age: or, Contemporary Portraits.* London, 1904.

MATHIESON, WILLIAM LAW. *Church and Reform in Scotland: A History from 1797 to 1843.* Glasgow, 1916.

—— *English Church Reform, 1815–1840.* London, 1923.

MORE, HANNAH. *Works.* 8 vols. London, 1801.

MOULE, HANDLEY C. G. *The Evangelical School in the Church of England: Its Men and Its Work in the Nineteenth Century.* London, 1901.

MURRAY, GILBERT. *Religio Grammatici: The Religion of a Man of Letters.* London, 1918.

NEWMAN, JOHN HENRY. *Apologia pro Vita Sua.* London, 1897.

OLIPHANT, MRS. *The Literary History of England in the End of the Eighteenth and Beginning of the Nineteenth Century.* 3 vols. London, 1882.

OVERTON, J. H. *The English Church in the Nineteenth Century (1800–1833).* London, 1894.

——— *The Evangelical Revival in the Eighteenth Century.* London, 1886.

OVERTON, J. H. and RELTON, FREDERIC. *The English Church from the Accession of George I to the End of the Eighteenth Century, 1714–1800.* London, 1906.

RATTENBURY, J. ERNEST. *Wesley's Legacy to the World: Six Studies in the Permanent Values of the Evangelical Revival.* London, 1928.

RUSSELL, GEORGE W. E. *Collections and Recollections.* London, 1898.

——— *A Short History of the Evangelical Movement.* London, 1915.

SEELEY, M. *The Later Evangelical Fathers, John Thornton, John Newton, William Cowper, Thomas Scott, Richard Cecil, William Wilberforce, Charles Simeon, Henry Martyn, Josiah Pratt.* London, 1879.

SHORTHOUSE, JOSEPH H. *Sir Percival: A Story of the Past and of the Present.* London, 1886.

SMITH, SYDNEY. *Works.* London, 1869.

SOUTHEY, ROBERT. *Essays, Moral and Political.* 2 vols. London, 1832.

STEPHEN, SIR JAMES. *Essays in Ecclesiastical Biography.* 2 vols. London, 1907.

STEWART, H. L. *A Century of Anglo-Catholicism.* London, 1929.

TEXTE, JOSEPH. *Jean Jacques Rousseau and the Cosmopolitan Spirit in Literature.* London, 1899.

THACKERAY, W. M. *The Newcomes.*

TREVELYAN, G. M. *Clio, a Muse, and Other Essays, Literary and Pedestrian.* London, 1913.

II. BIOGRAPHY AND LETTERS

BREADY, J. WESLEY. *Doctor Barnardo, Physician, Pioneer, Prophet: Child Life Yesterday and To-day.* London, 1930.

——— *Lord Shaftesbury and Social-Industrial Progress.* London, 1926.

BROUGHAM, HENRY, LORD. *Historical Sketches of Statesmen Who Flourished in the Time of George III,* First Series. London, 1839.

BUXTON, CHARLES, ed. *Memoirs of Sir Thomas Fowell Buxton, Baronet, with Selections from His Correspondence.* London, 1850.

BUXTON, TRAVERS. *William Wilberforce: The Story of a Great Crusade.* London, 1904.

CAREY, S. PEARCE. *William Carey.* London, 1923.

CARUS, WILLIAM, *Memoirs of the Life of the Rev. Charles Simeon.* Cambridge, 1847.

CASTLEREAGH, VISCOUNT. *Correspondence, Despatches, and Other Papers,* Third Series. See *Memoir and Correspondence of Viscount Castlereagh, Second Marquess of Londonderry.* Edited by his brother. 12 vols. London, 1848–53.

CHESTERTON, G. K. *William Cobbett.* London, 1925.

CLARKSON, THOMAS. *Strictures on a Life of W. Wilberforce, by the Rev. W. Wilberforce and the Rev. S. Wilberforce; with a Correspondence between Lord Brougham and Mr. Clarkson; also a Supplement Containing Remarks on the Edinburgh Review of Mr. Wilberforce's Life.* London, 1838.

COLE, G. D. H. *The Life of William Cobbett.* London, 1924.

COLQUHOUN, JOHN C. *William Wilberforce, His Friends and His Times.* London, 1867.

COUPLAND, R. *Wilberforce.* Oxford, 1923.

DALE, T. C. *Our Clapham Forefathers.* London, 1921.

Dictionary of National Biography.

FISHER, THOMAS. *A Memoir of the Late C. Grant, Esq., Member of Parliament for the Shire of Inverness.* London, 1833.

FITCHETT, W. H. *Wesley and His Century: A Study in Spiritual Forces.* London, 1906.

FURBER, HOLDEN, ed. *The Private Record of an Indian Governor-Generalship: The Correspondence of Sir John Shore, Governor-General, with Henry Dundas, President of the Board of Control, 1793–1798.* Cambridge, Mass., 1933.

GREVILLE, C. C. F. *The Greville Memoirs, a Journal of the Reigns of King George IV and King William IV.* 3 vols. Edited by H. Reeve. London, 1874.

GRIMSHAWE, T. S. *A Memoir of the Rev. Leigh* [sic] *Richmond.* London, 1829.

GURNEY, J. J. *Reminiscences of Chalmers, Simeon, Wilberforce, etc.* [*ca.* 1835.]

GRIGGS, EARL LESLIE. *Thomas Clarkson—the Friend of Slaves.* London, 1936.

HALDANE, ALEXANDER. *Memoirs of the Lives of Robert Haldane of Airthrey and of His Brother James Alexander Haldane.* London, 1827.

HAMMOND, J. LE B. *Charles James Fox, a Political Study.* London, 1903.

HAMMOND, J. L. and BARBARA. *Lord Shaftesbury.* London, 1923.

HARFORD, JOHN S. *Recollections of William Wilberforce during Nearly Thirty Years; with Brief Notices of Some of His Personal Friends and Contemporaries.* London, 1864.

HINTON, J. H. *Memoir of William Knibb, Missionary in Jamaica.* London, 1847.

HOARE, PRINCE. *Memoirs of Granville Sharp.* London, 1820.

HOBBES, R. G. *Reminiscences of Seventy Years' Life, Travel, and Adventure; Military and Civil; Scientific and Literary,* vol. I. London, 1893.

HOLLAND, LADY. *A Memoir of the Reverend Sydney Smith, by His Daughter.* London, 1855.

JENKINS, WILFRID J. *William Wilberforce, a Champion of Freedom.* London, 1932.

KINGSLEY, CHARLES. *Charles Kingsley: His Letters and Memories of His Life.* Edited by his wife. London, 1877.

KNIGHT, WILLIAM. *The Missionary Secretariat of Henry Venn.* London, 1880.

KNUTSFORD, VISCOUNTESS. *Life and Letters of Zachary Macaulay.* London, 1900.

LASCELLES, E. C. P. *Granville Sharp and the Freedom of the Slaves in England.* London, 1928.

MAITLAND, F. W. *The Life and Letters of Leslie Stephen.* London, 1906.

MARSHMAN, JOHN CLARK. *The Story of Carey, Marshman, and Ward, the Serampore Missionaries.* London, 1864.

MAURICE, JOHN FREDERICK, ed. *The Life of Frederick Denison Maurice, Chiefly Told in His Own Letters.* London, 1884.

MILNER, MARY. *The Life of Isaac Milner, Dean of Carlisle, . . . Comprising a Portion of His Correspondence and Other Writings Hitherto Unpublished.* London, 1842.

MORISON, J. COTTER. *Macaulay.* London, 1882.

MORLEY, JOHN. *The Life of Richard Cobden.* London, 1881.

——— *The Life of William Ewart Gladstone.* London, 1903.

MORRIS, HENRY. *The Governor-Generals of India.* London, 1907.

——— *The Life of Charles Grant.* London, 1904.

——— *Reginald Heber.* Madras, 1901.

MOULE, H. C. G. *Charles Simeon*. London, 1892.

MUDGE, Z. A. *The Christian Statesman: A Portraiture of Sir T. F. Buxton . . . with Sketches of British Antislavery Reform*. New York, 1865.

NEWTON, JOHN. *The Life of John Newton with Selections from His Correspondence*. London, 1855.

PEARSON, HUGH N. *Memoirs of the Life and Writings of the Rev. Claudius Buchanan, D.D.* 2 vols. Oxford, 1817.

PRATT, JOSIAH (the elder). *Sketch of the Life of the Late Right Honourable Lord Teignmouth*. London, 1834.

PRATT, JOSIAH (the younger) and JOHN HENRY. *Memoir of the Rev. Josiah Pratt, B.D.* London, 1849.

PUGH, S. S. *Sir Thomas Fowell Buxton, Bart.* London, 1899.

REID, STUART J. *A Sketch of the Life and Times of the Rev. Sydney Smith*. London, 1896.

ROBERTS, W. *Memoirs of the Life and Correspondence of Mrs. Hannah More*. London, 1834.

ROMILLY, Sir SAMUEL. *Memoirs of the Life of Sir Samuel Romilly, with a Selection from His Correspondence*. Edited by his sons. London, 1840.

ROSE, J. HOLLAND. *Pitt and Napoleon: Essays and Letters*. London, 1912.

——— *A Short Life of William Pitt*. London, 1925.

——— *William Pitt and National Revival*. London, 1911.

ROSEBERY, EARL OF. *Pitt*. London, 1891.

——— ed. *Pitt and Wilberforce* [Containing a "Sketch of Mr. Pitt" by Wilberforce and letters of Pitt and Wilberforce]. London, 1897.

RUDOLF, R. DE M. *et al. Clapham and the Clapham Sect.* Clapham, 1927.

RUSSELL, G. W. E. *The Household of Faith*. London, 1906.

——— *Sydney Smith*. London, 1905.

SEELEY, R. B. *Memoirs of the Life and Writings of Michael Thomas Sadler*. London, 1842.

SMITH, GEORGE. *The Life of William Carey, D.D., Shoemaker and Missionary*. London, 1895.

——— *Twelve Indian Statesmen*. London, 1895.

SOUTHEY, ROBERT. *The Life of Wesley, and the Rise and Progress of Methodism*. London, 1864.

STEPHEN, CAROLINE EMELIA. *The Right Honourable Sir James Stephen: Letters with Biographical Notes*. 1906.

STEPHEN, SIR LESLIE. *The Life of Sir James Fitzjames Stephen, Bart., K.C.S.I., a Judge of the High Court of Justice. London*, 1895.

STOUGHTON, JOHN. *Howard the Philanthropist and His Friends*. London, 1884.

——— *William Wilberforce*. London, 1880.

SHORE, CHARLES JOHN, BARON TEIGNMOUTH. *Memoir of the Life and Correspondence of John, Lord Teignmouth.* 2 vols. London, 1843.

—— *Reminiscences of Many Years.* 2 vols. Edinburgh, 1878.

THOMPSON, HENRY. *The Life of Hannah More; with Notices of Her Sisters.* London, 1838.

THORNTON, PERCY MELVILLE. *Some Things We Have Remembered.* London, 1912.

TREVELYAN, GEORGE M. *Lord Grey of the Reform Bill, being the Life of Charles, Second Earl Grey.* London, 1929.

TREVELYAN, SIR GEORGE O. *The Life and Letters of Lord Macaulay.* 2 vols. London, 1876.

URLIN, R. DENNY. *The Churchman's Life of Wesley.* London, 1880.

VENN, JOHN. *The Life and a Selection from the Letters of the Late Rev. Henry Venn.* Edited by the Rev. H. Venn, B.D. London, 1834.

VENN, JOHN. *Annals of a Clerical Family.* London, 1904.

WALLAS, GRAHAM. *The Life of Francis Place, 1771–1854.* London, 1898.

WALPOLE, HORACE. *Letters.* Edited by Mrs. Paget Toynbee. 16 vols. Oxford, 1903–1905.

WESLEY, JOHN. *Journal.* 4 vols. London, 1827.

WHEELER, H. M. *The Slaves' Champion: or, The Life, Deeds and Historical Days of William Wilberforce.* London, 1859.

WILBERFORCE, ROBERT ISAAC and SAMUEL. *The Life of William Wilberforce.* 5 vols. London, 1838. [This life is a poor biography, but it has one significant value: it includes almost everything of interest in Wilberforce's MS. diary. This diary, in the Wilberforce Museum at Hull, is extremely difficult to read. Moreover, the present writer thought it pedantic to refer to a MS. which is not readily available when reference could be made to a public though ancient biography. Hence the references to Wilberforce's diary may be found under the appropriate dates in the five volumes.]

WILBERFORCE, WILLIAM. *Correspondence.* Edited by R. I. and Samuel Wilberforce. 2 vols. London, 1840.

——MSS. Letters. Hull, Wilberforce Museum.

—— *Private Papers.* Edited by A. M. Wilberforce. London, 1897.

WILKS, SAMUEL C. *Memoirs of the Life, Writings and Correspondence of Sir William Jones; with the Life of Lord Teignmouth, Selections from Sir W. Jones's Works, and Occasional Notes by . . . S. C. Wilks.* 2 vols. London, 1835.

WOOLMAN, JOHN. *Journals of the Life and Travels of John Woolman.* Lindfield, 1832.

WORDSWORTH, CHARLES. *Annals of My Early Life, 1806–1846.* London, 1891.

III. CLAPHAM ENTERPRISES

Anti-Slavery

Anti-Negro Emancipation: An Appeal to Mr. Wilberforce. London, 1824.

BRIDGES, GEORGE W. *A Voice from Jamaica in Reply to William Wilberforce*. London, 1823.

BUXTON, THOMAS FOWELL. *The African Slave Trade and Its Remedy*. London, 1840.

The Claims for Fresh Evidence on the Subject of the Slave Trade Considered. London, 1807.

CLARKSON, THOMAS. *Address Presented to the Sovereigns of Europe and Their Representatives When They Met at Aix-la-Chapelle in 1818*. London, 1824.

———— *An Essay on the Impolicy of the Slave Trade*. London, 1788.

———— *The History of the Rise, Progress and Accomplishment of the Abolition of the African Slave-Trade by the British Parliament*. 2 vols. London, 1808.

———— *A Letter to the Clergy of the Various Denominations, and to the Slave-holding Planters in the Southern Parts of the United States of America*. London, 1841.

———— *Letters on the Slave Trade and the State of Natives in . . . Parts of Africa*. London, 1791.

Colonial Slavery (handbill). London, 1832.

COLONIST. *The Edinburgh Review and the West Indies; with Observations on the Pamphlets of Messrs. Stephen, Macaulay, etc. and Remarks on the Slave Registry Bill*. Glasgow, 1816.

East India Sugar: or, An Enquiry Respecting the Means of Improving the Quality and Reducing the Cost of Sugar Raised by Free Labour in the East Indies. London, 1824.

EDWARDS, BRYAN. *The History, Civil and Commercial, of the British Colonies in the West Indies*. 3 vols. London, 1793–1801.

———— *A Speech Delivered at a Free Conference between the Honourable Council and Assembly of Jamaica on the Subject of Mr. Wilberforce's Propositions in the House of Commons, concerning the Slave Trade*. Kingston, Jamaica, 1789.

FRANKLYN, G. *An Answer to . . . Mr. Clarkson's London Essay*. London, 1789.

FROUDE. J. A. *The English in the West Indies*. London, 1888.

GISBORNE, THOMAS. *Remarks on the Late Decision of the House of Commons Respecting the Abolition of the Slave Trade*. London, 1792.

HARRIS, R. *Scriptural Researches on the Licitness of the Slave-Trade, Shewing Its Conformity with the Principles of Natural and Revealed Religion Delineated in the Sacred Writings of the Word of God.* London, 1788.

KLINGBERG, FRANK J. *The Anti-Slavery Movement in England.* New Haven, Conn., 1926.

MACAULAY, ZACHARY. *East and West India Sugar: or, a Refutation of the Claims of the West India Colonists to a Protecting Duty on East India Sugar.* London, 1823.

—— *A Letter to His Royal Highness, the Duke of Gloucester, President of the African Institution.* London, 1815.

—— *Negro Slavery: or, A View of Some of the More Prominent Features of That State of Society, As It Exists in the United States of America and in the Colonies of the West Indies, Especially in Jamaica.* London, 1823.

MATHIESON, WILLIAM L. *British Slavery and Its Abolition, 1823–1838.* London, 1926.

A MERCHANT. *An Attempt to Strip Negro Emancipation of Its Difficulties, As Well As of Its Terrors: By Showing That the Country Has the Means of Accomplishing It with Ease, and Doing Justice to All Parties.* London, 1824.

NEWTON, JOHN. *Thoughts upon the African Slave Trade.* London, 1788.

PAYNE, ERNEST A. *Freedom in Jamaica: Some Chapters in the Story of the Baptist Missionary Society.* London, 1933.

A PLANTER AND MERCHANT of many years' residence in the West Indies. *West-India Trade and Islands: Commercial Reasons for the Non-Abolition of the Slave Trade, in the West-India Islands.* London, 1789.

RAMSAY, JAMES. *An Address on the Proposed Bill for the Abolition of the Slave Trade.* London, 1788.

—— *An Essay on the Treatment and Conversion of African Slaves in the British Sugar Colonies.* London, 1784.

RICHARDSON, J. M. *Anti-Slavery Emancipation: An Appeal to Mr. Wilberforce.* London, 1824.

SHARP, GRANVILLE. *An Essay on Slavery, Proving from Scripture Its Inconsistency with Humanity and Religion. . . .* West Jersey, 1773.

—— *Free English Territory in Africa.* 1790.

—— *The Just Limitation of Slavery in the Laws of God, Compared with the Unbounded Claims of the African Traders and British American Slaveholders.* London, 1776.

—— *The Sailors Advocate.* Preface. London, 1776.

—— *Serious Reflections on the Slave Trade and Slavery, Wrote in March 1797.* London, 1805.

—— *A Short Sketch of Temporary Regulations . . . for the Intended Settlement on the Grain Coast of Africa, near Sierra Leone.* London, 1786.

A Short Account of the African Slave Trade Collected from Local Knowledge. Liverpool, 1788.

SIMON, KATHLEEN. *Slavery.* London, 1930.

SOME GENTLEMEN OF ST. CHRISTOPHER. *An Answer to the Reverend James Ramsay's Essay on the Treatment and Conversion of Slaves in the British Sugar Colonies.* Basseterre, St. Christopher, 1784.

Statements Illustrative of the Nature of the Slave Trade. London, 1824.

STEPHEN, SIR GEORGE. *Antislavery Recollections: In a Series of Letters to Mrs. Harriet Beecher Stowe Written at Her Request.* London, 1854.

—— *A Letter to Sir Thomas F. Buxton on the Proposed Revival of the English Slave Trade.* London, 1849.

STEPHEN, JAMES. *A Defence of the Bill for the Registration of Slaves, in Letters to W. Wilberforce.* London, 1816.

—— *England Enslaved by Her Own Slave Colonies.* London, 1826.

—— *The Slavery of the British West-India Colonies Delineated, As It Exists Both in Law and Practice, and Compared with the Slavery of Other Countries, Antient and Modern.* 2 vols. London, 1824-30.

—— *Speech at the Annual Meeting of the African Institution, . . . , 26th March, 1817.* London, 1817.

—— *War in Disguise: or, The Frauds of the Neutral Flags.* London, 1805.

A Very New Pamphlet . . . Containing Some Strictures on the English Jacobins and the Evidence of Lord M'Cartney . . . Respecting the Slave Trade. 1792.

WILBERFORCE, WILLIAM. *Address to the Empress of Russia.* 1823.

—— *An Appeal to the Religion, Justice, and Humanity of the Inhabitants of the British Empire, in Behalf of the Negro Slaves in the West Indies.* London, 1823.

—— *A Letter on the Abolition of the Slave Trade, Addressed to the Freeholders and Other Inhabitants of Yorkshire.* London, 1807.

—— *A Letter to . . . the Prince of Talleyrand-Perigord on the Subject of the Slave Trade.* London, 1814.

—— *The Speeches of Mr. Wilberforce, Lord Penrhyn, Mr. Burke . . . on a Motion for the Abolition of the Slave Trade, in the House of Commons, May 12th, 1789; To Which are Added Mr. Wilberforce's Twelve Propositions.* London, 1789.

———— *Substance of the Proceedings in the House of Commons on Thursday, July 25, 1822, on the Occasion of Two Addresses to His Majesty: One Moved by Mr. Wilberforce, for Preventing the Extension of Slavery at the Cape of Good Hope.* . . . London, 1822.

Abridgement of Minutes of the Evidence Taken before a Committee of the Whole House to Whom It was Referred to Consider the Slave Trade. 1790.

African Institution. *Reports of the Committee.* London, 1807–24.

Association for Promoting the Discovery of the Interior Parts of Africa. *List of Members.* London, 1790.

———— *Proceedings,* London, 1790.

Extracts from the Report of the Commission Appointed for Investigating the State of the Settlements and Governments on the Coast of Africa. 1812.

London Anti-Slavery Society. *Proceedings of the First Anniversary Meeting, 1824.* London, 1824.

———— *Report of the Committee of the Society for the Mitigation and Gradual Abolition of Slavery throughout the British Dominions.* London, 1824.

A Plantation Inventory and Appraisement of All Negroes. MSS. Hull, Wilberforce Museum.

Society for Abolition of the Slave Trade. *List of the Society Instituted in 1787 for the Purpose of Effecting the Abolition of the Slave Trade.* London, 1788.

Report of the Lords of the Committee of Council Concerning the Present State of Trade to Africa and Particularly the Trade of Slaves. 1789.

Missions

BUCHANAN, CLAUDIUS. *Christian Researches in Asia.* Cambridge, 1811.

———— *Memoir of the Expediency of an Ecclesiastical Establishment for British India.* London, 1805.

CAMPBELL, DONALD. *A Journey Overland to India . . . in a Series of Letters to His Son.* London, 1795.

GRANT, CHARLES. *Observations on the State of Society among the Asiatic Subjects of Great Britain, Particularly with Respect to Morals; and on the Means of Improving It.* London, 1792.

HEADLAND, EMILY. *Brief Sketches of Church Missionary Society Missions.* London.

HOLE, CHARLES. *The Early History of the Church Missionary Society for Africa and the East to the End of Anno Domini 1814.* London, 1896.

KAYE, SIR JOHN WILLIAM. *Christianity in India: An Historical Narrative.* London, 1859.

PRATT, JOHN HENRY, ed. *Eclectic Notes: or, Notes of Discussions on Religious Topics, at the Meetings of the Eclectic Society, London, during the Years 1798–1814.* London, 1865.

SHORE, JOHN, LORD TEIGNMOUTH. *Considerations of the Practicability, Policy, and Obligation of Communicating to the Natives of India the Knowledge of Christianity.* London, 1808.

STOCK, EUGENE. *The History of the Church Missionary Society: Its Environment, Its Men and Its Work.* 4 vols. London, 1899–1916.

———— *One Hundred Years: Being the Short History of the Church Missionary Society.* London, 1898.

VENN, HENRY. *Retrospect and Prospect of the Operations of the Church Missionary Society.* London, 1865.

VENN, JOHN. *A Sermon Preached before the Society for Missions.* 1801.

WARING, MAJOR SCOTT. *Preface and Observations on the Present State of the East India Company.* 1806.

WILLIAMSON, CAPT. THOMAS. *The East India Vade-Mecum.* London, 1810.

Church Missionary Society. *Century Volume.* London, 1902.

———— *Church Missionary Society's African Missions* (Sierra Leone). London, 1863.

———— *Jubilee Volume.* London, 1849.

———— *The Missions of the Church Missionary Society* (Sierra Leone). London, 1899.

———— *The Present Position and Future Prospects of the Church Missionary Society.* London, 1846.

———— *Summary View of the Designs and Proceedings of the Society for Missions to Africa and the East.* London, 1812.

Society for Propagating the Gospel in Foreign Parts. *Classified Digest of the Records of the Society.* London, 1895.

Bible and Tract Societies

CANTON, WILLIAM. *A History of the British and Foreign Bible Society.* 5 vols. London, 1904-10.

DEALTRY, WILLIAM. "Speech . . . at the Twenty-Seventh Anniversary of the British and Foreign Bible Society." See *British and Foreign Bible Society Controversy.* London, 1831.

———— *A Vindication of the British and Foreign Bible Society.* London, 1810.

GREEN, SAMUEL G. *The Story of the Religious Tract Society for One Hundred Years.* London, 1899.

MACAULAY, ZACHARY. *The Substance of a Speech . . . Delivered . . . August 4, 1812, on the Formation of an Auxiliary Bible Society for Clapham and Its Vicinity.* London, 1812.

MORRIS, HENRY. *The Founders and First Three Presidents of the Bible Society.* London, 1890.

—— *A Memorable Room.* London, 1898.

OWEN, JOHN. *The History of the Origin and First Ten Years of the British and Foreign Bible Society.* 2 vols. London, 1816.

SHORE, JOHN, LORD TEIGNMOUTH. *A Letter to the Rev. Christopher Wordsworth, D.D., in Reply to His Strictures on the British and Foreign Bible Society.* London, 1810.

Naval and Military Bible Society. *Proceedings, May 11, 1875, with an Account of Its Origins.* London, 1875.

Prayer Book and Homily Society. *Proceedings.* London, 1814–25.

Religious Tract Society. *Brief View of the Plan and Operations of the Religious Tract Society, Instituted 1799.* London, ca. 1826.

—— Extracts from the Minutes of the Society. London, at the offices of the British and Foreign Bible Society.

Social and Philanthropic Movements

BERNARD, SIR T. *Of the Education of the Poor; being the First Part of a Digest of the Reports of the Society for Bettering the Condition of the Poor, etc.* London, 1809.

BUXTON, THOMAS FOWELL. *Severity of Punishment: Speech . . . in the House of Commons . . . May 23rd, 1821.* London, 1821.

—— *Speech . . . on the 26th November, 1816, on the Subject of the Distress in Spitalfields.* London, 1816.

—— *Substance of the Speech . . . in the House of Commons, March 2nd, 1819, on the Motion of Sir James Mackintosh, Bart., "that a select committee be appointed, to consider of so much of the criminal laws as relates to capital punishments or felonies."* London, 1819.

The Case of Thomas Spence . . . Who was Committed to Clerkenwell Prison . . . for Selling . . . Paine's Rights of Man. London, 1792.

CLARKSON, THOMAS. *The Grievances of Our Mercantile Seamen, a Rational and Crying Evil.* London, 1845.

—— ed. *An Account of the Charities Belonging to the Poor of the County of Norfolk.* By Zachary Clark. London, 1811.

DAY, WILLIAM. *Correspondence with the Poor Law Commissioners.* London, 1844.

—— *An Inquiry into the Poor Laws and Surplus Labour and Their Mutual Reaction.* London, 1833.

DEALTRY, WILLIAM. *The National Church a National Blessing.* London, 1835.

GISBORNE, THOMAS. *An Enquiry into the Duties of Men in the Higher and Middle Classes of Society in Great Britain, Resulting from Their Respective Stations, Professions, and Employments.* London, 1794.

—— *Friendly Observations Addressed to the Manufacturing Population of Great Britain, Now Suffering under the Difficulties of the Times.* London, 1827.

—— "On the Situation of the Mining Poor." See *Georgical Essays,* edited by A. Hunter, vol. 2. York, 1803.

HALCOMB, JOHN. *A Practical Measure of Relief from the Present System of the Poor-Laws.* London, 1826.

HAMILTON, ROBERT. *Address to the Inhabitants of Aberdeen on the Management of the Poor.* 1822.

HANWAY, JONAS. *A Comprehensive View of Sunday Schools.* London, 1786.

HILL, ROWLAND. *Village Dialogue between Farmer Littleworth and Thomas Newman, Rev. Messrs. Lovegood and Dolittle.* London, 1806.

JAMES, SIR WALTER. *The Poor of London: A Letter to the Lord Bishop of the Diocese.* London, 1844.

LEFROY, CHRISTOPHER EDWARD. *Letter to Sir Thomas Baring on the Subject of Allotments of Land to the Poor.* London, 1834.

LESLIE, JOHN. *Remarks on the Present State of the Poor Law Question.* London, 1834.

The Love of Christ the Source of Genuine Philanthropy: A Discourse Occasioned . . . by the Death of John Thornton. London, 1791.

MORE, HANNAH. *An Estimate of the Religion of the Fashionable World.* By one of the Laity. 1791.

—— *Thoughts on the Importance of the Manners of the Great to General Society.* 1788.

—— *Village Politics.* By Will Chip. 1792.

MORE, MARTHA. *Mendip Annals: or, A Narrative of the Charitable Labours of Hannah and Martha More . . . being the Journals of Martha More.* London, 1859.

SHARP, GRANVILLE. *An Address to the People of England, being the Protest of a Private Individual against Every Suspension of Law That is Liable to Injure . . . Personal Security, and Also Stating the Illegality of Impressing Seamen.* 1778.

—— *Letter to a Committee of the Corporation of London Appointed to Enquire into the State of the London Workhouse, 1791.* 1791.

—— *Plan for a Public Charity.* 1790.

—— *Remarks on the Opinions of Some of the Most Celebrated Writers on Crown Law, Respecting the Due Distinction between Manslaughter and Murder.* London, 1773.

—— *A Representation of the Injustice and Dangerous Tendency of Admitting the Least Claim of Private Property in the Persons of Men, in England, etc.* London, 1769.

SPENCE, THOMAS. *The Rights of Infants; . . . in a Dialogue between the Aristocracy and a Mother of Children.* London, 1797.

THORNTON, HENRY. *Family Prayers.* London, 1834.

URQUHART, THOMAS. *A Letter to William Wilberforce, Esq., M.P. on the Subject of Impressment.* London, 1816.

VENN, JOHN. *Agrarian Justice.* London, 1798.

—— *The Ground of Encouragement in the Present National Danger.* London, 1803.

—— *Rules and Regulations of the Society for Bettering the Condition of the Poor at Clapham, Surrey, Instituted February 11, 1799,* [with] *an Account of the Original Designs of the Society.*

WILBERFORCE, WILLIAM. *Advice Suggested by the State of the Times.* London, 1803.

—— *A Letter to the Gentlemen, Clergy, and Freeholders of Yorkshire.* London, 1807.

—— *A Practical View of the Prevailing Religious System of Professed Christians in the Higher and Middle Classes in This Country Contrasted with Real Christianity.* London, 1797.

Association for the Relief of the Manufacturing and Labouring Poor. *Report of the Committee Appointed by the Association . . . , Originally Constructed in the Year 1812.* London, 1816.

—— *Second Report of the Association . . . , Relating Chiefly to the General Supply of Fish in the Metropolis and the Interior.* London, 1815.

Philanthropic Society. *Report.* London, 1812.

Report from His Majesty's Commissioners for Enquiring into the Administration and Practical Operation of the Poor Laws. 1834.

Report of the Select Committee on Artisans and Machinery. 1824.

Society for Bettering the Condition and Increasing the Comforts of the
    Poor, Patron the King. *Report*. London, 1797.
—— *Report*. London, 1802.
Society for Educating the Poor of Newfoundland. *Report*. 1823.
Society for Giving Effect to His Majesty's Proclamation against Vice and
    Immorality. *Report of the Committee for the Year 1799*. London,
    1800.
Society for the Discharge and Relief of Persons Imprisoned for Small
    Debts. *An Account of the Rise, Progress and Present State of the
    Society*. London, 1777.
Society for the Suppression of Vice. *Proposal for Establishing a Society
    for the Suppression of Vice and the Encouragement of Religion and
    Virtue throughout the United Kingdom, to Consist of Members of
    the Established Church*. London, 1801.
Spitalfields Association. *Report*. London, 1816.
Sunday School Society. *Plan of a Society Established in London A.D.
    1785 for the Support and Encouragement of Sunday Schools*. London,
    1788.
Trinity Parish Church, Clapham. Clapham Vestry Minutes, 1792-1833.

IV. PERIODICALS

Anti-Slavery Monthly Reporter, 1825–1836.
British Critic, 1807–1833.
Christian Observer, 1802–1838.
Cobbett's Weekly Political Register, 1802–1833.
Edinburgh Review, 1802–1844.
Evangelical Magazine, 1795–1800.
Gentlemen's Magazine, 1785–1833.
Missionary Register, 1813–1833.
Quarterly Review, 1809–1833.
The Times (London).

Index